Palgrave Studies in Creativity and Culture

Series Editors
Vlad Petre Glăveanu
Department of Psychology
Webster University
Geneva, Switzerland

Brady Wagoner
Communication and Psychology
Aalborg University
Aalborg, Denmark

Both creativity and culture are areas that have experienced a rapid growth in interest in recent years. Moreover, there is a growing interest today in understanding creativity as a socio-cultural phenomenon and culture as a transformative, dynamic process. Creativity has traditionally been considered an exceptional quality that only a few people (truly) possess, a cognitive or personality trait 'residing' inside the mind of the creative individual. Conversely, culture has often been seen as 'outside' the person and described as a set of 'things' such as norms, beliefs, values, objects, and so on. The current literature shows a trend towards a different understanding, which recognises the psycho-socio-cultural nature of creative expression and the creative quality of appropriating and participating in culture. Our new, interdisciplinary series Palgrave Studies in Creativity and Culture intends to advance our knowledge of both creativity and cultural studies from the forefront of theory and research within the emerging cultural psychology of creativity, and the intersection between psychology, anthropology, sociology, education, business, and cultural studies. Palgrave Studies in Creativity and Culture is accepting proposals for monographs, Palgrave Pivots and edited collections that bring together creativity and culture. The series has a broader focus than simply the cultural approach to creativity, and is unified by a basic set of premises about creativity and cultural phenomena.

More information about this series at
http://www.palgrave.com/gp/series/14640

Constance de Saint-Laurent
Sandra Obradović • Kevin R. Carriere
Editors

Imagining Collective Futures

Perspectives from Social, Cultural and Political Psychology

palgrave
macmillan

Editors
Constance de Saint-Laurent
University of Neuchâtel
Neuchâtel, Switzerland

Kevin R. Carriere
Georgetown University
Washington, DC, USA

Sandra Obradović
London School of Economics and Political Science
London, UK

Palgrave Studies in Creativity and Culture
ISBN 978-3-319-76050-6   ISBN 978-3-319-76051-3   (eBook)
https://doi.org/10.1007/978-3-319-76051-3

Library of Congress Control Number: 2018939243

© The Editor(s) (if applicable) and The Author(s) 2018
This work is subject to copyright. All rights are solely and exclusively licensed by the Publisher, whether the whole or part of the material is concerned, specifically the rights of translation, reprinting, reuse of illustrations, recitation, broadcasting, reproduction on microfilms or in any other physical way, and transmission or information storage and retrieval, electronic adaptation, computer software, or by similar or dissimilar methodology now known or hereafter developed.
The use of general descriptive names, registered names, trademarks, service marks, etc. in this publication does not imply, even in the absence of a specific statement, that such names are exempt from the relevant protective laws and regulations and therefore free for general use.
The publisher, the authors, and the editors are safe to assume that the advice and information in this book are believed to be true and accurate at the date of publication. Neither the publisher nor the authors or the editors give a warranty, express or implied, with respect to the material contained herein or for any errors or omissions that may have been made. The publisher remains neutral with regard to jurisdictional claims in published maps and institutional affiliations.

Cover illustration: Jerome Mor / EyeEm / gettyimages

Printed on acid-free paper

This Palgrave Macmillan imprint is published by the registered company Springer International Publishing AG part of Springer Nature.
The registered company address is: Gewerbestrasse 11, 6330 Cham, Switzerland

Contents

1 Introduction: What May the Future Hold?   1
Constance de Saint-Laurent, Sandra Obradović, and Kevin R. Carriere

Section I   Imagining the Future   13

2 Imagining the Collective Future: A Sociocultural Perspective   15
Tania Zittoun and Alex Gillespie

3 Framing the Issue: Literature, Collective Imagination, and Fan Activism   39
Kevin R. Carriere

4 Thinking Through Time: From Collective Memories to Collective Futures   59
Constance de Saint-Laurent

5   Perspectival Collective Futures: Creativity
    and Imagination in Society   83
    Vlad Petre Glăveanu

Section II   Collective Imaginations   107

6   Imagining Collective Futures in Time: Prolepsis
    and the Regimes of Historicity   109
    Ignacio Brescó de Luna

7   Utopias and World-Making: Time, Transformation
    and the Collective Imagination   129
    Sandra Jovchelovitch and Hana Hawlina

8   Troubled Pasts, Collective Memory, and Collective
    Futures   153
    Cristian Tileagă

9   Imagining Collective Identities Beyond Intergroup
    Conflict   173
    Cathy Nicholson and Caroline Howarth

Section III   Creating Socio-Political Change   197

10 Creating Alternative Futures: Cooperative Initiatives
    in Egypt   199
    Eman A. Maarek and Sarah H. Awad

11 Remembering and Imagining in Human Development:
    Fairness and Social Movements in Ireland   221
    Séamus A. Power

12 Creating Integration: A Case Study from Serbia
    and the EU   237
    Sandra Obradović

13 History Education and the (Im)possibility of Imagining
    the Future   255
    Mario Carretero

14 Conclusion: Changing Imaginings of Collective Futures   273
    Ivana Marková

Index   295

Notes on Contributors

Sarah H. Awad is a PhD fellow at the Centre for Cultural Psychology, Aalborg University, Denmark. She received her MSc in social and cultural psychology from London School of Economics and Political Science and her BA in mass communication from the American University in Cairo. Her research interests are in the interrelations between the fields of cultural psychology, communication, and social development. She studies the process by which individuals develop through times of social change using signs to create alternative visions of social reality.

Mario Carretero is a professor at Autonoma University of Madrid, Spain, where he was Dean of the Faculty of Psychology, and Researcher at FLACSO, Argentina. He has carried out an extensive research on history education. His recent books are *History Education and the Construction of National Identities* (2012, co-ed.), *Constructing Patriotism* (2011, funded by the Guggenheim Foundation) and *Palgrave Handbook of Research in Historical Culture and Education* (2016). He has been Santander Fellow at Harvard University (DRCLAS) and Bliss Carnochan Visiting Professor at Stanford University (Humanities Center).

Kevin R. Carriere is a PhD candidate at Georgetown University, where he is examining the political psychology of perceived threat and its effects on support for human rights violations. His research focuses on how individuals understand, apply, and negotiate human rights and their violations through negotiation, education, and activism.

Ignacio Brescó de Luna is working as an associate professor at the Centre for Cultural Psychology, at Aalborg University (Denmark). He received his PhD from the Autonomous University of Madrid, where he worked as an associate professor until 2014. His research interests revolve around collective memory and identity, the teaching of history, positioning theory and the narrative mediation of remembering. He is working on memorials in relation to collective grief under the research project Sorgens kultur (Grief Culture) led by Svend Brinkmann and funded by the Obel Family Foundation.

Constance de Saint-Laurent is a research and teaching fellow at the University of Neuchâtel, Switzerland, where she recently finished a PhD on the sociocultural psychology of collective memory. Her research focuses on social thinking, imagination and the life course, and more generally on how we construct and understand the world we live in.

Alex Gillespie is Associate Professor in Social Psychology at the London School of Economics and Co-editor of the *Journal for the Theory of Social Behaviour*. His research focuses on communication, divergences of perspective, misunderstandings and listening. He studies these phenomena in a variety of empirical domains, including healthcare settings. He has co-edited the volumes *Trust and Conflict* (2012) and *Rethinking Creativity* (2014). He has recently finished a monograph with Tania Zittoun, entitled *Imagination in Human and Cultural Development* (2016).

Vlad Petre Glăveanu is an associate professor and the head of the Department of Psychology and Professional Counseling at Webster University Geneva in Switzerland, as well as an associated researcher at SLATE, University of Bergen in Norway, and LATI, Paris Descartes University in France. He received his PhD from the London School of Economics and has published extensively on creativity and culture, including the recently edited *Palgrave Handbook of Creativity and Culture Research* (2016) and co-edited *Oxford Handbook of Imagination and Culture* (with Tania Zittoun). Vlad is also Editor of *Europe's Journal of Psychology* (EJOP).

Hana Hawlina is a research assistant at the University of Ljubljana and the head of public engagement at the Slovenian Neuroscience Association. Her past work explores the relationship between perspective taking, multicultural experience and creativity, the role of perspective taking in facilitating collaborative creativity between culturally diverse individuals, and using process-oriented methods to study ideation. Another branch of her previous research investigates public perceptions of science, how new findings are circulated in the public sphere and the challenges of media reporting on science.

Caroline Howarth is Associate Professor in Social Psychology at the London School of Economics and Political Science. Her research and teaching seek to push social psychology in a more critical direction by addressing questions of intercultural relations, community, racism and resistance. This demanded the conceptualization of the role of re-presentation in identity formation, in the marginalization of specific communities, and in the possibilities of resistance and transformation. She was Associate Editor of *Political Psychology*, Consultative Editor for *Papers in Social Representations* and on the editorial boards of *British Journal of Social Psychology*, *Journal of Community and Applied Social Psychology* and P*sychologia*.

Sandra Jovchelovitch is Professor of Social Psychology at the London School of Economics, where she directs the MSc in Social and Cultural Psychology. Her research centers on human development under contextual adversity, the social psychology of community, and public spheres and social representations. Her books include *Social Representations and the Public Sphere: A study on the symbolic construction of public spaces in Brazil* (2000), *Knowledge in Context: Representations, community and culture* (2007), *Underground Sociabilities: Identity, culture and resistance in the favelas of Rio de Janeiro* (2013, with J Priego-Hernández).

Eman Maarek is an independent researcher with an academic background in political science from Cairo University. She has worked for over 15 years in the field of social development in Egypt, in projects affiliated to UNDP, EU, GIZ, and British Council, specializing in community development and youth empowerment. She has obtained several postgraduate certificates in the field of human rights and civil society, the most recent of which from the Cairo Institute for Liberal Arts and Sciences (CILAS). She has conducted research in topics related to social movements, community development, cooperatives, and women's role in revolution.

Ivana Marková is Professor Emeritus in Psychology, University of Stirling, and Visiting Professor in the Department of Psychological and Behavioural Science at the London School of Economics. Her research includes the theory of social representations, dialogicality, trust, responsibility, and the relation between common sense and other forms of knowledge. The latest books include: *The Dialogical Mind: Common Sense and Ethics* (2016); *Dialogue in Focus Groups: Exploring Socially Shared knowledge* (2007, with P. Linell, M. Grossen,

A. Salazar-Orvig); *Trust and Conflict: Representation, Culture, Dialogue* (2012, co-edited with A. Gillespie); *Dialogical Approaches to Trust in Communication* (2013, co-edited with P. Linell).

Cathy Nicholson is an independent researcher and visiting fellow in the Department of Psychological and Behavioural Science at the London School of Economics. Her interests are in the dialogical relationships across self-defined groups, particularly groups in conflict, as to the foundations of their perceived boundary formation and development, juxtaposed with perceptions of present-day social reality. Intergroup interdependence can be a vital, yet unseen, component of identification and solidarity, and yet the heterogeneity within groups leads to a complexity that can be explored, to further our knowledge in the social psychology of conflict research.

Sandra Obradović is a PhD candidate in the Department of Psychological and Behavioural Science at the London School of Economics and Political Science (LSE). Her research interests focus on exploring the connections between history, psychology and politics in times of sociopolitical change. Specifically, her research explores how processes of identity continuity, compatibility and recognition shape perceptions of supranational belonging and attitudes towards political change in the context of EU integration.

Séamus A. Power is a transdisciplinary scholar with expertise in social, cultural, and political psychology. He is a postdoctoral fellow in the Department of Comparative Human Development at the University of Chicago.

Cristian Tileagă is Senior Lecturer in Social Psychology at Loughborough University, the UK. He has research interests in social memory and transitional justice, social psychology of prejudice and discrimination, and issues around interdisciplinarity. He is the author of *The Nature of Prejudice: Society, Discrimination and Moral Exclusion* (2015) and *Political Psychology: Critical Perspectives* (2013), and co-author of *Discursive Psychology: Classic and Contemporary Issues* (2016) and *Psychology and History: Interdisciplinary Explorations* (2014).

Tania Zittoun is a professor at the Institute of Psychology and Education at the University of Neuchâtel (Switzerland). She develops a sociocultural psychology of the life course with a focus on the role of institutions and the dynamics of imagination. Her theoretical work is in dialogue with psychoanalysis and the critical social sciences. Her empirical work addresses mobility as well as ageing. She is Associate Editor of *Culture & Psychology*, and her latest books include *Imagination in Human and Cultural Development* (authored with Alex Gillespie, 2016) and the *Handbook of Culture and Imagination* (2018, co-edited with Vlad P. Glaveanu).

List of Figures

Fig. 2.1	1962 USA stamp, 4 cents, "U.S. Man in space. Project Mercury" (USA stamps no copyright before 1978. https://commons.wikimedia.org/wiki/File:Project_Mercury_1962_Issue-4c.jpg)	25
Fig. 2.2	1967 USSR stamp, 6 kopeks, "Space science fiction. On the moon" (No copyright on USSR stamps. https://commons.wikimedia.org/wiki/File:1967_CPA_3546_(2).jpg)	26
Fig. 2.3	"Smoke of chimneys is the breath of Soviet Russia" (1917–1921) (No copyright on Russia for posters before 1942, and per extension in the USA. https://commons.wikimedia.org/wiki/File:Smoke_of_chimneys_is_the_breath_of_Soviet_Russia.jpg)	28
Fig. 2.4	Cover to the propaganda comic book "Is This tomorrow" (1947) (Public domain, By Catechetical Guild (Catechetical Guild) [Public domain], https://commons.wikimedia.org/wiki/File:Is_this_tomorrow.jpg?uselang=fr)	30
Fig. 2.5	Trajectories of collective imagination of the future in a two-dimensional space (copyright authors)	32
Fig. 6.1	Prolepsis or bringing the future into the present through the reconstruction of the past	116
Fig. 9.1	Themata to denote kernels of embedded social representations	185
Fig. 10.1	Recurring themes in the data	212

1

Introduction: What May the Future Hold?

Constance de Saint-Laurent, Sandra Obradović, and Kevin R. Carriere

We have, both individually and collectively, always tried to imagine what the future may hold. From Athen's Pythia to modern-day algorithms trying to predict our shopping behaviours, we have always sought ways to anticipate what tomorrow may be like. On the one hand, there is tremendous power associated with being able to see the future, because of what it could allow us to do: gather riches, control others by anticipating what they may do, avoid death (at least temporarily), or, in the best of cases, even change the course of time. It is quite literally called a "power" in fiction, and there are whole industries claiming to be able to show us what

---

C. de Saint-Laurent (✉)
University of Neuchâtel, Neuchâtel, Switzerland

S. Obradović
London School of Economics and Political Science, London, UK
e-mail: S.Obradovic@lse.ac.uk

K. R. Carriere
Georgetown University, Washington, DC, USA
e-mail: krc58@georgetown.edu

the future may hold—from very serious consultancy firms and data companies to the medium in the local ad section of the newspaper claiming to have "a third eye". On the other hand, there is something both fascinating and terrifying about being able to know what will come next, in lifting the mystery and being able to go against the course of time. Even in fiction, characters who are given the power to look into the future can only see very limited parts of it—as Frodo looking down Galadriel's mirror (Tolkien, 2009)—or it is at the price of their safety and sanity—as the "precogs" in Philip K. Dick's *Minority Report* (Dick, 2002).

Indeed, much energy and effort has been devoted to the question of the future. In the literature, science fiction and the anticipation genre have considered where technology may bring us, exploring what the future may look like some thousands of years down the line. Asimov, one of the most prolific and brilliant science fiction authors of our time, even imagined the emergence of a science that would use psychology and history to predict the future (Asimov, 2004). Utopias and dystopias, with their decisively more political perspective, have tried to imagine the best and the worst human societies that could await us. In science, modelizations and statistical analyses have tried to predict everything from the weather to the characteristics of the world population in a hundred years. Behavioural sciences, attempting to predict how we may conduct ourselves in different situations, have been on a constant rise, becoming once more the most prominent form of psychology. Their findings have been applied in economics, marketing, and politics, and have changed the way we understand the world. And at a more mundane level, newspaper and media outlets have tried to predict anything from the result of upcoming elections—with more and more surprises—to the new features of the latest iPhone.

This tendency is not new, and not all attempts have been equally successful. On the one hand, the sales of 1984 have rocketed in the United States since the last presidential election, and some have argued that Orwell forecasted post-truth when he wrote:

> For, after all, how do we know that two and two make four? Or that the force of gravity works? Or that the past is unchangeable? If both the past and the external world exist only in the mind, and if the mind itself is controllable – what then? (Orwell, 2003/1949, p. 162)

On the other hand, Herbert Hoover, the then president of the United States, famously said in June 1930: "Gentlemen, you have come sixty days too late. The depression is over." If we must admit that people are not always extremely good at predicting the future, looking at how past generations have imagined how we would live is as fascinating as it can be, at times, hilarious or surprisingly accurate.

In 1900, John Elfreth Watkins Jr. collected the predictions for the next hundred years of eminent scientists of his time, and they are a wonderful example of the wide spectrum on which (informed) guesses about the future can be placed. It is a heteroclite list of forecasts, although many seem to be oriented towards science and technology and none predicted the important social changes of the twentieth century, including the fact that it would no longer be acceptable to have only men participate in the elaboration of such a list. Some predicted "peas as large as beats", that "university education [would] be free for everyone", or that we would all be able to "walk ten miles", and that someone who could not do so would be "regarded as a weakling". Others imagined that "stores purchases [would be made] by tube", that "vegetables [would be] grown by electricity" because "winter [would be] turned into summer", or, almost anticipating the internet, that "man [would] see around the world [because] persons and things of all kinds [would] be brought within focus of cameras connected electrically with screens at opposite ends of circuits, thousands of miles at a span" (Elfreth Watkins, 1900, p. 8). What becomes clear, when reading these predictions, is that the future tends to be imagined as the prolongation of current changes one is experiencing—hence the fact that many of the examples above would very well fall within the area of expertise of the scientists interviewed by Elfreth Watkins. In other words, how we imagine the future is frequently bound to existing social knowledge of the present, and it is either seen as a prolonging—or alternative—to the current reality.

The Question of the Future in Psychology

In 1968, Maslow argued that "no theory of psychology will ever be complete which does not centrally incorporate the concept that man has his future within him, dynamically active at this present moment." (p. 15).

Yet, despite the centrality of the future in particular, and temporality in general, to human thought and behaviour, less work has explored the explicit role of imagining the future within the field of psychology. Among those who have, concepts such as "mental time travel" (MTT; Epstude & Peetz, 2012; Storm & Jobe, 2012; Tulving, 2002), "futuring" (Sools & Mooren, 2012) or "anticipatory representations in the making" (Philogene, 1999) have been developed to help us understand the complexities of future-oriented thinking. Perhaps this lack of focus comes from a poor understanding of what imagining the future actually *does* for individuals and social groups. As Zittoun (2013) argues, "[a] person who imagines some future event is not doing something useless. Just the contrary – imagining potential future events makes it possible to strive towards them or – in the case of adverse imaginary events – to try to avoid them." (p. 3). This process of imagination extends not only to how we anticipate the development of our personal lives, but also how we envision the future of our social groups, be they micro-groups such as families, or macro-groups such as nations or even the fate of humanity itself. Imagination thus plays a crucial part in human thinking and behaving. Within research on memory, for example, Storm and Jobe (2012) draw on a series of experiments to illustrate that there are important differences in the consequences that remembering the past and imagining the future have on the memory. Namely, their study illustrates that "under conditions in which remembering and experienced event does cause forgetting, imagining a non-experienced event does not." (Storm & Jobe, 2012, p. 233). Thus, it becomes crucial to consider imagining the future as linked to representing the past, but not identical in terms of the underlying psychological processes and consequences.

However, while research such as that mentioned above is crucial and moves us in the right direction in terms of understanding "futuring" or "mental time travel", they remain focused on the individual, disregarding the extent to which individual imagination is influenced, and shaped by, the larger social world in which he exists. For example, imagining the future becomes possible by drawing on the semiotic resources available to us from our sociocultural contexts, which vary from one place to the next. Equally, in contexts of conflict and war, the ways in which individuals imagine their personal future becomes intimately linked with the anticipations they hold for their social groups, whether these relate to changing intergroup relations, power dynamics, or political ideology.

Consequently, while it seems that literature, natural and behavioural sciences, popular culture, and the media have all attempted to imagine (and more importantly, predict) what our future may be like, less has been said about the role of the social sciences, especially in their more critical forms, as may be embodied in social, cultural, and political psychology. Have we left future predictions in the hands of data scientists and experimentalists, looking down at their attempts to model a reality that we believe eludes them? Or to the mediums and other adepts of the occult, observing them as the exotic remnants of superstitious practices? In this introduction, we would like to argue that quite the contrary, much of the social sciences and humanities—including social, cultural, and political psychology—have been as intrigued and fascinated with the future as other fields, but they have done so more indirectly. First, they have been primarily interested in how we construct collective futures—and not so much in predicting these futures themselves. Second, they have often approached this question indirectly, through topics such as collective memory, social identity, collective action, or imagination. This is reflected in the contributions to this book, where each chapter takes (at least) one of these topics as a point of departure. Let us consider each in turn and how they relate to the construction of collective futures.

First, collective memory—and more generally, memory—has frequently been connected to the imagination of the future on two grounds: that memory has a directive function and may actually be more about the future than about the past (e.g., Bartlett, 1932; Schacter & Addis, 2007), and that both remembering and imagining share, as psychological processes, many characteristics (Mullally & Maguire, 2013). While very few empirical studies had so far directly explored the links between the two, it is quite commonly accepted, in collective memory studies, that they are deeply connected (Szpunar & Szpunar, 2016). This is, we believe, because collective memory answers, for people, a question that is fundamental to understand and imagine where the future may lead us: Where are we from? Indeed, knowing where we come from means knowing the road travelled to the present, helping us to project where it may take us in the future. Being aware, for instance, of the tremendous changes agriculture brought, compared to the hunter-gatherer lifestyle, can help us anticipate that advances in the way we deal with our resources can fundamentally change our social organization, and thus, to imagine such changes in the future and the consequences they may have. As a result, the relations between collective memory and the imagination of the collective future are at the heart of the works presented in Chap. 4 (by Constance de Saint-Laurent), Chap. 6 (by Ignacio Brescó de Luna), Chap. 8 (by Cristian Tileăga), and Chap. 13 (by Mario Carretero).

Second, studies on social identity—and more generally, how we construct a sense of self and belonging—implicitly emphasize the importance of the future, as identities are seen as continuous and projected on to the future (Sani et al., 2007). In other words, those researchers working on social identities often consider these as fluid constructs in constant state of "becoming", where imagining the future can, at times, be an active process of resistance and positive social change (Cinnirella, 1998). Indeed, answering the question of "who we are" has consequences in terms of which actions and choices become desirable, necessary, or possible in the future. Considering humanity to be essentially belligerent, for instance, would make it difficult to imagine a peaceful future. And seeing one's social group as fundamentally different than others may encourage some to believe that their community would need to become independent to thrive. Furthermore, how we construct a sense of in-group belonging and continuity also has implications for intergroup relations, and who is considered a friend or a foe. These complex interrelations between social identity, intergroup relations, and collective futures are explored in Chap. 9 (by Caroline Howarth & Cathy Nicholson) and Chap. 12 (by Sandra Obradović).

Third, research on collective action—whether it is on protests, grassroots movements, cooperatives, and so on, or at a smaller scale, on collaboration and joint intentionality—has also proven to be future-oriented. On the one hand, it generally focuses on coordinated action as it unfolds, and thus, also in how participants anticipate and plan for the more or less immediate future (Jasper, 1998). On the other hand, participants in collective movements often come to realize the "power of the crowd"—one of the exhilarating aspects of protests and demonstrations—and thus to revise what they think may be possible in the future. That is, it may lead people to reverse the question of where may the future lead us to ask: Where could we take the future? At a more fundamental level, then, collective action raises the question of what we believe that we could collectively do, with tremendous consequences for how we imagine the future. Indeed, believing that the crowd has the power, for instance, to overthrow the global economic tendency would allow one to imagine a very different—and probably brighter—future than one could imagine by believing that the crowd would never come together and achieve such an aim. Collective action and how people who engage in it imagine the collective future is the focus of Chap. 5 (by Vlad Petre Glăveanu), Chap. 10 (by Eman Maarek & Sarah H. Awad), and Chap. 11 (by Seamus Power).

Fourth, and quite unsurprisingly, researchers working on imagination have also been interested in how people construct representations of the collective future. In particular, they have been concerned with what resources people use and what they are able to imagine; that is, in understanding how we construct what we believe to be possible. Looking back at the predictions for the next hundred years proposed by those Elfreth Watkins interviewed, for instance, we can see that most relate to the technological advances of the late 1890s, and propose more a continuation of the changes that were going on at the time than a real anticipation of radical novelty. Understanding how people imagine what is not there, and how they open up possibilities that were not imaginable before, is thus crucial to the study of how collective futures are imagined. These questions are discussed in Chap. 2 (by Tania Zittoun & Alex Gillespie), Chap. 3 (by Kevin R. Carriere), and Chap. 7 (by Sandra Jovchelovitch & Hana Hawlina).

What this brief overview has aimed to show is twofold. First, it was to outline the fundamental questions that are connected to the imagination of the collective future, and how it resonates with profound human interrogations, making of it both a complex and fascinating topic. These questions are: Where are we from? (Collective memory); Who are we? (Social identity); What can we collectively do? (Collective action); What is possible? (Imagination). The second aim of this overview was to highlight that the question of how we imagine the future, especially in its collective form, is linked to important fields of study in social, cultural, and political psychology. And it is, in large parts, what led us to this choice of disciplinary delimitation, beyond our own expertise and interests: Because we believed that these three types of psychology—that are deeply interconnected—all had much to contribute to the discussion of the imagination of collective futures. As these four categories are not mutually exclusive, they do not serve as the basis for the structure of this book. However, they represent the four main topics from which the various authors have explored the question of the collective future.

Structure and Outline of the Book

This book is divided into three sections of four chapters, each reflecting the area of expertise of the authors and the perspective from which they have approached the question of how we imagine the collective future. The first section regroups contributions from researchers working primarily on the processes of imagination, creativity, and memory, and who have explored their role in the construction of collective futures. The second section includes chapters from scholars studying the collective dynamics of society. Each chapter investigates how social phenomena and representations shape how the collective future is—or can be—imagined. Finally, in the third section, researchers working on specific collective movements or social issues developed case studies exploring the role of the imagination of the future in the creation of new initiatives and actions in the present.

Chapter 2, by Tania Zittoun & Alex Gillespie, presents a sociocultural model of imagination, and applies it to the imagination of collective futures. This model is illustrated with two historical cases studies—the landing on the moon and socialism—showing how these collective imaginations became concretized. In Chap. 3, Kevin R. Carriere uses two case studies—the history of the book *The Jungle* and the Harry Potter Alliance—to show the power of literature in the construction of the future. In particular, he shows how literature can help us imagine futures that previously seemed impossible, and can serve as the basis for collective action. In Chap. 4, Constance de Saint-Laurent explores the relations between memory and imagination, both in their individual and collective forms. Building on different studies on collective memory, she argues that collective memory frames collective imagination, provides contents and examples, and participates in the construction of generalized representations of the world, that in turn guide the imagination. In Chap. 5, Vlad-Petre Glăveanu builds on his work on creativity and activism to develop a perspectival model of how we imagine the collective future. Using three case studies from the United States, Columbia, and Turkey, he shows how the future is always constructed from a certain perspective and with a certain representation of the other.

In Chap. 6, Ignacio Brescó introduces the concept of "prolepsis" to explore how imagining the future relates to collective memory. He explores not only how the past shapes the present, but also how processes of imagining a certain future allow us to reconstruct the past, thus making of imagination a tool to move through time. In Chap. 7, Sandra Jovchelovitch and Hana Hawlina consider the function of utopias and utopian thinking in relation to how we understand our selves and social worlds. They discuss how imagination is a part of both the mental activities of humans as well as our capabilities of socially organizing the world. They explore the necessity, but also the dangers, of utopian thinking, highlighting its role in opening up avenues for social change to take place in the present. Cristian Tileagă, in Chap. 8, considers the role of experts in dealing with troubles past with the intention of constructing a different, more progressive future. Focusing on Romania and how the communist past was dealt with by experts in the Tismaneanu Report, Tileagă argues that the process of constructing communism as an "Other" allowed for the construction of a positive representation of the Romanian people in the past, present, and future. Lastly, in the final chapter of this section, Chap. 9, Cathy Nicholson and Caroline Howarth consider how imagining the future occurs in contexts of intergroup conflict, where collective imagination becomes intimately bound to not just the in-group, but also the out-group. The authors question whether imagining the future in this context always entails a future where conflict continues, or whether there are ways in which alternative, more peaceful, representations can be developed. As the authors argue, concepts such as thema and narratives can help unravel these complexities that define intergroup relations and meaning-making in the context of imagining the future.

In Chap. 10, Eman A. Maarek and Sarah H. Awad focus on how imagination can be used to maintain momentum in times of rupture and social change. Their work follows three case studies of cooperatives in Egypt and how imagining the future assisted in a decentralized form of resistance against the state. Seamus Power, in Chap. 11, provides a reflection on the links between moral psychology and collective imagination within collective action. Using narratives from Irish protesters during a debate on the privatization of water, he links up the interaction of morality and imagination and shows an imagination through a drive for justice. In Chap. 12, Sandra Obradović identifies a case of how collective imagination can come in conflict with collective identity through its representation as a discontinuity (or rupture) from the past. She draws on empirical work from Serbian to examine how citizens represent their nation's future in times of socio-political change, illustrating how imagining the future can tell us a lot about the present, and the fears which underlie political attitudes towards change. Mario Carretero presents his work on formal and informal historical education and its relation to imagination in Chap. 13. Using the novel *1984* as a backdrop, Carretero argues that control of the past by historical education, both in classrooms and museums, directly constricts how we imagine the future.

Finally, Ivana Marková provides a synthesis of these works in her conclusion. Her insight into the contributions delineate two different approaches to our discussion of collective imagination—of either removing ourselves from the current moment or being constantly active in the present moment of our lives. Her discussion on imagination through the view of Heidegger focuses on how imagination transverses through societal transformation and guides the generation of images.

This project started as an imaginative idea—can we bring together contributors from a wide range of perspectives to weigh in on how they see collective imagination playing out in their work? By drawing together works from social, cultural, and political psychology, the authors of this volume provide valuable theoretical and empirical insights into the topic of imagining collective futures, hopefully convincing the readers of this volume of the significance of both imagination and the future in the psychology of human thought and behaviour.

We are thankful to Jaan Valsiner, whose inspirational encouragement at the onset of this project was critical in getting this volume off the ground, and to Joanna O'Neill, from Palgrave Macmillan, for all her help.

References

Asimov, I. (2004). *Foundation and Empire*. New York: Random House Publishing Group.
Bartlett, F. C. (1932). *Remembering. A study in experimental and social psychology*. Cambridge: Cambridge University Press.
Cinnirella, M. (1998). Exploring temporal aspects of social identity: The concept of possible social identities. *European Journal of Social Psychology, 28*(2), 227–248. https://doi.org/10.1002/(sici)1099-0992(199803/04)28:23.0.co;2-x.
Dick, P. K. (2002). *The minority report: And other classic stories*. New York: Citadel Press.
Elfreth Watkins, J. (1900). What may happen in the next hundred years. *The Ladies' Home Journal, XVIII*(December), 8.
Epstude, K., & Peetz, J. (2012). Mental time travel: A conceptual overview of social psychological perspectives on a fundamental human capacity. *European Journal of Social Psychology, 42*(3), 269–275.
Jasper, J. M. (1998). The emotions of protest: Affective and reactive emotions in and around social movements. *Sociological Forum, 13*(3), 397–424.
Mullally, S. L., & Maguire, E. A. (2013). Memory, imagination, and predicting the future. A common brain mechanism? *The Neuroscientist, 20*(3), 220–234. https://doi.org/10.1177/1073858413495091.
Orwell, G. (2003). *Animal farm and 1984*. London: Houghton Mifflin Harcourt.
Philogène, G. (1999). *From Black to African American: A new social representation*. Westport, CT/London: Praeger.
Sani, F., Bowe, M., Herrera, M., Manna, C., Cossa, T., Miao, X., et al. (2007). Perceived collective continuity: Seeing groups as entities that move through time. *European Journal of Social Psychology, 37*(6), 1118–1134. https://doi.org/10.1002/ejsp.430.

Schacter, D. L., & Addis, D. R. (2007). Constructive memory. The ghosts of past and future. *Nature, 445*(7123), 27–27. https://doi.org/10.1038/445027a.

Sools, A., & Mooren, J. H. (2012). Towards narrative futuring in psychology: Becoming resilient by imagining the future. *Graduate Journal of Social Science, 9*(2), 203–226.

Storm, B. C., & Jobe, T. A. (2012). Retrieval-induced forgetting predicts failure to recall negative autobiographical memories. *Psychological Science, 23*(11), 1356–1363. https://doi.org/10.1177/0956797612443837.

Szpunar, P. M., & Szpunar, K. K. (2016). Collective future thought. Concept, function, and implications for collective memory studies. *Memory Studies, 9*(4), 376–389. https://doi.org/10.1177/1750698015615660.

Tolkien, J. R. R. (2009). *The lord of the rings*. London: HarperCollins.

Tulving, E. (2002). Chronesthesia: Conscious awareness of subjective time. In D. T. Stuss & R. T. Knight (Eds.), *Principles of frontal lobe function* (pp. 311–325). New York: Oxford University Press.

Zittoun, T. (2013). *Human development in the life course: Melodies of living*. Cambridge: Cambridge University Press.

Section I

Imagining the Future

2

Imagining the Collective Future: A Sociocultural Perspective

Tania Zittoun and Alex Gillespie

The present chapter examines how groups imagine their future from a sociocultural perspective. First, we present our sociocultural model of imagination and its three dimensions, before building on it to account for how collectives imagine the future. We maintain that it is a mistake to assume that because imagination is "not real", it cannot have "real" consequences. Imagination about the future, we argue, is a central steering mechanism of individual and collective behaviour. Imagination about the future is often political precisely because it can have huge significance for the activities of a group or even a nation. Accordingly, we introduce a new dimension for thinking about collective imagination of the future—namely, the degree of centralization of imagining—and with it, identify a related aspect, its emotional valence. Based on two examples, we argue that collective imaginings have their own developmental trajectories as

T. Zittoun (✉)
University of Neuchâtel, Neuchâtel, Switzerland
e-mail: tania.zittoun@unine.ch

A. Gillespie
London School of Economics, London, UK
e-mail: a.t.gillespie@lse.ac.uk

they move in time through particular social and political contexts. Consequently, we suggest that a sociocultural psychology of collective imagination of the future should not only document instances of collective imagining, but also account for these developmental trajectories—specifically, what social and political forces hinder and promote particular imaginings.

A Sociocultural Model of Imagination

Psychology has mainly studied imagination among children (e.g., Harris, 2000; Singer & Singer, 1992), adults (i.e., training creativity; Karwowski & Soszynski, 2008), and in small groups (i.e., brainstorming and innovation; Brown & Paulus, 2002). In contrast to these approaches, that tend to focus on the outcomes of imagination, and based on a large review and synthesis of the literature, we have adopted a sociocultural perspective on imagination; building on the works of L. S. Vygotsky, G. H. Mead, but also D. W. Winnicott and many others, we have progressively defined the core dynamics of imagination. In this first section, we present our basic model of imagination, the sequence of imagination, and the three analytical dimensions we have proposed to account for its variations.

We conceive of imagination as the process by which a person temporarily decouples his or her flow of experience from the here-and-now of his or her proximal sphere of experience. This decoupling can be described as a loop, a little voyage to a distal sphere of experience, before looping back to the proximal sphere of experience and recoupling with the immediately present socially shared reality (Zittoun & Gillespie, 2016). For instance, a child in math class dreamingly looks out of the window and imagines building a hut in a tree, a dragon that comes to attack, and his glorious defence; he comes back from his daydream with a smile on his face, which leads the teacher to ask what was so funny. A teenager comes back upset from a meeting with friends, locks herself up in her room, listens to her preferred rock band, and is deeply moved again and again when listening to the lyrics or certain melodic phrases; she comes to dinner calmed down. A scientist needs to conceptualize the consequences of time-space relativity, and imagines sitting on a beam of light; his clarity of conceptualization convinces a sceptical audience. A novelist is dissatisfied with his current life, and engages in an exploration of his lost childhood, re-experiencing the tastes and smells of his childhood home; with time, he writes a novel which will be considered a milestone in European literature. An older person sees her mobility decline, and she imagines life in a nursing home and possible rearrangements of her life; this leads to practical changes in the layout of her home and the introduction of assistive devices.

In all these examples, imagination involves a three-step sequence. First, there is a *trigger*—usually, disruptions of some kind questioning a person's involvement in a current conduct that initiate the person's uncoupling from the proximal sphere of experience (boredom in class, frustration with friends, limits of physical explanation, etc.). Second, the burgeoning loop of imagination utilizes *resources*—drawn from a wide range of semiotic and material elements previously internalized by the person along the life course, or present in the immediate environment, through the presence of others, the affordances of the setting, or the power of guidance of complex artefacts. For example, the child's imagination utilizes the view of the tree out of the window, his experience of tree-climbing, and stories about dragons; the teenager uses the recording of the rock band; and the elderly person uses stories and images of assisted living. Regarding the semiotic processes of imagining, we agree with other authors that imagination demands a complex decomposition and rearrangement of all this semiotic material, loaded with emotions and embodied experiences, into new synthesis (Vygotsky, 1933). The dynamics of imagination thus resemble dream work (Freud, 2001; Singer & Singer, 1992; Winnicott, 1996). The fact that imagination occurs in distal spheres of experiences implies that it is liberated from the laws (social, logical, material, temporal, spatial, etc.) that govern proximal spheres of experiences located in specific social and material settings. When imagining, causality can be undone; children can fly; scientists can sit on beams of light; and one can regain lost abilities. Third, the sequence ends with a *return*—when the person loops out of imagining, and recouples with her proximal circumstances, a few seconds or hours older. Although no dragons will lay slain, there will always be outcomes. These outcomes can be temporary emotional changes (e.g., in the example with the teenager), they can be important life decisions (e.g., choosing not to go to a nursing home), or the outcomes can be the production of new semiotic or material elements (e.g., new theories or the basis for a new novel). Hence, some people's imaginings are crystallized into cultural artefacts (e.g., novels, films), which then can guide the imagining of others (Zittoun & Gillespie, 2016). In that sense, imagination can feed into an expansion of our collective experience (Pelaprat & Cole, 2011; Zittoun & Cerchia, 2013).

To build a theoretical integration, we have identified three core dimensions to describe the variety of imaginings in which people engage. The first dimension is that of *time orientation*: imagination can be oriented towards the past (such as when one re-experiences aspects of one's childhood in the taste of a cake); the future (such as when imagining a future life in a nursing home); or alternative presents (such as defending the tree-hut from a dragon). The second dimension is the *semiotic distance* of the imagining, some being rather concrete and close to embodied experiences (such as imagining climbing a tree) while others demand generalized experiences (such as imagining the speed of light). The third dimension is *plausibility*; this accounts for the fact that in certain social, cultural, and material conditions, imaginations can have a more or less degree of likelihood or possible realization. Hence, fighting a dragon is impossible for most children; yet, there is a small degree of plausibility if that child lives in Indonesia, habitat of the Komodo dragon. Imagination about living in a nursing home is very plausible for many people in contemporary society.

Theorizing imagination in terms of three steps and dimensions allows for a rich description and analysis of diverse instances of imagination. It also allows us to understand the complex cultural guidance shaping people's imagination of the past and people's future life trajectories. For instance, Welzer and colleagues have shown that social discourses have so much attributed the responsibility of WWII German war crimes to the "bad" Nazis, that younger generations can only end up remembering their parents' or grandparents' actual implication in the war as heroic resistance (Welzer, 2005, 2008; Welzer, Moller, & Tschuggnall, 2013). In a very different context, we have shown how a young woman's imaginings of herself and her possible future are selectively validated or rejected by her immediate social environment (parents, friends, school), thus shaping the plausibility or nonplausibility of her possible future selves. Eventually, the young woman finds herself guided into certain life path, which she reinterprets in the light of her past imagining of her future, creating a new synthesis and imagining of herself (Zittoun & de Saint-Laurent, 2015). Our model thus shows the sociocultural nature of imagining in terms of origin, process, material, guidance, and outcomes. But what happens when imagining is done collectively?

Collective Imagination of the Future: Centralization and Emotional Valence

Our initial theorization of imagination as sociocultural dynamic has been developed mainly considering the diversity of imagination of single persons, in interaction and dialogue with others and their environment. Our approach can also be used to account for dialogical imagination; that is, the capacity to imagine the perspective of the other (Gillespie, Corti, & Heasman, 2018; Marková, 2016). However, imagination can also be social in the sense of being shared or distributed; many people can collaboratively imagine, as in the case of group discussion, or imagination can emerge collectively, as in the case of the shared imagination of life on other planets, where the outputs of one person or groups imagining are resources in the next person or group's imagination. Collaborative imagination can be accounted for within our initial model with some fitting. For instance, we have shown that children in a classroom attempt to explain where stones come from; through their exploratory discussion, each child brings some elements of knowledge, personal experiences, or bits of demonstration, building on what the others have said, until one child can formulate a quasi-scientific explanation. Collaboratively, the children have imagined the origins of stones (Hilppö, Rajala, Zittoun, Kumpulainen, & Lipponen, 2016). However, in order to account for collective imagination, which takes place between more people and over a longer time span, we have to make some additions to our model. For instance, the imagination of the end of communism was developed by many people in Czechoslovakia during communism. Some people, then called "dissidents", expressed these imaginations in songs, theatre plays, and novels (Havel, 1988; Klíma, 2013; Zantovsky, 2015). The government of the time arrested them, censored their work, and punished their families, while producing state-compatible cultural elements (Bren, 2010). However, using these dissident songs and novels as crystallized imaginations that circulated illegally, as well as the knowledge of these arrests, many more people could build on these outputs to imagine that an alternative life was possible (Bilefsky, 2009; Day, 1999). Such dynamics of maintaining an imagined alternative, while a centralized power controlled the availability and the circulation of cultural elements and the expression of imaginations, entailed strong psychological and social tensions, until, in changing historic-political conditions (the Perestroïka, fall of the Wall, etc.), the whole society came to a tipping point, and the political regime in place lost its legitimacy in what was called the "Velvet Revolution" in 1989 (Zittoun, 2018).

To account for these societal dynamics, we define the collective imagination as loops of imagination distributed among many people over time, with partly shared and crystallized outputs of imagination being the resources utilized in subsequent imaginings. Also, we assume that collective imaginations can have large-scale outcomes, which not only affect one person, but a community or a society at large. It is this consequential aspect of collective imagining that can make such imaginings political, such as when people imagine alternative possible social arrangements. Accordingly, considering collective imagining and the future requires a consideration of social control and valence, or emotional guidance.

Before considering these new aspects of imagination, let us review how our previously proposed dimensions fit the phenomenon of collectives imagining their future. First, the temporal dimension remains central. Like individual imaginations, the collective imagination can be oriented towards the past (i.e., spontaneous memories of the collective past, as well as history or other more controlled versions of the past), or towards alternative realities, or towards the future. Here, however, we will only consider collective imaginations of the future. Second, the dimension of semiotic distance becomes less relevant here, because collective imaginations are diffused and distributed in many minds, using a wide variety of resources, and each of them may be more or less concrete or distanced. For example, the collective imagination of a socialist future involves very concrete ideas, such as equal income, and very abstract ideas, such as the idea of equality; it is thus impossible to define an overall or "average" semiotic distance. The third dimension—plausibility—is central, as it is the place through which groups and entities can exert their free determination or their power: deciding what is plausible is to decide the orientation of progress of a group. Of course, plausibility is changeable and different in various zones of the social field.

Now, we can consider our new dimension—namely, the extent to which a collective imagination is centralized or distributed, and thus, the social control exerted. At the extreme, control of imagination is centralized in a small number of social or political entities, which have a strong and unilateral power to define what can, should or should not be imagined by the other members of the society. At this extreme, they would control the production, availability, and circulation of cultural elements usable for imagining, and the social spaces in which imagination can be achieved. Their control would be unilateral, in the sense that the public sphere would be deprived of dialogical imagination: it ignores or does not tolerate the fact that members of the group or society have the capacity to imagine, using cultural elements in divergent ways or in spaces that escape from its control, and that these imaginings might be divergent from the one promoted by these sources of control. Techniques of control include censorship, a climate of fear leading to self-censorship, and at the extreme, silencing by incarceration. At that extreme, collective imagination is an imagination asymmetrically promoted by a few on the many; we call it "monological". Examples include imaginations controlled by a central party, an ultra-liberal market economy, an ideological hegemony, or a bureaucratic entity (Marková, 2016). At the other extreme, control is largely distributed among participants of the given sociocultural field. People can engage their personal and dialogical imagination with others, in the social settings of their choice, and produce and identify the cultural elements they wish. They may also question, contradict, or refuse certain elements or imaginings. Because of the distributed nature of the control and the symmetrical dynamics amongst actors, at this extreme, control is dialogical and collective imagination is an emergent property of a field (Marková, 2016). This dimension of control does have an affinity with Habermas's (1970, p. 205) concept of the public sphere in the sense that collective imaginations that are produced in a non-ideal public sphere could be described as "systematically distorted".

The second aspect that we need to introduce concerns the "valence" of these imaginings; that is, how these imaginings are attractive for a given group of people in a different field. Valences are relational and motivational; they designate how people will tend towards these imaginations, and therefore, organize their conduct so as to maintain and cultivate certain imaginations and even turn them into projects. Imaginations with positive valences for certain persons are utopian; imaginations of the future with negative valences are dystopian—that is, futures to be avoided. For instance, the projects of "urban garden" that are developed in many urban centres are carried by individual and collective initiatives, and are plausible enough for people to get committed to it and be attracted by the utopia of a green city.

Imaginations are always located in a specific time and context: we need to place collective imaginings in their historical sequences, within sociocultural fields that have their own historicity. In that sense, imaginations develop and die, and utopias can become dystopias. Accordingly, our argument is that collective imaginations have their own developmental trajectories within the multidimensional space of collective imagination that we have described. To illustrate our argument, we will present two examples: travel to the moon and socialism in the first half of the twentieth century.

Travelling to the Moon: From Distributed and Implausible to Centralized and Plausible

The moon has long been a projective canvas for human's collective imagination. The Ancient Greeks imagined the moon in terms of a goddess named Selene, daughter of Hyperion and Theia, and protagonist in several love affairs with both gods and mortals. A more plausible set of imaginations about the moon were introduced with the invention of the telescope. In 1609, Galilei observed that the moon is not smooth, and instead, had ravines, mountains, and craters. The idea that the moon was a landscape led to the quite concrete and positive imagination of being on the moon, walking on the moon, and inhabiting the moon.

Initially the imagined mode of transport to the moon was magical, including, dreams, magic and transportation by a flock of swans (Godwin, 1638/1971). However, it became much more plausible with Jules Verne's *From the Earth to the Moon* (1865/1993) and *Around the Moon* (1870/2012), which had a huge impact on the popular imagination of the moon. Specifically, Verne speculated that huge cannons might be able to shoot humans beyond the earth's gravity and thus to the moon. He also introduced the idea, later put into practice, of steering space projectiles by means of rocket power (McCurdy, 2011). The ideas introduced by Jules Verne were made visual and vivid by Georges Méliès, in his 1902 film, *Le Voyage dans la Lune* (Méliès, 1902). In his film, Méliès used a cannon to shoot his protagonists onto the moon. Once on the moon, these discovered a rugged and mountainous landscape, as described by Galilei. Incorporating prior ideas of new fauna and alien species, Méliès' film also included rapidly growing mushrooms and Selenites who exploded when hit. Méliès also had his protagonists observe the earth rise over the lunar landscape—a future defining feature of space imagination (Farr, 1999).

As with previous imaginings of the New World or alien worlds, *Le Voyage dans la Lune* was also a reflexive social comment on the society from which it emerged. Specifically, it can be seen as a comment on the attitude underlying scientific progress and imperialism. The explorers encounter an alien species, from which there could be so much to learn. However, rather than engage in any meaningful dialogue with the Selenites, the explorers discover that they are easily killed. They proceed to kill several, then they kill the Selenite king, and they return to earth with a Selenite—who is paraded and ridiculed in the streets, while the explorers are handed oversized medals for their triumph. The superior and aggressive attitude of the explorers, their disregard for everything of interest on the moon, and their disrespect of the Selenites is arguably a critique of European colonialism. *Le Voyage dans la Lune* reveals the stages of the loop of imagination. First, there are triggers, such as telescope imagery, the emerging techniques of film, and concerns about colonialism. Second, cultural resources are utilized, such as specific ideas and tropes about the moon and space travel. Third, we see how the imagination of an individual—in this case, Georges Méliès—exists within a larger collective imagination which spans many decades. The consequences of this loop of imagination range from the short to the long term. In a most immediate sense, Méliès' film excited audiences across Europe and the United States. However, over a longer term, with its positive valence, it provided an early template for thinking about a moon landing.

The anxieties of the Cold War period provided another trigger for a much more programmatic imagination about the moon and space in general. During the 1930s and 1940s, technological advances in rocketry moved science closer to travelling to the moon, but the idea did not fully catch the public imagination. However, in 1957, the Union of the Soviet Socialist Republics (USSR) successfully put a satellite into orbit. The impact on the global imagination was unexpectedly immense. Sputnik 1 was not designed to gather data; rather, it was designed to broadcast an open-channel radio signal, to prove that the USSR had a satellite in orbit. Orbiting the Earth every hour and a half, its verifiable signature sound heralded the start of the space race. This unknown quantity hurtling above at 29,000 kilometres per hour was an open canvas (McCurdy, 2011): Was the satellite spying? Could it fall from the sky? Was the satellite carrying a nuclear weapon? In the United States, the Dow Jones fell over 10% and Eisenhower saw his popularity fall over 20 points. The number of UFO sightings in the United States in the months before Sputnik 1 was 46 per month, while immediately after, it was over 200 sightings per month (Condon, 1969). In short, Cold War anxieties provided a massive trigger, or spur, to the imagination of manned space flight.

The emergence of the space race marked the shift of imaginings about the moon from being distributed and unregulated towards becoming more centralized and guided. When, in 1961, President Kennedy announced that the United States would put a person on the moon (despite there being little more practical or scientific benefit to such an achievement than using sensors or remote devices), he was leading the charge in a governmental interest in how the moon was imagined. The space race led the governments in both the United States and the USSR to invest money in promoting, on the one hand, the utopic dream of conquering space, and on the other hand, the dystopic fear of losing the "space race".

The technologies that the United States and USSR utilized to generate particular imaginings around space and to propagate these through their respective communities were diverse. Posters, television programmes, leaflets, children's toys, educational courses, celebrity status, awards, medals, ceremonies, art, and even stamps were used to stabilize and focus the collective imagination. Figure 2.1 shows a 1962 stamp from the United States. Project Mercury was the national plan to have an astronaut orbit Earth. Although the United States succeeded in this task, the USSR was the first to achieve this milestone by a narrow margin. Figure 2.2 shows a 1967 stamp from the USSR. This stamp depicts people on the moon, a milestone to be achieved by the United States in 1969.

The trigger to the centralized imaginings about the moon in the USA and the USSR was the Cold War in general, and the space race in particular. This trigger, when combined with the rich resources of previous imaginings (i.e., Verne, Miles, etc.) and the technological potentials of the post-war period (i.e., computing and rockets), led to huge investments to make the implausible plausible. It is estimated that, normalized to 2010 values (i.e., adjusted for inflation), the USA invested more than 100 billion dollars in the moon landing (Lafleur, 2010). Such investments could

Fig. 2.1 1962 USA stamp, 4 cents, "U.S. Man in space. Project Mercury" (USA stamps no copyright before 1978. https://commons.wikimedia.org/wiki/File:Project_Mercury_1962_Issue-4c.jpg)

Fig. 2.2 1967 USSR stamp, 6 kopeks, "Space science fiction. On the moon" (No copyright on USSR stamps. https://commons.wikimedia.org/wiki/File:1967_CPA_3546_(2).jpg)

only be made because the public participated in the collective imagination of the space race and the future possible significance of the moon landing.

Our collective imagination of the moon, in the context of the space race, reveals how centralized collective imaginations can grow out of decentralized distributed imaginations, and in turn, how these centrally promoted imaginations can feed back into more distributed imaginations. For example, the moon landings have been the focus of alternative interpretations and conspiracy theories. Also, thinking specifically of the space race, it is evident that utopian visions go hand in hand with dystopian imaginings. While the imagination of the moon was certainly attractive, the idea for either side of losing the space race was repelling.

Imagining Socialism: From Distributed to Centralized but with Polarizing Valence

Another trajectory of collective imagination is that related to socialism as a political programme. Socialism as a project for a class-free, equalitarian society can be seen as, initially, an emergent utopia. Present in many novels and stories, the possibility of a life where people would all be equal, cooperating and sharing their resources, was developed in the work of authors such as Gerrard Winstanley in the seventeenth century, Jean-Jacques Rousseau in the eighteenth century, and in the first quarter of the nineteenth century, by Charles Fourier in France (Fourier, 1829) and Robert Owen in the United Kingdom (Owen, 1991). These authors were part of general intellectual movements developed in Germany, France, and the United Kingdom that inspired authors such as Karl Marx and Friedrich Engels—both widely read in Greek philosophy. Hence, for a very long time, experiences of cooperative or equalitarian communities were either imagined and debated, or freely experienced by small groups, among which religious communities. To develop these shared yet collective imaginations, a strong conceptual analysis was provided by Karl Marx and Friedrich Engels's reflexion on the emerging capitalist society. They then wrote their *Communist Manifesto* in 1847, and had it published in 1848 for a meeting of the, at that time, secret German Communist party (Marx & Engels, 1969).

When, later, the Russian Revolution started in 1917, first to overthrow Emperor Nikolai II, then under the command of the Bolsheviks, to install a proletarian power in place, the ideas promoted by Marx and Engels became an inspiration for a political system—although the practicalities of the system had to be fully defined. Various attempts were made and different policies implemented, supported by a strongly future-oriented ideology. To shape the imagination of the future, the political authorities reedited various science fiction books, both local and foreign (such as works by G. Orwell and Jules Verne; Lovell, 2009, p. 20). Under Stalin from 1928 on, the materialization of these ideas became stronger, and also more centrally controlled; alternative cultural elements were suppressed (e.g., Churches destroyed), and the semiosphere started to be built in a redundant manner—from urban architecture to official arts. Writers, film-makers, and artists had to narrate and make the "Soviet dream" convincingly imaginable (Lovell, 2009, pp. 22–23). In the 1930s, the history of the beginning of the Soviet society started to be rewritten according to political goals, and Soviet communism redefined as a national project, rather than an international movement. Next to this work of imagination, of course, the communist regime implemented important industrial reforms, and a very strong controlling apparatus—first, the Tcheka; then, the KGB, whose role was to identify people that did not fit with the system (because of their background, opinions they may have expressed, or different imaginings they might have externalized), and to isolate, control, or transform them (in prisons, the Gulag, etc.). Yet, even so, until the end of communism, the political regime sponsored (e.g., in science and art) and promoted (e.g., in education and propaganda) versions of the radiant, equal, and advanced future to come (for example, in Fig. 2.3 the chimneys are valorized as leading to a glorious future).

In this example, the trigger for change is a combination of long-standing wars and inequalities in Russia, dissatisfaction with the emperor, and a series of complex political events, together with the long-standing presence of revolutionary literature. Communism developed as collective imagination—first, diffuse and spontaneous, and progressively, more and

Fig. 2.3 "Smoke of chimneys is the breath of Soviet Russia" (1917–1921) (No copyright on Russia for posters before 1942, and per extension in the USA. https://commons.wikimedia.org/wiki/File:Smoke_of_chimneys_is_the_breath_of_Soviet_Russia.jpg)

more controlled by a centralized power. The future to come was meant to attract and motivate the whole of society, and accordingly, the utopic imagery organized the whole field.

Although the USA and USSR were allies during WWII, in the post-war years a strong anti-communist imagination was cultivated in the USA. This period was called the "Second Red scare" (the first one taking place during the Great Depression in the early 1930s) and referred to as McCarthyism after Wisconsin Senator Joseph McCarthy (Storrs, 2015, p. 2). McCarthyism was a centralized and emotionally charged imagination of a communist infiltration of American society (see, for instance, Fig. 2.4), in great part fostered by a State-commissioned institution, the FBI. During the Cold War, McCarthyism led to systematic screenings of the population, with many people being blacklisted, censured, and interned on suspicion of espionage or collaboration with the Soviet Union: "During the program's peak between 1947 and 1956, more than five million federal workers underwent loyalty screening, resulting in an estimated 2,700 dismissals and 12,000 resignations" (Storrs, 2015, p. 8). Authorities especially screened the Arts; a list of suspect cinema artists was created, known as the "Hollywood blacklist", denying access to work to actors, directors, and other cinema professionals. Interviews with suspects appear totally scripted and staged, denying people the right to defend themselves. Also, librarian activities were controlled and books burned (Storrs, 2015).

Hence, in this case, we could say that the collective imagination in Russia triggered a counter-imagination in the USA. There, we can observe another variation of controlled, monological collective imagination of the future. Only this time, the future has to be avoided—a possible communist USA is the repelling organizer of the sociocultural field. Ironically, some of the mechanisms by which this communist-free imagination was implemented were very similar to the mechanisms used by the USSR to foster the utopian imagination of communism: control of the production of cultural elements, control of their mode of diffusion, and control over their access, as well as silencing people who maintained a different voice.

To summarize, the collective imagination of the future of socialism can be described as having undertaken a series of mutations and bifurcations. Starting as an emerging, distributed and dialogical utopia, socialism

Fig. 2.4 Cover to the propaganda comic book "Is This tomorrow" (1947) (Public domain, By Catechetical Guild (Catechetical Guild) [Public domain], https://commons.wikimedia.org/wiki/File:Is_this_tomorrow.jpg?uselang=fr)

encouraged people and groups to work for a better society, producing a great number of texts presenting these ideas. Then, after the trigger of the revolution, once implemented as political regime in the USSR, socialism became a controlled collective imagination, creating and diffusing the cultural elements nourishing that imagination, and suppressing and destroying the possibility of alternatives; even so, it remained a positive utopia, a goal to achieve. Interestingly, from the perspective of the USA, the valence was flipped over: the "same" content of an imagination appeared as radically repelling, and another centralized control shaped it as dystopia, being the future that must be guarded against.

Discussion

Humans are actively oriented towards goals, understood as a broad range of imagined future states, and as such, any understanding of human behaviour needs to take account of human imagination of the future. Imagining the future, however, is only in a narrow sense a solitary cognitive act. Each individual's imagination of the future is a reconfiguration of past experiences and imaginations; the horizon of our individual futures is set by our community of imagination (Zittoun & Gillespie, 2016).

So powerful is the imagination of the future in corralling human behaviour that it inevitably becomes political and potentially ideological. Accordingly, when considering the collective imagination of the future, it is imperative to interrogate the provenance of an imagination, the resources used in its construction, the institutions promoting it, and its consequences. Arguably, a core concern should always be evidence of a narrowing of the collective imagination; that is, any closing off of the alternatives that might become resources either for future imaginings or critique. In this sense, a healthy community of imagination is diverse, a rich treasure trove of cultural elements, the building blocks of human potential.

In the present chapter, we have used a sociocultural model of imagination, focused on the collective imagination of the future, to describe and analyse two case studies. Figure 2.5 depicts the movement of these collective imaginations in a two-dimensional space of distributed-centralized and implausible-plausible. Both imaginings began as implausible and distributed, both became more plausible as they were centralized and

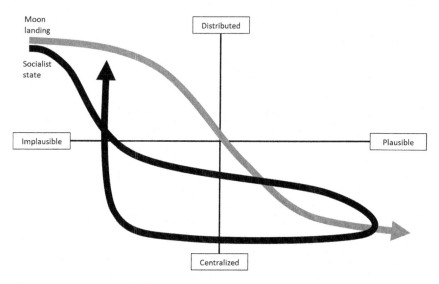

Fig. 2.5 Trajectories of collective imagination of the future in a two-dimensional space (copyright authors)

resources were put behind instituting the given imagination. Both imaginations were achieved, but the trajectory of socialism arguably became more implausible through its institutionalization and centralization, ultimately collapsing back into a distributed and implausible set of imaginings. Of course, Fig. 2.5 is highly simplistic. Arguably, we should have separate lines for imaginings in the USA and USSR (or indeed, separate lines for the heterogeneous groups within each society). However, the aim of Fig. 2.5 is not to represent these collective imaginings exhaustively, but rather, to illustrate how trajectories of collective imagination can be conceptualized using the proposed multidimensional model. For example, one could point out the role of key moments in history (e.g., the Sputnik orbit, President Kennedy's speech committing to a moon landing, or Glasnost) that shape the trajectory.

Sociocultural psychology is particularly suited for studying how groups imagine their own future. First, the imagined future, despite exerting material changes on the present, is an entirely semiotic construction (Salvatore, 2016; Toomela, 2003; Valsiner, 1999, 2009; Zittoun et al., 2013). Accordingly, any understanding of imagined futures needs to focus on the content and semiotic dynamics of those imaginings, including how embodied feelings and images combine and recombine to create images of the future that motivate behaviour. Second, to understand how groups imagine their future requires a model of how individual subjectivities (loops of imagination) are related to and supported, hindered, or subtly guided by broader social factors such as the cultural elements available, the social valences ascribed to given images of the future, and technologies of imagination that can selectively cultivate, amplify, and project particular imaginings (Zittoun & Gillespie, 2016). Again, sociocultural psychology has the conceptual tools for understanding this intersection between individual subjectivities and societal forces. Third, sociocultural psychology has a methodological toolkit that enables both the close and detailed study of semiotic processes at the level of the individual, as they unfold in a specific context and time, and also the more macro-structure of ideas as they relate to collectives and broader sociocultural processes (Toomela & Valsiner, 2010; Valsiner, Marsico, Chaudhary, Sato, & Dazzani, 2016). However, although sociocultural psychology is moving towards more complex phenomena, it has so far been very hesitant to address social and political changes (but see Wagoner, Jensen, & Oldmeadow, 2012).

Within the frame of sociocultural psychology, we have argued that the study of collective imagination, especially of the future, needs to be attuned to the political forces shaping the trajectory of imagination. Finance, uprising, propaganda, censorship, and silencing dissenting voices are all techniques used to centralize and institutionalize particular imaginings about the future. We have also tried to emphasize, in the case studies, how collective imaginations do not occur in isolation. In both case studies, the imaginations cultivated in the USA and the USSR were reacting to each other. The imagination of the moon landing, which became particularly strong in the USA, was a reaction to the USSR having an early lead in the "space race". The case of socialism is even more striking; the same phenomenon (i.e., socialism) was represented with entirely opposing valences in the USA and USSR. While there was broad agreement on the positive valence of landing on the moon, there was outright opposition to the valence of socialism. This demonstrates, as mentioned above, that valence is more about the relation that an individual or group has to an imagination than a quality of the imagination itself (although, of course, such strong valences shape how the phenomenon is imagined).

In this chapter, we have used the theoretical assumptions, concepts, and methods of sociocultural psychology to conceptualize collective imaginations of the future. Although we have here examined two cases of past collective imaginations, we call for more careful studies of current emerging imaginations of the future, and the social forces that are supporting, channelling, or silencing these trajectories. In this way, sociocultural psychology can use its strengths to address the mutual construction of individual and collective trajectories of imagination in the contemporary world, with all its ideological and political underpinnings, and perhaps help us to foster an imagination of the future that has positive valences for all.

References

Bilefsky, D. (2009, November 15). Czechs' Velvet Revolution paved by plastic people. *The New York Times*. Retrieved from http://www.nytimes.com/2009/11/16/world/europe/16iht-czech.html

Bren, P. (2010). *The Greengrocer and his TV: The culture of communism after the 1968 Prague Spring*. Ithaca, NY: Cornell University Press.

Brown, V. R., & Paulus, P. B. (2002). Making group brainstorming more effective: Recommendations from an associative memory perspective. *Current Directions in Psychological Science, 11*(6), 208–212.

Condon, E. U. (1969). *Scientific study of unidentified flying objects* (E. U. Condon & D. S. Gillmor, Eds.). New York: Bantam Books, 1. Retrieved from http://adsabs.harvard.edu/abs/1969ssuf.book.....C

Day, B. (1999). *The velvet philosophers*. London: Continuum.

Farr, R. M. (1999). *The curved nature of the earth's surface: The Apollo 11 mission to land a man on the moon*. Paper presented at the London School of Economics, Department of Social Psychology, London.

Fourier, C. (1829). *Le nouveau monde industriel et sociétaire: ou Invention du procédé d'industrie attrayante et naturelle distribuée en séries passionnées* [The new industrial and societary world. Or: invention of an attractive and natural industrial procedure distributed in passionate series]. Paris: Bossange père.

Freud, S. (2001). On dreams (1901). In *The complete psychological works of Sigmund Freud* (Vol. 5, New ed., pp. 631–714). London: Vintage Classics.

Gillespie, A., Corti, K., & Heasman, B. (2018). Imagining the self through cultural technologies. In T. Zittoun & V. P. Glăveanu (Eds.), *Handbook of imagination & culture* (pp. 301–318). Oxford: Oxford University Press.

Godwin, F. (1971). *The man in the moon* (Original 1638). Menston: Scolar press.

Habermas, J. (1970). On systematically distorted communication. *Inquiry, 13*, 205–218.

Harris, P. L. (2000). *The work of the imagination*. Oxford: Blackwell Publishing.

Havel, V. (1988). *Letters to Olga*. New York: Knopf.

Hilppö, J. A., Rajala, A., Zittoun, T., Kumpulainen, K., & Lipponen, L. (2016). Interactive dynamics of imagination in a science classroom. *Frontline Learning Research, 4*(4), 20–29.

Karwowski, M., & Soszynski, M. (2008). How to develop creative imagination?: Assumptions, aims and effectiveness of Role Play Training in Creativity (RPTC). *Thinking Skills and Creativity, 3*(2), 163–171.

Klíma, I. (2013). *My crazy century. A memoir* (C. Cravens, Trans.). New York: Grove Press.

Lafleur, C. (2010). *The space review: Costs of US piloted programs [The space review]*. Retrieved from http://www.thespacereview.com/article/1579/1

Lovell, S. (2009). *The Soviet Union: A very short introduction* (1st ed.). Oxford/New York: Oxford University Press.

Marková, I. (2016). *The dialogical mind: Common sense and ethics*. Cambridge, UK: Cambridge University Press.

Marx, K., & Engels, F. (1969). Manifesto of the Communist Party. In S. Moore (Trans.), *Marx/Engels selected works* (Orignal publication 1848, Vol. 1, pp. 98–137). Moscow: Progress Publishers. Retrieved from https://www.marxists.org/archive/marx/works/download/pdf/Manifesto.pdf

McCurdy, H. E. (2011). *Space and the American imagination*. Baltimore: Johns Hopkins University Press.

Méliès, G. (1902). *Le voyage dans la lune*.

Owen, R. (1991). *A new view of society and other writings* (G. Claeys, Ed.). London/New York: Penguin Classics.

Pelaprat, E., & Cole, M. (2011). 'Minding the gap': Imagination, creativity and human cognition. *Integrative Psychological and Behavioral Science, 45*, 397–418. https://doi.org/10.1007/s12124-011-9176-5.

Salvatore, S. (2016). *Psychology in black and white. The project of a theory driven science*. Charlotte, NC: Information Age Publishing, Incorporated.

Singer, D. G., & Singer, J. L. (1992). *The house of make-believe: Children's play and the developing imagination* (Reprint). Cambridge, MA: Harvard University Press.

Storrs, L. R. Y. (2015, July 2). McCarthyism and the second red scare. In J. Butler (Ed.), *Oxford research encyclopedia of American history*. New York: Oxford University Press. Retrieved from http://americanhistory.oxfordre.com/view/10.1093/acrefore/9780199329175.001.0001/acrefore-9780199329175-e-6

Toomela, A. (Ed.). (2003). *Cultural guidance in the development of the human mind*. Westport, CT: Ablex Publishing Corporation.

Toomela, A., & Valsiner, J. (Eds.). (2010). *Methodological thinking in psychology: 60 years gone astray?* Greenwich, CT: Information Age Publishing.

Valsiner, J. (1999). I create you to control me: A glimpse into basic processes of semiotic mediation. *Human Development, 42*(1), 26–30. https://doi.org/10.1159/000022606.

Valsiner, J. (2009). Between fiction and reality: Transforming the semiotic object. *Sign System Studies, 37*(1/2), 99–113.

Valsiner, J., Marsico, G., Chaudhary, N., Sato, T., & Dazzani, V. (Eds.). (2016). *Psychology as the science of human being: The Yokohama Manifesto*. Cham: Springer International Publishing. Retrieved from http://link.springer.com/10.1007/978-3-319-21094-0.

Verne, J. G. (1993). *From the earth to the moon* (Original 1865). New York: Bantam Classics.

Verne, J. G. (2012). *Around the moon* (Original 1870). New York: Kassock Book.

Vygotsky, L. S. (1933). *Play and its role in the mental developmental of the child*. Retrieved July 22, 2010, from http://www.cddc.vt.edu/marxists/archive/vygotsky/works/1933/play.htm

Wagoner, B., Jensen, E., & Oldmeadow, J. A. (Eds.). (2012). *Culture and social change: Transforming society through the power of ideas*. Charlotte, NC: Information Age Pub.

Welzer, H. (2005). *Grandpa wasn't a nazi: The Holocaust in German family remembrance*. New York: American Jewish Committee.

Welzer, H. (2008). Collateral damage of history education: National Socialism and the Holocaust in German family memory. *Social Research, 75*(1), 287–314.

Welzer, H., Moller, S., & Tschuggnall, K. (2013). *'Grand-père n'était pas un nazi'. National-socialisme et Shoah dans la mémoire familiale* (Original German edition 2002). Paris: Gallimard.

Winnicott, D. W. (1996). *Therapeutic consultations in child psychiatry* (New ed.). London: Karnac Books.

Zantovsky, M. (2015). *Havel: A life.* London: Atlantic Books.

Zittoun, T. (2018). The Velvet revolution of land and minds. In B. Wagoner, F. M. Moghaddam, & J. Valsiner (Eds.), *The psychology of radical social change: From rage to revolution* (pp. 140–158). Cambridge: Cambridge University Press.

Zittoun, T., & Cerchia, F. (2013). Imagination as expansion of experience. *Integrative Psychological and Behavioral Science, 47*(3), 305–324. https://doi.org/10.1007/s12124-013-9234-2.

Zittoun, T., & de Saint-Laurent, C. (2015). Life-creativity: Imagining one's life. In V. P. Glăveanu, A. Gillespie, & J. Valsiner (Eds.), *Rethinking creativity: Contributions from cultural psychology* (pp. 58–75). Hove/New York: Routledge.

Zittoun, T., & Gillespie, A. (2016). *Imagination in human and cultural development.* London: Routledge.

Zittoun, T., Valsiner, J., Vedeler, D., Salgado, J., Gonçalves, M., & Ferring, D. (2013). *Human development in the lifecourse. Melodies of living.* Cambridge: Cambridge University Press.

3

Framing the Issue: Literature, Collective Imagination, and Fan Activism

Kevin R. Carriere

In this chapter, I examine how literature is a tool under which the collective can frame their imagination, leading to social change. In doing so, it is perhaps best to start our discussion of imagination with a quote from a novel. In the quote below, our main character, Harry Potter, is in an imagined dream world with a teacher, perplexed if his current experience is real or not. The teacher responds:

> *Of course it is happening inside your head, Harry, but why on earth should that mean it is not real?* (Rowling, 2007, p. 723)

They share this mental space together, and together, they mold the present and future Harry will inevitably face in the pages to come. Through this imaginative process in reflecting about his life, his friends, and his foes, Harry makes decisions about his future alongside others. His imagination of the future—of the friends waiting for him, of those

---

K. R. Carriere (✉)
Georgetown University, Washington, DC, USA
e-mail: krc58@georgetown.edu

© The Author(s) 2018
C. de Saint-Laurent et al. (eds.), *Imagining Collective Futures*, Palgrave Studies in Creativity and Culture, https://doi.org/10.1007/978-3-319-76051-3_3

who died to save him, of those who are not yet born—is shared not only by the speaker, but by everyone who existed with him. Harry is at the same time alone but yet completely surrounded by others. His vision of a new world is necessarily collective, and together with the rest of the Wizarding World, Harry will create a new vision for a future without his mortal enemy.

How do we define this kind of imaginative process Harry embarked on? We imagine what life would have been like, could have been like, will soon be like—all without moving a muscle. Secluded and silent, it stays within our minds. Yet, the quote above reminds us that just because something happens inside of ourselves does not negate its reality. Instead, our imagination, as both individuals and groups, fosters real action—real change. We imagine the mind of the other and we adjust our interactions based on how we imagine they will respond. We imagine the future and then build huge skyscrapers and works of art. Imagination is completely within, yet at the same time, tied intricately to the social world (Zittoun & Gillespie, Chap. 2, this volume).

In this chapter, I will focus on the collective imagination and its relation to literature. First, I will define *collective imagination* as a contextualized, socialized, and historical psychological process by which groups make meaning of an uncertain world across the past, present, and future. I will use two case studies—a historical reflection on *The Jungle*, as well as qualitative interviews with members of the *Harry Potter Alliance*. Both cases will be used to show how literature can create and maintain collective imaginations by providing readymade schemas under which we can interpret and understand the present and reimagine the future.

Imagination

Imagination has been defined around a psychological function that enables manipulation of meanings within experiences (Tateo, 2015). Yet, imagination also expands our experience (Pultz & Hviid, 2018) through creativity and aesthetics (Glaveanu, Karwowski, Jankowska, & de Saint-Laurent, 2017; Zittoun & Gillespie, 2016). When Vygotsky wrote on imagination, he wrote that "the richer a person's experiences, the richer is the material his imagination has access to" (Vygotsky, 1990, p. 15).

But imagination is not based on a single individual's experiences. We imagine the future as told to us by our leaders. We imagine the wonders and terrors promised by campaigns. We demonize the other and rally to restore humanity. There is a systemic structure—a political, social, cultural, historical system of prior imaginations that inform our current and future imaginations. We imagine not merely as single units living in side-by-side realities, but a collective whole that engages, challenges, and develops alongside millions of other imaginations (Glaveanu & de Saint-Laurent, 2015).

Imagination develops not simply alongside the collective, but *with and through* the collective. While we can find similarities in collective imaginations across time (for example, the terminology within nationalistic rhetoric is easily traced through the years with slight variations), the makeup of that imagination is ever changing. While technological advancements may change the nature of our fears of spying from the neighbor across the street, to surveillance, and now, email security, the imaginative overtones of "loose lips sink ships" continues throughout time. We cross the border between what is, what was, and what could be. We grapple with the uncertainty of not knowing which future will arise, and allow our imagination to contextualize these meanings in a way that makes sense (Abbey & Valsiner, 2005).

When we imagine, we are shifting our perspectives. Whether it is a time-based perspective, an individual-perspective, or a collective-group perspective, we use these new perspectives to consider future outcomes in our lives (Mead, 1938). These perspectives are built around and with others (Martin, 2006). It is not simply two individuals listening to the same political rhetoric, but our combined understanding and display of this rhetoric while listening and being an engaged social creature surrounded by other social creatures. This duality of simultaneously experiencing the same imagination is a building block of intersubjective understanding (Rommetveit, 1992).

Perspective-taking and perspective-making are important for imaginative processes (c.f. Glăveanu, Chap. 5, this volume). We learn how to take the perspective of the other in a variety of ways beyond imagination. We observe our parents, our friends, and media characters. Our children form parasocial relationships with characters (Schmid & Klimmt, 2011), where they gain one-sided, emotionally tinged friendships that assist in children's development (Calvert & Richards, 2014) and increase feelings of belonging. One of the areas in which parasocial relationships can form is literature.

Imagination as Literature

Literature can be many things. It can be autobiographical, where the writer tells us about their own lives. It can be fantasy worlds filled with dragons and sorcerers and medieval knights. Even research is literature (Lordelo, 2015)—a story is told to explain a given outcome and potential reasons for why that outcome occurred. Literature shapes and influences our perspectives through continuous expansions on the meanings of literature. Movie theaters play the screen adaptation of *Nineteen Eighty-Four* in protest of a government against the media. Sarah Palin, a vice-presidential candidate in 2004, was lambasted for being unable to name a newspaper she frequently read. Propaganda, written media, even religious texts are constantly reinterpreted for an individual's own goals to do great, selfless deeds on one end or horrible acts of suicide bombings on the other end.

We learn how we are meant to act alongside literature. We learn empathy and guilt as the characters deal with complex moral issues (Nikolajeva, 2012). We learn of being open to novelty in *Green Eggs and Ham*, of providing a voice to the voiceless in *Horton Hears a Who*, and of the tragedy of love in *Romeo and Juliet*. For example, take the passage below from *The Kite Runner*, where the main character hides in his war-torn country.

> We stayed huddled that way until the early hours of the morning. The shootings and explosions had lasted less than an hour, but they had frightened us badly, because none of us had ever heard gunshots in the streets. They were foreign sounds to us then. The generation of Afghan children whose ears would know nothing but the sounds of bombs and gunfire was not yet born. Huddled together in the dining room and waiting for the sun to rise, none of us had any notion that a way of life had ended. (Hosseini, 2003 p. 36)

We understand the terror of war and the life-changing experiences it can have on our children by taking the perspective of Amir. Literature facilitates these feelings of continuity and strength, self-esteem and courage, uniqueness and group cohesion (Lyons, 1996). While we may have no actual experience of war, we can use literature to explore these boundaries and imagine what it would be like to be Amir, to be huddled in the corner, scared of the loud explosions so nearby. We learn of group relations, of caring for others, of the effects our actions can have on others.

This is not to say that literature is unidirectional in its nature—strictly influencing human action as an independent variable. The authors of literature are influenced by the culture they live in. The experiences, emotional states, and personal opinions of the authors all come in to mediate the eventual outcome and meanings within a piece of work. Fact or fiction, literature teaches us about who we (as readers) are, and who they (as writers and characters) were (c.f. Moghaddam, 2004).

But beyond all of that, literature shows us who we are as imaginative beings. As a cultural carrier, it provides a pathway through which the values and normative ideals of a society are handed down to the next generation (Jaspal, Carriere, & Moghaddam, 2016). From the *Odyssey* to *Shakespeare* to *Of Mice and Men*, the novels and writings of a culture expose us not only to what was important at that moment of creation, but at the same time, provide lessons to the reader that stand the test of time. They anchor us to both the past, present, and future by providing lessons that define the normative systems that develop and influence further imaginations. Texts such as fairy tales serve a heuristic function in our society as ways to manage typical anxieties and problems (Jones, 2002). The exposure to mythical (or realistic) worlds of various complexities teaches the nature of the social norms that surround us (Manderson, 2003).

Literature as Future-Forward Imagination

Literature enables us to explore the unknown—to test new boundaries and taboos (c.f. Parry & Light, 2014, on *Fifty Shades of Grey*), to imagine a changed future if history had been different (*Nineteen Eighty-Four* was written as if communist Russia had taken over Britain c.f. Shelden, 1996), or to travel into magical worlds and escape reality (Usherwood & Toyne, 2002). The ability to imagine utopias (Jovchelovitch & Hawlina, Chap. 7, this volume) can push us to consider new (and many times, taboo) ways of life. In Ireland, *Brave New World* was at one point banned for its portrayal of sexual promiscuity (Sova, 2006). In the United States, heavy influences around educational policies has created severe arenas of censorship in the education of our children and the literature they are exposed to (Lehr, 2010).

Expanding on this, Collie (2011) argues that science fiction can be used to explore futuristic urban planning. Urban planning should "engage with communities and connect them through story-telling to both the history and the future of the places" (Collie, 2011, p. 430). Her analysis of cyberpunk stories of author William Gibson develops the border from what currently *is* to considerations of what *could be*. The border-crossing nature of literature (Lordelo, 2015) allows us to re-reflect on what we thought was real—both in space, and ourselves. We develop our self-concept (how we see ourselves) by comparing ourselves to others, and characters in literature are no different in this regard. For example, in one study, women who were engaged in a fictional story about motherhood, and who had no children of their own, increased their reported femininity compared to those who were not engaged in the story or those who were mothers (Richter, Appel, & Calio, 2014). More than spaces or individuals, we can use literature to reflect on our collective self-concept. Reflection is an impetus for social change, pushing us to make changes we want to see in ourselves and the greater world.

The power of dystopian novels lies in their ability to make us consider the benefits and dangers of the world we currently live in—the perfections of imperfection. Whether that is our knowledge of pain and suffering that does not exist in *The Giver*, the importance of self-restraint and truth in the hedonistic *Brave New World*, or the value of a free press and democratic government in *Nineteen Eighty-Four*, literature helps us reflect on the positives and negatives of our world. We seek the love found in *Romeo and Juliet*, admire the adventurous eye of *Don Quixote*, and try and gain the wisdom of Atticus in *To Kill a Mockingbird*. By imagining the characters of these stories, groups can see both the good and the bad of both the imagined world and the world they live in.

Imagination's power is in its ability to help us clarify uncertainty in our lives. And when we live in a socially constructed world with limited information, even the most basic of facts—what are we eating—can be inherently ambiguous and uncertain. In the following section, I will highlight a case in which literature helped the collective imagine their own lives as they were living it. This case of self-reflection through literature brought the collective together in a single voice to express their outrage, demand change, and then achieve it.

The Case of The Jungle

In 1906, Upton Sinclair published *The Jungle*. The novel is about a Lithuanian immigrant, Jurgis Rudkus, who attempts to live the American dream in Chicago. Yet, the world is not what Jurgis thought—his job at the local meat factory cannot pay the rent and his family struggles to survive. His father dies from unsafe conditions, his child dies from malnourishment, and the conditions at work cause further tension and conflict within his family. The novel ends with Jurgis alone, a laborer still struggling to survive. A harrowing tale of the struggles of the working class, *The Jungle* speaks to the American worker and the cycle of poverty that is so difficult to escape.

Yet, even as Sinclair tried to highlight the plight of workers, his eye-opening descriptions of the conditions at the factory were what caught the public's eye. Sinclair had spent two months in 1904 in Chicago, observing the meat factories and conditions that existed at the time (Bloodworth, 2008). In his quest to engage the reader with the struggles of the factory life, Sinclair's descriptions of the meat-handling process, such as the one below, were enough to make even the strongest stomach queasy.

> The meat would be shoveled into carts, and the man who did the shoveling would not trouble to lift out a rat even when he saw one—there were things that went into the sausage in comparison with which a poisoned rat was a tidbit. There was no place for the men to wash their hands before

they ate their dinner, and so they made a practice of washing them in the water that was to be ladled into the sausage... Every spring they did it; and in the barrels would be dirt and rust and old nails and stale water—and cartload after cartload of it would be taken up and dumped into the hoppers with fresh meat, and sent out to the public's breakfast. (Sinclair, 1906a, pp. 161–162)

Some authors claim Sinclair's depiction of the factory standards were overdramatized and untrue (Wade, 1991, 2008). While the Department of Agriculture eventually released the famous Reynolds-Neill Report (H.R. Rep. No 59-873, 1906) under which they outlined many of the deficiencies that Sinclair wrote about, Reynolds himself was unable to corroborate the stories of any of the witnesses Sinclair had sent to the investigators (Conditions in Chicago Stock Yards, 1906). Yet, even if the truth is debatable and the lines between fact and fiction become blurred, the fact is that the public responded. Letters poured into the White House, demanding investigation into the allegations made by Sinclair (Davis, 2010), and Sinclair soon became an international bestseller, receiving praise from Winston Churchill (Churchill, 2008), and bringing attention to the factory conditions in Chicago and around the United States (Schlosser, 2008).

When Sinclair wrote his tale, he wrote to emphasize the benefits of socialism. Jurgis, at the end of the book, finds himself joining a socialist party and observing political victories—at the tune of "an increase [in votes] of something like three hundred and fifty percent in four years" (Sinclair, 1906a, p. 411). And yet, when the collective read his work, the benefits of socialism were not the target of their imaginative futures. Instead, the public responded against the outcry of the working conditions, demanding a future in which they would know what was in the food they were consuming. *The Jungle* was a pivotal piece in moving the American public to construct a new version of their consumerist identity. No longer were they willing to be ignorant of their products, but instead demanded that the knowledge of what they were putting inside their bodies be made available for all citizens (Pickavance, 2003).

And their rights were indeed fulfilled. Only six months after the release of *The Jungle*, The Pure Food and Drug Act (1906) was enacted into law.

This law made it a misdemeanor for failure to truthfully brand and label the ingredients in all food products, and it was soon followed by the Meat Inspection Act (1907), which required visual inspection of any animal carcass that crossed state lines. This chapter is not meant to be a legal debate on the efficacy of these laws (for further, see Roots, 2001), but instead, to exemplify how literature can assist the public in making real change. Only six months were required—and only 26 days after President Roosevelt wrote a letter to Congress (H.R. Rep. No 59-873, 1906) to enact the law.

In this case, *The Jungle* helped the public imagine a new future—one with proper labelling of what they were eating. While earlier, the nature of their food was left to the public's imagination, the (possibly pseudo)-realities of the conditions of the factories captured this imagination and flipped it on its head. Imagination shifted their perspective of reality, creating a case of cognitive dissonance. On the one hand, they believed their food was healthy, but on the other hand, their experiences reading *The Jungle* forced them to face the fact that this may not be an accurate belief. This created a need to change the present in order to properly align their original beliefs with reality.

Ironically, this case also reveals the potential limits of imagination. Sinclair's goal in writing this literary work was to inspire a collective imagination of socialism. While imagination can motivate collective action, it cannot immediately change the status quo if the status quo is as rigid as the political system. Capitalism's pressure, and hardships faced by the working class, were not the concern in the eyes of the public—instead, it was just a backdrop for the more pressing concern of food processing and handling. While we can look at cases such as the Arab Spring as examples of collective imagination attempting to make significant change, sometimes even they fail and new measures must be taken instead (c.f. Maarek & Awad, Chap. 10, this volume).

While for *The Jungle*, literature was able to shift the perspective of its readers to be more critical of the food in their lives, many times, the point of literature is to move us outside of our perspectives entirely and into magical worlds and advanced technology. We take these new, unique, and imaginative worlds and apply them to our own lives, collectively imagining new meanings toward a new future. In this way, when we imagine, it is not simply imagining through reading the text and picturing the story, but instead, we can imagine new lives through the meanings and messages gained from the literature itself.

The Case of Fan Activism

In the prior section, I illustrated a case in which literature itself informed individuals to imagine collective futures by highlighting the tragedies of factory life in the 1900s. However, literature does not simply act on individuals—we act *through* literature. Many times, it is not the reality of literature that assists in creating new futures, but instead, the fantasy of literature that facilitates the exploration of new possibilities in the real world.

Literature provides us with the ability to critically analyze our own lives, solving problems from which we demand resolutions (Mageo, 2002). The story of Cinderella shows the right to housing and proper standards of living as she is taken away from her abusive home (Todres & Higinbotham, 2016, chapter 6). We read the story of *The Lorax*, and learn the devastation that industries can have on the environment. We understand the importance in protecting equal rights for all individuals as Horton tries to give a voice to the Whos of *Horton Hears a Who!* All these stories emphasize the importance of securing rights for all individuals, and help us find resolutions to our own lives.

And many times, these literature-led lessons show up in current events. Palestinian activists protesting the West Bank used the *Avatar* movie—by painting themselves blue like the characters who try and fight the invading colonizers—to explain and exemplify their struggles (Brough & Shresthova, 2012). These activists took the themes of the movie—of colonization, of relocation of individuals, and of threats to one's way of life—and imagined it for their own purposes and stories. *Avatar* provided a common cultural marker for external others observing the conflict to imagine and contextualize the Palestinian victimhood and history.

This trend of taking from literature and popular culture toward collective action is increasing in popularity, so much so that it has generated its own subfield of scholarship called fan activism. Fan activism, defined as "forms of civic engagement and political participation that emerge from within fan culture itself... often framed through metaphors that are drawn from ... participatory culture" (Jenkins & Shresthova, 2012, p. 217), is an important outcome from literary sources.

The power of fan activism revolves around its ability to target the cultural interests of a group alongside the issues that directly face the group at the present moment. This cultural acupuncture (Slack, 2011) provides us the ability to bridge the border of imagined and real, pinpointing an association between our imagined worlds and the real world. Fans who take part in fan activism use their collective imagination to act between the border of *as is* and the *as could be*. It uniquely engages members in civic action while permitting a simplified, more common frame to the general public from which one should view the issue. While we may not understand the complex details surrounding the Palestine-Israeli conflict, we can comprehend the plot of the *Avatar* movie and clearly place the activists into the roles provided by the movie scripts.

One such example of fan activism is the Harry Potter Alliance (HPA). The HPA is a nonprofit organization that stemmed from the work of J.K. Rowling's *Harry Potter* series. The nonprofit organization has donated over 100,000 books worldwide, enforced fair-trade chocolate from Warner Brothers studios (Rosenberg, 2015), and donated over $123,000 worth of goods to Haiti after the 2010 earthquake (Martin, 2012). In each fundraising campaign, they draw on different aspects of the fictional Wizarding world to bridge the connection that enables their base, brings the topic down to a more palatable level, and directs the collective's imagination to imagine comparisons between fiction and reality.

In one of the larger campaigns, the HPA petition Warner Brothers to use fair-trade chocolate in all of its parks and merchandise that involve Harry Potter, ensuring that the workers were being paid fair wages in harvesting the cocoa beans for the chocolate. The beauty of the campaign was in its simplicity. Chocolate, in the Harry Potter universe, brings happiness and is a cure for despair and depression. It is so critical that there is always some on hand in the hospital wing of the school. In explaining the importance of the need for fair-trade chocolate, organizer Andrew Slack framed the issue in the sense that both Hermione and Dumbledore, two main characters, would be abhorrent to the conditions of the workers (Slack, 2011).

In order to get a better understanding of how fan activism is driven by literature and its imaginative properties, three semi-structured interviews were conducted over Skype between November 2014 and April 2016 between the author and either past or current members of the Harry Potter Alliance National. Interviews lasted between 45 minutes and 75 minutes, and were recruited from a mix of snowball sampling as well as advertising on the National Harry Potter Alliance's volunteers' email list service. As data collection is ongoing, this is a preliminary analysis of the data. The aim was to explore how these individuals understood their relations with the Harry Potter universe, their involvement with the HPA, their perceptions of social justice, and their beliefs in the power of fan activism as a way to improve and support human rights and a more humane society.

Activism: Shifting Perspectives on Ourselves

> I think because people saw it as, like coming from within the Harry Potter world. Like, yeah they had those connections to house elves and labor issues and things, but I think people saw it coming from the fandom. (Participant 1)

This participant, while reflecting on her experiences with the fair-trade chocolate campaign, notes how cultural acupuncture played out within the organization. While there were human rights issues that were important to consider, it was the unification of the group—a collective imagination of fiction, facts, and fandom coming together to move the group toward a new idea. Fan activism provides a shift in perspectives—from *just another cause* to something that was being driven by the whole group. A second participant brought up this idea of coming from within and how it made it more approachable to her when she was trying to find ways to get involved in the world.

> This is an important issue you should care about this too, but it feels like unapproachable... And I just felt that way with most other organizations. And the Harry Potter Alliance really wasn't. It was like, everything mattered if you want to be a Harry Potter Alliance member you are.... The only cost of entry essentially is like, reading a book. Or knowing of the book. Or seeing the movie of it... It was a mixture of like, me reading

> Harry Potter, and then caring about all these other issues that were apparent in our world as well as the wizarding world, and being around fans that had their own stake in it. (Participant 2)

The Harry Potter books empowered Participant 2 to gain entry into the arena of activism. It helped shift their perspective on activism as something that was "unapproachable", and too big and large an effort to take on, to something they find more manageable and real. And it helped expand their collective group to anyone who had experienced this cultural phenomenon with them. Literature expanded their in-group through finding other fans, other activists, who also were passionate and wanted to find ways to relate Harry Potter with the real world.

> I mean with not in Harry's Name it was relating unfair labor to house elves. Anything where some character is being treated poorly because of who they are from Hagrid being a half giant to Lupin being a werewolf. To blood status you can relate that to any kind of inequality that you see in the world… So yeah I think they were really able to harness that to an active group of fans. (Participant 3)

The collective imagination of the HPA, in combination with the literature, is able to move forward at very low cost to oneself. Literature ties us from the fictional to the factual. Social justice is a big problem. Worker's rights are a huge problem, and attempting to make a difference in equal, fair pay when facing a corporation seems unattainable. Yet, by linking literature with real-world issues, the collective was able to imagine a new future where changing the business model of a multibillion dollar corporation was possible.

On their website, discussing one of their campaigns—"Neville Fights Back"—they say, "sometimes, it can feel like problems are just too big – like we can't influence policy, or like hatred and bigotry are too powerful. At those times, we remember Neville Longbottom" (Neville Fights Back, 2015). They frame this campaign as the driving force that will always be there—the social activist who would never give up, who resists and pushes back even when all odds seem against them. Their focus is on individual-level change and through framing activism on one of the more minor characters, the HPA is able to highlight that everyone, not simply the hero, can do good.

Activism: Shifting Perspective on Other Issues for Themselves and Others

Another theme that came forward in the interviews was the reach and extent of the HPA. While the activists may have joined for a single reason, they quickly became educated and were surprised how many different issues there were and how they all could relate in different ways to the stories. One participant states:

> I think it's exposed me to a lot of different issues that maybe I wouldn't have been as aware of. At one point I remember phone banking for marriage equality which is something I would have never done on my own. I don't like talking on the phone. Very happy about the cause, but talking on the phone – not so much. Learning about fair trade chocolate I didn't know anything about that or anything about you know, Dafur, all those years ago. I hadn't know anything about that. (Participant 3)

In this way, the HPA widens their imagination by teaching them about new things and expanding the ways in which they can make changes. While most activist groups are focused on single issues, the HPA uses its breadth of magical ability to touch on a litany of potential areas for social justice. In one of their online flyers, "Fantastic Tools And Where to Find Them: A fan's guide for fighting climate change", the HPA uses the newly emerging *Fantastic Beasts* series to frame the problem of deforestation and climate change. They write:

> Newt is trying to educate his magical peers about protecting, rather than destroying, magical creatures. In 1926, he was worried about the human impact on animals. Today, Newt would be fighting climate change. (The Harry Potter Alliance Fandom Forward, n.d., p. 13)

The HPA uses this imaginary character to contextualize what the hero should be fighting for in this time period. They use Harry Potter as a way to actively engage in political imagination (Glaveanu & de Saint-Laurent, 2015). Literature becomes a way to seek political goals—mass emailing senators to oppose a bill in light of the free healthcare of the Wizarding World, to inspire fundraising, and to promote climate science. In using

Harry Potter, they attempt to change the narrative from something highly complex (the issues of health care or climate change) to something that everyone can comprehend. They shift the perspective of the issue, which reduces the cost of entry into taking a stand. Instead of needing to be an expert to understand the topic, by using literature, the HPA is able to change the entry toward needing to have watched a movie or read a book.

Conclusion

In the prior section, I examined two cases. In the first case, the novel *The Jungle* exposed individuals to think more critically about the state of their food packing industry. Its graphic depictions of the improper handling of meat and unsanitary work space, with questionable additions to the meat, caused Americans to write letters in protest to the United States Government, which lead to drastic changes in food policy and food safety. In this way, *The Jungle* assisted in changing the perspective of the public's view on food, and created a connection between *what we imagined it was* to *what it was really like*, causing cognitive dissonance that needed to be resolved. In the second case, the activism group *The Harry Potter Alliance* was discussed as a way in which literature bridges a connection between imagined and real worlds, reducing the border between *what we imagine in fiction* to clarify the troubles of *what exists out in the world*. The use of literature in this way helped root the lofty aims of policy change into something more concrete and coherent for the average individual.

What can we say then, about collective imaginations and literature? I believe we can conclude on two main points.

There Are Limits to the Direction of Imagination

Sinclair's goal was not to change the food processing industry. He was famously quoted as saying, "I aimed for the public's heart, and by accident I hit it in the stomach" (Sinclair, 1906b, p. 594). Whether this was a limit of the public being able to imagine a new system or the public deciding the larger concern was not what Sinclair believed it was—imagination is only as strong as the actions it can produce, which cannot be determined by a single actor. When politicians give speeches, they have a goal under which they hope the speech will be read and understood, but many times, this can backfire and cost them dearly if the collective imagination does not bind to what the individual hoped it would, or we disagree with the framing of the fan activism context, and the collective imagination may not inspire to the same degree as one would hope.

Literature Can Be Used to Direct Imaginations

However, it does not mean that we will never buy into the schema. Beyond transporting us to the fictitious worlds of Dante or Hercules, literature helps us be critical on what is "fake" in our own lives. In a post-truth world (de Saint-Laurent, Bresco, Awad, & Wagoner, 2017), literature can be used as a schema under which we can collectively imagine and reframe our worldviews on current-day issues. Whether it is through creating cognitive dissonance in the battle over fake news or food labeling, or by simplifying complex policies into an imagined good versus evil, literature roots us in a shared imaginative world. We may be unable to fully relate to the historical, cultural, social, and even academic complexities of the Palestine-Israel conflict or the costs of universal healthcare, but we can relate to the narratives provided by literature. When fan activists use literature, they are not only providing the schema from which we should understand the conflict, but also directing us to view certain sides as good, and certain sides as bad. In this way, collective imagination toward the future is done not only alongside literature, but through literature.

References

Abbey, E., & Valsiner, J. (2005). Emergence of meanings through ambivalence. *Forum: Qualitative Social Research, 6*(1), 1–18.

Bloodworth, W. A. (2008). The life of Upton Sinclair. In G. Wiener (Ed.), *Workers' rights in Upton Sinclair's The Jungle* (pp. 20–30). Detroit: Greenhaven Press/Gale.

Brough, M. M., & Shresthova, S. (2012). Fandom meets activism: Rethinking civic and political participation. *Transformative Works and Cultures, 10.* http://journal.transformativeworks.org/index.php/twc/issue/view/12

Calvert, S. L., & Richards, M. N. (2014). Children's parasocial relationships. In A. B. Jordan & D. Romer (Eds.), *Media and the well-being of children and adolescents* (pp. 187–200). New York: Oxford University Press.

Churchill, W. (2008). The Jungle and workers' rights. In G. Wiener (Ed.), *Workers' rights in Upton Sinclair's The Jungle* (pp. 86–91). Detroit: Greenhaven Press/Gale.

Collie, N. (2011). Cities of the imagination: Science fiction, urban space, and community engagement in urban planning. *Futures, 43*(4), 424–431.

Conditions in Chicago Stock Yards, 59th Cong., 5-369 (1906) (testimony of Thos. E. Wilson, Charles P. Neill, and James B. Reynolds).

Davis, M. C. (2010). *Jungle redux: Meat industry reform in the progressive era and contemporary applications* (Unpublished master's thesis). Ohio University, Athens, OH.

De Saint-Laurent, C., Bresco, I., Awad, S., & Wagoner, B. (2017). Collective memory and social sciences in the post-truth era. *Culture & Psychology, 23*(2), 147–155.

Glăveanu, V. P. (2018, this volume). Perspectival collective futures: Creativity and imagination in society. In C. de Saint-Laurent, S. Obradović, & K. R. Carriere (Eds.), *Imagining collective futures: Perspectives from social, cultural, and political psychology* (pp. 83–105). London: Palgrave Macmillan.

Glaveanu, V. P., & De Saint-Laurent, C. (2015). Political imagination, otherness and the European crisis. *Europe's Journal of Psychology, 11*(4), 557–564.

Glaveanu, V. P., Karwowski, M., Jankowska, D. M., & De Saint-Laurent, C. (2017). Creative imagination. In T. Zittoun & V. P. Glaveanu (Eds.), *The Oxford handbook of imagination and culture*. Oxford, UK: Oxford University Press.

Hosseini, K. (2003). *The kite runner*. New York: Riverhead Books.

H.R. Rep. No. 59-873 at 1-11 (1906).

Jaspal, R., Carriere, K. R., & Moghaddam, F. M. (2016). Bridging micro, meso, and macro processes in social psychology. In J. Valsiner, G. Marsico, N. Chaudhary, M. V. Dazzani, & T. Sato (Eds.), *Psychology as the science of human being: The Yokohama Manifesto* (pp. 265–276). Cham: Springer International Publishing.

Jenkins, H., & Shresthova, S. (2012). Up, up, and away! The power and potential of fan activism. *Transformative Works and Culture, 10*. http://journal.transformativeworks.org/index.php/twc/issue/view/12

Jones, S. S. (2002). *The fairy tale: The magic mirror of the imagination*. New York: Routledge.
Jovchelovitch, S., & Hawlina, H. (2018, this volume). Utopias and world-making: Time, transformation and the collective imagination. In C. de Saint Laurent, S. Obradovic, & K. R. Carriere (Eds.), *Imagining collective futures: Perspectives from social, cultural, and political psychology* (pp. 129–151). London: Palgrave Macmillan.
Lehr, S. S. (2010). Literacy, literature, and censorship: The high cost of no child left behind. *Childhood Education, 87*(1), 25–34.
Lordelo, L. (2015). Research is literature: Exploring borders between arts and sciences. *Psychology & Society, 7*(2), 6–14.
Lyons, E. (1996). Coping with social change: Processes of social memory in the reconstruction of identities. In G. M. Breakwell & E. Lyons (Eds.), *Changing European identities: Social psychological analyses of social change* (pp. 31–40). Oxford: Butterworth-Heinemann.
Maarek, E., & Awad, S. H. (2018, this volume). Creating alternative futures: Cooperative initiatives in Egypt. In C. de Saint-Laurent, S. Obradović, & K. R. Carriere (Eds.), *Imagining collective futures: Perspectives from social, cultural, and political psychology* (pp. 199–219). London: Palgrave Macmillan.
Mageo, J. M. (2002). Intertextual interpretation, fantasy and Samoan dreams. *Culture & Psychology, 8*(4), 417–448.
Manderson, D. (2003). From hunger to love: Myths of the source, interpretation, and constitution of law in children's literature. *Law and Literature, 15*(1), 87–141.
Martin, C. E. (2012, March 21). *From young adult book fans to wizards of change*. Retrieved from http://opinionator.blogs.nytimes.com/2012/03/21/from-young-adult-book-fans-to-wizards-of-change/?_r=0
Martin, J. (2006). Reinterpreting internalization and agency through G.H. Mead's perspectival realism. *Human Development, 49*(2), 65–86. https://doi.org/10.1159/000091333.
Mead, G. H. (1938). *The philosophy of the act* (C. W. Morris, Ed.). Chicago: University of Chicago Press.
Meat Inspection Act, Pub. L. No. 59-242, 34 Stat. 1260, (1907).
Moghaddam, F. M. (2004). From 'psychology in literature' to 'psychology is literature': An exploration of boundaries and relationships. *Theory & Psychology, 14*(4), 505–525.
Neville Fights Back. (2015). Retrieved July 3, 2017, from http://www.thehpalliance.org/nevillefightsback

Nikolajeva, M. (2012). Guilt, empathy and the ethical potential of children's literature. *Barnboken, 35*, 1–13.

Parry, D. C., & Light, T. P. (2014). Fifty shades of complexity exploring technologically mediated leisure and women's sexuality. *Journal of Leisure Research, 26*(1), 38–57.

Pickavance, J. (2003). Gastronomic realism: Upton Sinclair's The Jungle, the fight for pure food, and the magic of mastication. *Food and Foodways, 11*(2–3), 87–112.

Pultz, S., & Hviid, P. (2018). Imagining a better future: Young unemployed people and the polyphonic choir. *Culture & Psychology, 24*(1), 3–25.

Pure Food and Drug Act, Pub. L. No. 59-384, 34 Stat. 768, (1906).

Richter, T., Appel, M., & Calio, F. (2014). Stories can influence the self-concept. *Social Influence, 9*(3), 172–188.

Rommetveit, R. (1992). Outlines of a dialogically based social-cognitive approach to human cognition and communication. In A. H. Wold (Ed.), *The dialogical alternative: Towards a theory of language and mind* (pp. 19–44). Oslo: Scandinavian University Press.

Roots, R. I. (2001). A muckraker's aftermath: The Jungle of meat-packing regulation after a century. *William Mitchell Law Review, 27*(4), 2413–2433.

Rosenberg, A. (2015, January 13). *How 'Harry Potter' fans won a four-year fight against child slavery*. Retrieved from https://www.washingtonpost.com/news/act-four/wp/2015/01/13/how-harry-potter-fans-won-a-four-year-fight-against-child-slavery/

Rowling, J. K. (2007). *Harry Potter and the deathly hallows*. London: Bloomsbury.

Schlosser, E. (2008). Conditions depicted in The Jungle are returning. In G. Wiener (Ed.), *Workers' rights in Upton Sinclair's The Jungle* (pp. 138–148). Detroit: Greenhaven Press/Gale.

Schmid, H., & Klimmt, C. (2011). A magically nice guy: Parasocial relationships with Harry Potter across different cultures. *International Communication Gazette, 73*(3), 252–269.

Shelden, M. (1996). *Orwell: The authorised biography*. London: Heinemann.

Sinclair, U. (1906a). *The Jungle*. Cambridge, MA: R. Bentley.

Sinclair, U. (1906b). What life means to me. *Cosmopolitan, 594.*

Slack, A. (2011, May 25). *Making all Harry Potter chocolate fair trade*. Retrieved from http://www.huffingtonpost.com/andrew-slack/making-all-harry-potter-c_b_784116.html

Sova, D. B. (2006). *Literature suppressed on social grounds*. New York: Infobase Pub.

Tateo, L. (2015). Giambattista Vico and the psychological imagination. *Culture & Psychology, 21*(2), 145–161.

The Harry Potter Alliance, Fandom Forward. (n.d.). *Fantastic tools and where to find them* [Press release]. Retrieved July 3, 2017, from http://www.thehpalliance.org/fandomforward

Todres, J., & Higinbotham, S. (Eds.). (2016). *Human rights in children's literature: Imagination and the narrative of law*. Oxford: Oxford University Press.

Usherwood, B., & Toyne, J. (2002). The value and impact of reading imaginative literature. *Journal of Librarianship and Information Science, 34*(1), 33–42.

Vygotsky, L. S. (1990). Imagination and creativity in childhood. *Journal of Russian and East European Psychology, 28*(1), 84–96.

Wade, L. C. (1991). The problem with classroom use of Upton Sinclair's The Jungle. *American Studies, 32*(2), 79–101.

Wade, L. C. (2008). Sinclair distorted conditions in packingtown. In G. Wiener (Ed.), *Workers' rights in Upton Sinclair's The Jungle* (pp. 79–85). Detroit: Greenhaven Press/Gale.

Zittoun, T., & Gillespie, A. (2016). *Imagination in human and cultural development*. London: Routledge, Taylor & Francis Group.

Zittoun, T., & Gillespie, A. (2018, this volume). Imagining the collective future: A sociocultural perspective. In C. de Saint-Laurent, S. Obradović, & K. R. Carriere (Eds.), *Imagining collective futures: Perspectives from social, cultural, and political psychology* (pp. 15–37). London: Palgrave Macmillan.

4

Thinking Through Time: From Collective Memories to Collective Futures

Constance de Saint-Laurent

Introduction

Being able to imagine the future, in a world in constant change, is more than a necessity for action. Imagining where society might be going or should be going can shed new light on the present: imagining, for instance, a world were men and women are fully equal can highlight the road left to travel and what remains to be done, while imagining the consequences of climate change can be a powerful drive to rethink our relation to the environment. As Asimov (1978, p. 6) stated,

> It is change, continuing change, inevitable change, that is the dominant factor in society today. No sensible decision can be made any longer without taking into account not only the world as it is, but the world as it will be. [...] This, in turns, means that our statesmen, businessmen, our every men must take on a science fictional way of thinking.

C. de Saint-Laurent (✉)
University of Neuchâtel, Neuchâtel, Switzerland

The way we imagine collective futures—a form of political imagination (de Saint-Laurent & Glăveanu, in press; Glăveanu & de Saint-Laurent, 2015)—is thus of tremendous importance to understand how we act as members of society and how we represent the world we live in. However, as we do for our personal lives, we do not imagine where we may be going solely based on inferences made from the present; we build on past experiences to construct a plausible image of what the future might hold. In the case of collective futures, then, this implies that the way we represent history—our collective memory—plays a fundamental role in the way we can imagine the future. It is precisely this relation between collective memory and imagination of the collective future that this chapter sets to explore.

In a first section, the links between memory and imagination will be explored, initially in general, and then, in the specific cases of collective memory and collective imagination. This will lead me to argue that collective memory provides the frame and materials from which to imagine the collective future. In the second section, three cases from different studies will be presented to illustrate this claim, each showcasing a different function of collective memory for imagination: (1) collective memory as framing the content of collective imagination; (2) collective memory as a source of experience and examples for collective imagination; and (3) generalisations from collective memory in the form of "Personal World Philosophy", which, in turn, shapes how the future can be imagined. Finally, I will argue that our representations of the world are characterised by "temporal heteroglossia", that is the simultaneous presence of different times, and that it is by connecting the past and future that we can understand the world we live in and act within it.

Memory and Imagination

The deep links between memory and imagination can be summarised by the idea of "Mental Time Travel", as proposed by Tulving (2002). For him, memory and imagination both grant us the uniquely human ability to mentally travel through time, to experience events that are not anymore or that have not yet been. Although the notion of mental time travel is problematic in more than one respect—I will come back to this in the conclusion—it remains that imagination and memory are deeply associated processes: whether it is because they both involve scene construction (Mullally & Maguire, 2013), interacting with distal experiences (Zittoun & Gillespie, 2015), or moving away from the present (Berntsen & Bohn, 2010), these processes are similar in many ways. To the point that some have gone to suggest that this is because they are one and the same process (Berntsen & Bohn, 2010; Zittoun & Gillespie, 2015), highlighting the complex relation between the two.

On the one hand, imagination does rest on past experiences: memory provides the "material" transformed by imagination to produce something new (Vygotsky, 2004; Zittoun & de Saint-Laurent, 2015). Indeed, although we often suppose that children's imagination is the most fertile, it is not the case: experiences add content, thickness, and richness to our imagination, and children's play cannot rival, for instance, with the works of proficient science fiction authors (Vygotsky, 1991). Furthermore, some types of imagination that anticipate the future can take the form of reminiscence of a past that is directly relevant to the situation, what Mattli, Schnitzspahn, Studerus-Germann, Brehmer, and Zöllig (2014) have called "prospective memory". Finally, some imaginations can become so rehearsed that they blur the line with memory. It is the case, for instance, of some imaginations of the future during adolescence that are engaged with regularly as one plans for one's life (Zittoun & de Saint-Laurent, 2015).

On the other hand, memory is not the mere repetition of the past but a reconstruction (Bartlett, 1932) that requires some form of imagination (de Saint-Laurent & Zittoun, 2017). This is because memory is not ultimately oriented towards the past, but towards the future: it allows us to adapt to what is and what will be by flexibly reconstructing past experiences (Bartlett, 1932). This prospective function of memory, considered by many its most important one (Dudai & Carruthers, 2005; Schacter & Addis, 2007), has been mainly studied in relation to autobiographical memory. It has been found, for example, that remembering one's life gives it direction (Habermas, 2012); that autobiographical memory and future imagination develop in parallel and interdependently (D'Argembeau, 2012); or that there is a continuity, for instance, between the way parents remember their past and imagine the future of their children (Cole, 2007). Moreover, memory itself can be imaginative: giving meaning to the past and integrating experiences in a coherent narrative also involves keeping a distance from what happened in a way that is very similar to the work of imagination (de Saint-Laurent & Zittoun, 2017).

What transpires from memory and imagination research is that one of the primary functions of memory is to provide material for imagination and to help us anticipate the future. Furthermore, imagination as a process participates in the reconstructive nature of memory. How does this, however, apply to collective memory and collective imagination?

Remembering History and Imagining the Future

Before we turn to the relations between collective memory and collective imagination, it is important to make clear what we mean by "collective". In both cases, the "collective" aspects can refer to two different dimensions: memory or imagination can be about collective events or societal issues (e.g., remembering World War II or imagining alternatives to a political regime), or the dynamics underlying them can themselves be collective (e.g., remembering with friends where you were when you learned about 9/11 or imagining with colleagues the future of your organisation). Although one does not exclude the other, this chapter focuses more directly on the former, considering that imagination and memory are, in any case, social and cultural activities (de Saint-Laurent, 2018a; Zittoun & Gillespie, 2016; Chap. 2, this volume). This means, however, that collective memory is not directly a mnemonic activity, as it does not exclusively concern *our* past but the past in general (de Saint-Laurent, 2018a). How do collective memory and collective imagination relate to each other in this context?

In collective memory studies, it is generally considered that representations of history shape how the collective future is imagined (Szpunar & Szpunar, 2016), although little attention has been given to how and whether this actually takes place (Merck, Topcu, & Hirst, 2016). There have been, however, a few notable exceptions. Brescó de Luna (2017; Chap. 6, this volume), for instance, has adapted Cole's (2007) ideas on prolepsis to collective memory, to argue that it is the stories we tell about the past that in themselves "announce" what will come next—a form of "end into the beginning" (Brescó de Luna, 2017) due, among other things, to the way we anticipate the end of stories with a well known narrative frame. Szpunar and Szpunar (2016), on the contrary, have argued that although collective memory serves as the basis for collective imagination, the relation is not unidirectional: the way we understand the past is shaped by how we imagine the future. They explain how, for instance, imagining a future characterised by technological progress versus by pollution changes how people represent the invention of the car, either as a major progress or a the origin of unprecedented pollution. Such a mechanism has also been used in political campaigns, where the past is presented in such a way that it justifies the future candidate's vision (de Saint-Laurent, Brescó de Luna, Awad, & Wagoner, 2017).

Studies of collective memory from a sociocultural perspective have also focused on the role of imagination in remembering, insisting on the constructive—and creative—aspects of collective memory (Wagoner, 2017). Understanding global events, for which we often have only partial and indirect accounts, does involve some form of collective imagination to fill in the gaps of experience (de Saint-Laurent & Glăveanu, in press; Glăveanu & de Saint-Laurent, 2015). Moreover, imagining how one would have acted during historical events, or how it was like to live in a different period, participates in the creation of a sense of connection with the past and plays an important role in how it is represented (de Saint-Laurent, 2018b).

There have been, on the other hand, very few studies of collective imagination (Merck et al., 2016), and even fewer on the links between collective imagination and collective memory (Szpunar & Szpunar, 2016). Nonetheless, we can infer from the existing literature on memory and imagination in both their individual and collective forms that: (1) collective memory (at least) sometimes relies on collective imagination (e.g., imagining how life was at a certain period of time); (2) collective memory provides the basis for collective future imagination (e.g., providing the experiences from which to imagine what could be possible for future societies), and (3) that collective future imagination, in turn, shapes how the past is remembered (e.g., by making some aspects of the past more relevant than others). It is on these two last points that the rest of this chapter will focus. In particular, I will attempt to answer the two following questions: How does collective memory participate in the imagination of collective futures? And how does the resulting imagination affect how the collective past is remembered?

Collective Memory to Imagine Collective Futures

In order to better understand how collective memory provides the basis for how we imagine collective futures, I propose to now look at three cases illustrating different relational dynamics between these two processes. The cases come from previous studies that primarily focused either on collective memory or where collective imagination also played a central role. For the purposes of this chapter, a secondary analysis was carried out, looking at how collective memory is mobilised to imagine what the collective future will be or should be. Three main dynamics emerged: (1) history as a frame of reference, determining the main actors and the roles they should play in the future; (2) history as a source of experiences and examples from which we can draw to imagine what is likely, possible, or desirable; and (3) history as generalisable experience from which global representations of the world can be built, which in turn, inform the imagination of collective futures. Although these dynamics can be found in all three cases, albeit unequally, they are each illustrated in what follows with reference to the case they feature in most prominently.

Frames of Reference in Parliamentary Debates on Immigration

The first role that collective memory can play for the imagination of collective futures is that of a frame of reference. Indeed, understanding the past as the interactions between different national groups that have, at times, cooperated and at others been at war will make it likely that the future is imagined as involving nation states as central actors and their changing interactions as the main events (see for instance Obradović, Chap. 12, this volume). Understanding, on the contrary, nation states as a recent historical development—and thus, their role as transient—will probably lead to a very different imagination of the future, possibly without nations but with very different actors. This is, for instance, what made Foucault's method so successful (e.g., Foucault, 1993): discussing the historical roots of categories that seem natural to us makes it possible to imagine a world without them, for they have not always been there. More generally, however, collective memory provides frames that determine what is "normal", expected, and possible, whether it is in terms of actors, events, or the general circumstances of life. Using collective memory to frame the future does not mean, however, imagining the future as a perpetual repetition of the past, but quite the contrary: ideas of progress, evolution, or development (as well as their opposites) are not only historically rooted but often used to organise the past as a crescendo (or diminuendo) that culminates in the more or less distant future.

One particularly prominent way in which the past frames the future is through the use of *grand narratives*, which are highly general historical narratives that cover broad periods of time (de Saint-Laurent, 2014). They differ from the *narrative templates* often found in collective memory: narrative templates are general storylines repeated over multiple historical events (Wertsch, 2008), while *grand narratives* are storylines used to bring together a multitude of events, often spanning centuries. The narrative of scientific progress, for instance, is a *grand narrative* that can be made to start as early as Antiquity and that presides over the organisation of many "sub-stories" about science. Although they are quite close to the notion of *charters* (Liu & Hilton, 2005), they diverge from them in the sense that *charters* are supposed to determine and underlie—in an almost unconscious way—how the past, present, and future are understood, while *grand narratives* are general storylines constructed in discourse and mobilised in certain contexts for specific purposes.

Grand narratives were found, for instance, in a previous study on the use of collective memory in political discourses on immigration (de Saint-Laurent, 2014). This study explored the references made to history by French politicians during the parliamentary debates that led to the adoption of the 2006 bill on "Immigration and Integration". In particular, it examined how the way different political groups represent the past of the country changes how they see the nation and who should be part of it. Although the original analysis stopped there, it is possible to see how such representations change politicians' imagination of the future of the nation, particularly regarding immigration. This is reflected in the way they position themselves towards the bill and its many amendments. How do the *grand narratives* proposed by politicians, then, frame how they imagine the collective future?

In these parliamentary debates, two main grand narratives emerged, representing each side of the political spectrum, and both narrating the history of France since the Revolution. On the left side of the political spectrum (Socialists and Radical Left), the main narrative is one of ongoing political struggle between "humanists" and their opponents. This position is well illustrated in the following excerpt[1]:

> Jean-Pierre Brard (Radical Left): Really, two Frances are in confrontation, as throughout History: the one of Coblence against the one of the Revolution; [...] The one that supported Franco, Salazar, Mobutu (protestations on the Right's benches) against the one that defended Grimau, Cunhal, Lumumba,[2]... [...] the France that supported the colonial wars against the France in solidarity with the oppressed populations! [...] We will fight you with every fibre and ounce of strength we have! [02.05.2013, third session]

One of the examples of such struggles evoked frequently in the debates and concluding this quote is colonisation. Many comparisons are also made between the Right's desire to select immigrants based on "compe-

---

[1] All the transcripts come from the French Parliament website. The only additions are the political inclination in brackets after the name of the speaker, and [...] to signal that parts of the quote were removed to shorten it, although always while being careful not to alter meaning. Political affiliations were simplified for clarity (see de Saint-Laurent, 2012, 2014 for full details). All the transcripts are identified by date and parliamentary session, and all the translations were made by the author.

[2] All the names in the quote work in opposite pairs, one representing humanist ideals and the other their oppressors. The original quote, rather long, can be found in de Saint-Laurent, 2014, and includes more of such oppositions.

tencies and talents" and slavery or the World War II Vichy regime. However, the references to colonisation are the ones that the Members of Parliament (MPs) linked most directly with how they envision the future of the country with regard to immigration. This is made clear, for instance, in an intervention from the same deputy, the next day:

> Jean-Pierre Brard (Radical Left): When I fight against your bill, I am faithful to my anticolonial tradition. That others remain faithful to the opposite tradition, agreed, but they must take responsibility for it! When you see the state of the countries who have been victims of colonisation [...] we evidently understand that France has a duty to redress the wrongs done and a duty of solidarity. [03.05.2006, first session]

The Left's representations of history define the main actors of history: humanists, oppressors, and victims. These are "traditional" positions they wish to preserve, although with the hope that the humanists will win: there is a duty to redress, in the future, what was done.

The Right's narrative of French history paints a quite different picture: it presents the French nation as the product of the Enlightenment philosophy, and more specifically, as the result of a form of Republican or civic pact concluded between the citizens of the country. This is made especially clear when they argue for the bill they proposed. This "Immigration and integration" bill, discussed in these debates, was centred on two main proposals: prioritising immigration of "talented" people and creating an "Integration Contract" immigrants would have to sign upon arrival, insisting on the need to learn French and to respect French values. In order to justify their positions, several Right-winged MPs referred to Enlightenment philosophers, and in particular, Rousseau. One Left-winged MP argued that Rousseau would have been against these "Integration Contracts", as he believed in the good nature of people, and here is how a Right-winged deputy clarified his position:

> Christian Vanneste (Right): Reread Rousseau! [...] It is precisely the social contract that is at the basis of good societies. [04.05.2006, first session]

Similarly, when the Left reacted to the Right's desire to prioritise "talented" immigrants—comparing it to a colonial plundering—here is how a Right-winged MP responded:

> Thierry Mariani (Right): Please allow me to remind you of the Article VI of a text you will probably recognise: 'Law is the expression of the general will. [...] All citizens being equal in its eyes, they are equally admissible for all dignities, places and public employment, without any other distinctions than their virtues and talents.' This is the Article VI of the Declaration of Human and Citizen Rights, dating from 1789. The idea isn't new! [04.05.2006, third session]

What they propose is a narrative that puts the French Revolution and its constitution—product of the Enlightenment—at the root of the French nation. If a Republican pact is what founded the country, and if this pact is now in danger because newcomers do not respect the "French values", then a simple way to protect the country in the future is to ask immigrants to agree to such a pact. By the same token, it becomes acceptable—reasonable, even—to select only those deemed worthy of becoming part of this social contract.

In both of these examples, we can see how a broad historical narrative frames what kind of future can be imagined. In the first case, for the Left, the past tells a story of struggle between humanists and their opponents, who oppress populations for their own interest. The future, then, can only be imagined in terms of either reparation for the victims, which would mean a victory for the humanists, or as a continuation of the wrongs done—something comparable to past oppressions, such as colonial plundering and slavery—and thus, a victory for their opponents. In the case of the Right, the *grand narrative* tells the story of a contract signed between different parties who wished to live together. Newcomers, then, have a duty to respect such a pact if they wish to join the country, because not doing so would threaten the future of the nation: without a social contract, we cannot be a "good society" anymore. In conclusion, the historical narratives found in these parliamentary debates frame the future, but they also make it look like the logical conclusion to the story being told, especially when they are broadly shared with one's social group, as was the case in this study. However, supposing that collective memory does more, in this case, than give general lines—a frame—would be forgetting that these accounts were also constructed by the participants to justify the policies they were advocating for. Looking at how politicians referred to the French Revolution elsewhere, for instance, revealed that although the general frame remains the same, the specifics of the story are adapted to the needs of the situation (de Saint-Laurent, 2014).

Analogies in Historical Reasoning

The second role collective memory plays for collective imagination is to provide examples and experiences from which to infer what is possible, probable, or desirable for the future. Although there are many ways to build on past events to imagine possible future outcomes, one of the most frequent ones is through the use of *historical analogies*. Analogies work by using a source, that is usually well known, and mapping out the similarities with a target—usually less known—in order to infer things about the target (Holyoak, 2005). They are, thus, particularly adapted to infer things about the future (the target) by mapping out similarities between the present and a past situation (the source), and looking at how the events unfolded in the past to predict what might happen. Research on the topic has found that we do use historical analogies to draw conclusions about present situations (Spellman & Holyoak, 1992), but it has not looked at how they are used to imagine the future. What has been found, however, is that although people are not always very efficient in finding analogies, they are very good at mapping existing ones (Holyoak, 2005). Once given an analogy between World War II and the first Gulf War, for instance, research participants were easily able to map out the correspondence between the two situations, although they did not all do so in the same way (Spellman & Holyoak, 1992). Research on the links between social representations and analogies has also showed that analogies can help people make diffuse and abstract ideas more concrete, serving both as a form of "anchoring" of the unfamiliar into more familiar elements and as a way of illustrating one's ideas (Marková, Linell, Grossen, & Salazar Orvig, 2007).

In our own research, we found that historical analogies are very frequently used to infer information not only about the present and the future, but also about the past itself. Indeed, people employ historical analogies to reason about history, what I have termed elsewhere *historical reasoning* (de Saint-Laurent, 2018b, in preparation). This process does not only allow people to infer information about less known targets, but perhaps more importantly, to transfer *meaning* from one event to the other, using history as a form of *symbolic resource* (Zittoun, 2006; Zittoun, Duveen, Gillespie, Ivinson, & Psaltis, 2003). For instance, in the examples presented in the previous section, comparing the bill proposed to slavery and colonisation is not just done to imply that it would have disastrous consequences were it to be adopted, but mainly to give value and sense to what is being done: a horribly wrong policy for which future generations will judge us. And although such processes are present in all three cases presented in this chapter and used for quite various purposes, they become especially salient in cases where, similarly to the example earlier, participants imagine where a present situation might lead.

And indeed, in a research on historical reasoning (de Saint-Laurent, 2018b, in preparation), analogies were regularly used by the participants to infer about the present and the future.[3] In this study, using a qualitative and dialogical experiment, participants from Poland were asked to react to statements about the Ukrainian conflict, illustrating different perspectives on the situation (see de Saint-Laurent, 2018b for a full description). One of the vignettes was about the presence of Russian soldiers in Ukraine, to which one of the participants replied by saying that she thinks Russia is invading Ukraine, and that people call Putin the "new Hitler". I then asked:

C: where did you hear people call him "new Hitler"? Is it something that people say here?

I: yes, yes, and I heard it from some people, we… Often also on TV people compare Hitler and compare what happened before World War II

---

[3] The participants in this study used a variety of processes to reason about history. However, analogies were employed quasi systematically when the participants were discussing the future, which was the case for no other process. For a full description, however, see de Saint-Laurent, 2018.

and compare the lack of reaction of other countries, of Alliance and it's very often said here that it's, it's new Hitler and it may be the same scenario, like… and I'm very, very afraid about it. And also, my mother often recalls how her mother told that for years before the war, people were talking about war. And also in books like Gone with the wind… I remember Scarlett O'Hara says boys you are boring, you talk about the war all the time and it's not the war, yet. But they are talking, and talking and… I feel it's what we do now, we talk… We observe in the news and we are almost bored with news from Ukraine. But it happens and it's closer and closer to our borders and borders of *the* European Union and I wonder what must happen to make us *react* and I'm afraid it will be too late to react. If we react. […] I'm afraid it's the beginning, I hope it will not be the war as World War III would be much quicker than Second World War and with nuclear weapons it would be quick and rather many people would die immediately. […] I don't know but I'm afraid it will be that. The war.

In this excerpt, the participant uses the analogy proposed between Putin and Hitler to more broadly compare the situation in Ukraine with World War II. These successive analogies lead her to conclude that World War III may be coming, because of the similarities between what she knows of the discourses before World War II, the American Civil War, and the current situation. Four elements are particularly striking here. First, the interviewee refers to several historical analogies—Putin/Hitler, pre-World War II/discourses on Ukraine, Gone with the Wind/discourses on Ukraine—illustrating how widespread the use of analogies is, and how easily they can be mobilised and combined. Second, she borrows from different sources—books, TV, family narratives—either using the analogies proposed by others (for the comparisons with World War II) or that she constructs herself (American Civil War), showing once more their frequency and flexibility. Third, the use of analogies is, in itself, never justified by the participants, neither here nor in any of the data collected: although people do discuss and contest the use of specific analogies, the process is never questioned in itself. Fourth, the analogies are not just used to imagine what may happen, but also to "learn" from the past what course of action may be desirable, and thus, to transfer meaning from one event to the other: when she compares the reactions of the European Union with the ones of the Allies during World War II, she is not just anticipating what may happen, but also, implicitly, how our own (lack of) actions may be judged in the future.

What we can conclude from this example is that collective memory provides a breadth of experiences from which people can draw to imagine the future, in particular by finding analogies between the past and the present and mapping out their consequences. These analogies allow the transfer of information between a past event and an unfolding one, but also of meaning and value (see also Marková et al., 2007). Indeed, history does not only provide examples of how things went in the past, but also of how, with time and distance, we came to judge what happened.

Generalisations: Metamemory and Personal World Philosophies

The third way in which collective memory participates in the imagination of collective futures is through the generalisation from past events into *metamemory* or *Personal World Philosophies*. In the first case, representations of history are used to develop a general understanding of how collective memory works (de Saint-Laurent, 2017c). This is, for instance, what expressions such as "those who do not learn from the past are doomed to repeat it" capture. Second, collective memory can be used to develop *Personal World Philosophies* (PWP). The term is derived from the notion of *Personal Life Philosophies* (PLP), which are maxims, philosophies, and other culturally shared wisdoms that are given a personal significance through generalisations from life experiences. Although they often take the form of culturally shared ideas (such as "actions speak louder than words" or "after a storm comes a calm"), these become PLP when they take on a personal meaning for people, through life experiences (Zittoun et al., 2013). PWP work in a similar way: they are general understandings of the way the world works, derived from past historical events and social experiences. They usually refer to commonly shared ideas about the world, but also take on a more or less personal form. For instance, one can generalise from history that "man is a wolf for man" (shared representation) or that, as one of our research participants did, wars were started when there was a deficit of jobs or of women (more unique construction). These beliefs are, in turn, used to imagine the future: in the first case, the future will necessarily be imagined in terms of violent relations between people; in the second, the participant imagined that a war would necessarily happen with China, because they had a "dude overpopulation".

This second example comes from a study on people's relation to history, where participants were asked, among other things, to describe their relation to history and how it had changed over time (de Saint-Laurent, 2017a, 2017b, 2017c). One of the final questions asked the participants to imagine where they thought the world was going. This is where Robert,[4] in the example above, explained being afraid of a war with China and justified his answer with the idea that wars were started by unbalanced populations and by low employment rates. Another participant, Marc, replied to this question by saying that we are heading "straight into a wall". When asked what would cause it, here is what he responded:

> I think the economic stakes, and I think that the Middle Ages are a bit of a [...] turning point where ideals shifted. I don't remember who said that but [...] let's say that man before the Middle Ages is Homo Politicus. And after that, he truly becomes Homo Economicus. And I think are still in this history primarily governed by trade. [...] I have the impression that maybe through trade we don't have anymore the question of how to live together. Maybe during Antiquity we were wondering about living together. [...] It was not all pink, but we were thinking about it, and I have the impression that since the Middle Ages what connects us is only trade. [...] I don't know where it's going but [...] Maybe if we discovered another planet, for instance with other living people, who would not necessarily be human but who would have a conscience like us, maybe at the beginning we would wonder about how to live together, you see? We are here, in the Universe, but we are two now. And maybe once we would have found a kind of a compromise between our forms of intelligent life, maybe then we would start having commercial relations, and then, maybe at one point one would need to dominate the other or I don't know.

In this excerpt, Marc proposes a very general understanding of history: while during Antiquity we wondered about how to live together, since the

---

[4] All names have been changed.

advent of trade in the Middle Ages mercantile relations are what characterise humanity. This representation of the world is shared with others ("I don't remember who said that") and yet Marc appropriated it ("Let's say that...") in a way that allows him to think about the world and its future, fitting the above description of PWP. Marc imagines first that we are going "straight into a wall", but when asked to elaborate, he proposes an alternative: maybe if we encountered a completely new "Other", then we would think about how we can best live together. However, his PWP leads him to conclude that even in such a case, we would possibly end up in the same situation as today, and one group would "dominate the other".

In these examples, we can see how collective memory participates in the elaboration of representations of the world—PWP—that provide general understandings of how the world, societies, and human beings are or should be. These can in turn be used to imagine what the future might hold. In a sense, PWP are a form of *hyper generalised grand narrative*—Marc's narrative covers the whole of human history in two sentences—that may both employ and produce historical analogies—Robert's PWP allows him to draw an analogy between past wars and the situation in China, but was also probably constructed by building analogies between multiple past conflicts. The three roles collective memory plays for the imagination of collective futures—framing, exemplifying, and generalising—are thus interdependent and they all participate in the creation and maintenance of general representations of the world, in particular PWPs.

Thinking Through Time: Temporal Heteroglossia in Our Representations of the World

I have, in the three cases presented in this chapter, mainly focused on how collective memory shapes how the future can be imagined. What about our second question, then: How do collective futures shape how the past is remembered? Before attempting to answer this question, two shortcomings need to be clarified. First, it is difficult, both in discourse and in the analysis, to reverse the course of time. Even at times when what we imagine about the future directly determines what we remember from the past—as in prospective memory, for instance—there is a sort of natural logic in presenting our thinking as following the irreversible flow of time. Second, it is more convincing, both for ourselves and for others, to start from what we believe actually happened and go towards what we think might happen. The first carries the aura of truth, while the other stinks of speculation. I could, for instance, imagine a future with flying cars, and justify its probability by a consideration of the evolution of personal vehicles over time, when the truth is that I watched the Fifth Element too many times as a child. However, I would not believe everything I have seen in science fiction movies to be possible in the future. The idea of flying car fits quite well with my general representation that technological progress, especially if it leads to more autonomy and potential financial gain, is one of the characteristics of the societies we live in. But I would not imagine a future with light sabres as probable, because it does not fit with my representation of the world as building more and more violent and destructive weapons—I would, for that matter, more easily believe in a Death Star.

What this example points at is the fact that PWPs, as general representations of the world, mediate the relations between the imagination of collective futures and the memory of the collective past by allowing us to alter the course of time. Indeed, what appears in the cases presented in this chapter is that the way we understand the world is not bound to a specific period of time, but, on the contrary, it is developed at the crossroad between multiple historical periods and temporalities. PWP are thus characterised by *temporal heteroglossia*, the simultaneous presence of multiple periods of time. Heteroglossia is a Bakhtinian concept (Bakhtin, 1981) that refers to how "any discourse contains the traces of previous discourses, is made of different genres (rhetoric, journalistic, literary, scientific, etc.), and echoes discourses (or voices) uttered by other people in different places at different times" (Grossen, 2010, p. 10). *Temporal heteroglossia*, then, refers to how discourses on the world, society, humanity, and so on are characterised by the simultaneous presence of multiple periods of time, and it is through this consideration of several temporalities that they are constituted. Indeed, even in cases where the representation seems to apply to only one period of time, it is done against the backdrop of other historical periods. For instance, current discourses on society and mass media seem to apply only to the present. However, they are built in contrast with other periods, where mass communication did not exist, and often in anticipation of a future of which we imagine they will be part. The alternative representation—of a world without mass media, as we used to have—is thus part of the representation itself (Gillespie, 2008).

In the first case presented in this chapter, the way the MPs represent French society is done, for the Left, by considering simultaneously the various periods of time when "two Frances are in confrontation". Doing so is what allows politicians to develop a representation of the country as torn by a social struggle, and it assumes enough similarity between all of these periods for them to be comparable. For the Right, the contrast is made between the period before the French Revolution and everything that came after, which still applies to the present. These representations of French society provide the basis from which the future can be imagined, but also the frame within which the past should be remembered— encouraging Left-winged MPs to focus on past oppositions in French politics and Right-winged MPs to overlook setbacks in the constitution of the French Republic, for instance, the Terror or Napoleon.

In the second study, a participant discusses the future of the Ukrainian crisis by comparing it to World War II, implicitly assuming that humanity has not significantly changed in the meantime. Indeed, what makes the comparison possible is the supposition that the behaviour of the different actors is today what it was in the past. This is what allows her to infer from the past—people talked a lot about the possibility of a war before World War II—something about the present circumstances: if we talk a lot about a possible war, it may indeed be coming. Representations of how human beings behave in society and in the world in general are thus built on the assumption that we can learn about human nature from any given period of time and that our conclusions would globally be valid at any time. Although we usually accept that different circumstances produce different behaviours, it is still assumed that human nature remains generally unchanged, what Gergen criticised by calling social psychology "history" (Gergen, 1973). While we would generally agree that society widely changed with regard to authority in the past half-century, Milgram's findings do remain, for instance, an important part of how many people represent the "natural" relation of human beings to authority.

In the third study, participants similarly draw from multiple periods of time to build personal representations of the world and where it is going. In doing so, they assume that what happened in the past remains relevant to the present because humanity did not change in ways that would invalidate the comparison, making it irrelevant to the present or the future. PWP thus provide a sense of continuity across vast periods of time, making the past and the future not only familiar—the world and its inhabitants were essentially the same—but also a source of knowledge for the present. It is because the past and the future bear enough similarity that we can use them to know how to behave in the present, learning from the past and anticipating what may happen.

Would this be, then, a form of mental time travel (Tulving, 2002)? Quite the contrary, actually. Where the notion of mental time travel implies that we can leave the here and now, in a rather dualist fashion,[5] the temporal heteroglossia of PWPs means that we can bring the past and the future into the present because our representations of the world are not bound to a specific time or a specific place. Representations of the world, crystallised into PWPs, thus allow us to think through time and to use the past in answering one fundamental question: Where are we going?

References

Asimov, I. (1978). Foreword. In R. Holdstock (Ed.), *Encyclopedia of science fiction* (pp. 6–8). London: Octopus Books.
Bakhtin, M. M. (1981). *The dialogic imagination: Four essays*. Austin, TX: University of Texas Press.
Bartlett, F. C. (1932). *Remembering. A study in experimental and social psychology*. Cambridge: Cambridge University Press.

---

[5] The idea of time travel also employs a spatial metaphor, which has been shown to be deeply problematic for memory (Brockmeier, 2010).

Berntsen, D., & Bohn, A. (2010). Remembering and forecasting: The relation between autobiographical memory and episodic future thinking. *Memory & Cognition, 38*(3), 265–278. https://doi.org/10.3758/MC.38.3.265.

Brescó de Luna, I. (2018, this volume). Imagining collective futures in time: Prolepsis and the regimes of historicity. In C. de Saint-Laurent, S. Obradović, & K. R. Carriere (Eds.), *Imagining collective futures: Perspectives from social, cultural, and political psychology* (pp. 109–128). London: Palgrave Macmillan.

Brescó de Luna, I. (2017). The end into the beginning. Prolepsis and the reconstruction of the collective past. *Culture & Psychology, 23*(2), 280–294. https://doi.org/10.1177/1354067X17695761.

Brockmeier, J. (2010). After the archive. Remapping memory. *Culture & Psychology, 16*(1), 5–35. https://doi.org/10.1177/1354067X09353212

Cole, M. (2007). Phylogeny and cultural history in ontogeny. *Journal of Physiology-Paris, 101*, 236–246.

D'Argembeau, A. (2012). Autobiographical memory and future thinking. In D. Bernsten & C. Rubin (Eds.), *Understanding autobiographical memory* (pp. 311–330). New York: Cambridge University Press. Retrieved from https://doi.org/10.1017/CBO9781139021937.022.

de Saint-Laurent, C. (2012). *Dialogue in democratic institutions. A dialogical analysis of the French parliamentary debates on immigration of 2006* (Unpublished dissertation). London: London School of Economics.

de Saint-Laurent, C. (2014). "I would rather be hanged than agree with you!". Collective memory and the definition of the nation in parliamentary debates on immigration. *Outlines. Critical Practice Studies, 15*(3), 22–53.

de Saint-Laurent, C. (2017a). Staying on topic: Doing research between improvisation and systematisation. In C. Wegener, N. Meier, & E. Maslo (Eds.), *Cultivating creativity in methodology and research. In praise of detours* (pp. 143–152). London: Palgrave.

de Saint-Laurent, C. (2017b). Personal trajectories, collective memories. Remembering and the life-course. *Culture & Psychology, 23*(2), 263–279.

de Saint-Laurent, C. (2017c). Trajectories of resistance and historical reflections. In N. Chaudhary, G. Marsico, P. Hviid, & J. Villadsen (Eds.), *Resistance in everyday life: Constructing cultural experiences*. Singapore: Springer.

de Saint-Laurent, C. (2018a). Memory acts. A theory for the study of collective memory in everyday life. *Journal of Constructivist Psychology, 31*(2), 148–162. https://doi.org/10.1080/10720537.2016.1271375.

de Saint-Laurent, C. (2018b). *Beyond collective memory. A sociocultural perspective on historical representations*. Unpublished PhD Thesis. Université de Neuchâtel, Neuchâtel.

de Saint-Laurent, C. (In preparation). *Social thinking and history. A sociocultural perspective on how we represent the past.* London: Routledge.

de Saint-Laurent, C., Brescó de Luna, I., Awad, S. H., & Wagoner, B. (2017). Collective memory and social sciences in the post-truth era. *Culture & Psychology, 23*(2), 147–155. https://doi.org/10.1177/1354067X17695769.

de Saint-Laurent, C., & Glăveanu, V. P. (in press). Cultural psychology and politics. Otherness, democracy and the refugee crisis. In B. Wagoner, I. Brescó de Luna, & V. P. Glăveanu (Eds.), *The road to actuliazed democracy.* Charlotte, NC: Information Age Publishing.

de Saint-Laurent, C., & Zittoun, T. (2017). Memory in life transitions. In B. Wagoner (Ed.), *Handbook of memory and culture* (pp. 209–236). Oxford: Oxford University Press.

Dudai, Y., & Carruthers, M. (2005). The Janus face of Mnemosyne. *Nature, 434*(7033), 567–567. https://doi.org/10.1038/434567a.

Foucault, M. (1993). *Surveiller et punir. Naissance de la prison.* Paris: Gallimard.

Gergen, K. J. (1973). Social psychology as history. *Journal of Personality and Social Psychology, 26,* 309–320.

Gillespie, A. (2008). Social representations, alternative representations and semantic barriers. *Journal for the Theory of Social Behaviour, 38,* 375–391. https://doi.org/10.1111/j.1468-5914.2008.00376.x.

Glăveanu, V. P., & de Saint-Laurent, C. (2015). Political imagination, otherness and the European crisis. *Europe's Journal of Psychology, 11*(4), 557–564. https://doi.org/10.5964/ejop.v11i4.1085.

Grossen, M. (2010). Interaction analysis and psychology. A dialogical perspective. *Integrative Psychological and Behavioral Science, 44*(1), 1–22. https://doi.org/10.1007/s12124-009-9108-9.

Habermas, T. (2012). Identity, emotion, and the social matrix of autobiographical memory. A psychoanalytic narrative view. In D. Bernsten & D. Rubin (Eds.), *Understanding autobiographical memory. Theories and approaches* (pp. 33–53). New York: Cambridge University Press.

Holyoak, K. J. (2005). Analogy. In K. J. Holyoak & R. G. Morrison (Eds.), *The Cambridge handbook of thinking and reasoning* (pp. 117–142). New York: Cambridge University Press.

Liu, J. H., & Hilton, D. (2005). How the past weighs on the present. Social representations of history and their role in identity politics. *British Journal of Social Psychology, 44,* 537–556. https://doi.org/10.1348/014466605X27162.

Marková, I., Linell, P., Grossen, M., & Salazar Orvig, A. (2007). *Dialogue in focus groups. Exploring socially shared knowledge.* London: Equinox.

Mattli, F., Schnitzspahn, K. M., Studerus-Germann, A., Brehmer, Y., & Zöllig, J. (2014). Prospective memory across the lifespan. Investigating the contribution of retrospective and prospective processes. *Neuropsychology, Development, and Cognition. Section B, Aging, Neuropsychology and Cognition, 21*(5), 515–543. https://doi.org/10.1080/13825585.2013.837860.

Merck, C., Topcu, M. N., & Hirst, W. (2016). Collective mental time travel. Creating a shared future through our shared past. *Memory Studies, 9*(3), 284–294. https://doi.org/10.1177/1750698016645236.

Mullally, S. L., & Maguire, E. A. (2013). Memory, imagination, and predicting the future. A common brain mechanism? *The Neuroscientist, 20*(3), 220–234. https://doi.org/10.1177/1073858413495091.

Obradović, S. (2018, this volume). Creating integration: A case study from Serbia and the EU. In C. de Saint-Laurent, S. Obradović, & K. R. Carriere (Eds.), *Imagining collective futures: Perspectives from social, cultural, and political psychology* (pp. 237–254). London: Palgrave Macmillan.

Schacter, D. L., & Addis, D. R. (2007). Constructive memory. The ghosts of past and future. *Nature, 445*(7123), 27–27. https://doi.org/10.1038/445027a.

Spellman, B. A., & Holyoak, K. J. (1992). If Saddam is Hitler then who is George Bush? Analogical mapping between systems of social roles. *Journal of Personality and Social Psychology Journal of Personality and Social Psychology, 62*(6), 913–933. https://doi.org/10.1037/0022-3514.62.6.913.

Szpunar, P. M., & Szpunar, K. K. (2016). Collective future thought. Concept, function, and implications for collective memory studies. *Memory Studies, 9*(4), 376–389. https://doi.org/10.1177/1750698015615660.

Tulving, E. (2002). Episodic memory. From mind to brain. *Annual Review of Psychology, 53*(1), 1–25. https://doi.org/10.1146/annurev.psych.53.100901.135114.

Vygotsky, L. S. (1991). Imagination and creativity of the adolescent. *Soviet Psychology, 21*(1), 73–88.

Vygotsky, L. S. (2004). Imagination and creativity in childhood. *Journal of Russian and East European Psychology, 42*(1), 7–97.

Wagoner, B. (2017). *The constructive mind. Bartlett's psychology in reconstruction.* New York: Cambridge University Press.

Wertsch, J. (2008). The narrative organization of collective memory. *Ethos, 36*, 120–135. https://doi.org/10.1111/j.1548-1352.2008.00007.x.

Zittoun, T. (2006). *Transitions. Development through symbolic resources.* Greenwich: Information Age Publishing.

Zittoun, T., & de Saint-Laurent, C. (2015). Life-creativity. Imagining one's life. In V. P. Glăveanu, A. Gillespie, & J. Valsiner (Eds.), *Rethinking creativity. Contributions from cultural psychology* (pp. 58–75). Hove/New York: Routeldge.

Zittoun, T., Duveen, G., Gillespie, A., Ivinson, G., & Psaltis, C. (2003). The use of symbolic resources in developmental transitions. *Culture & Psychology, 9*, 415–448. https://doi.org/10.1177/1354067X0394006.

Zittoun, T., & Gillespie, A. (2018, this volume). Imagining the collective future: A sociocultural perspective. In C. de Saint-Laurent, S. Obradović, & K. R. Carriere (Eds.), *Imagining collective futures: Perspectives from social, cultural, and political psychology* (pp. 15–37). London: Palgrave Macmillan.

Zittoun, T., & Gillespie, A. (2015). Integrating experiences. Body and mind moving between contexts. In B. Wagoner, N. Chaudhary, & P. Hviid (Eds.), *Integrating experiences. Body and mind moving between contexts* (pp. 3–49). Charlotte, NC: Information Age Publishing.

Zittoun, T., & Gillespie, A. (2016). *Imagination in human and cultural development*. London: Routledge.

Zittoun, T., Valsiner, J., Vedeler, D., Salgado, J., Gonçalves, M. M., & Ferring, D. (2013). *Human development in the life course. Melodies of living*. Cambridge: Cambridge University Press.

5

Perspectival Collective Futures: Creativity and Imagination in Society

Vlad Petre Glăveanu

Collective futures are a product of both imagination, helping us envision beyond the here and now of our existence, and creativity, acting on imaginative constructions in ways that bring the future closer and make it possible. The story I propose here of how we construct collective futures has its origin in a basic observation: the fact that we imagine and create—I will use these terms interchangeably for the time being—*in relation to other people*. For as basic as this observation is, it is rarely acknowledged or, at least, seriously engaged with. Against it stand both a long cultural tradition of individualising genius (for a critique see Montuori & Purser, 1995) and a more recent scientific one of studying creativity and imagination as mainly intra-psychological processes (increasingly contested as well, see Hanchett Hanson, 2015; Zittoun & Gillespie, 2016). The sociocultural approach I am building on in theorising both phenomena takes me away from the isolated self and towards self–other relations and interactions. The paradigm of distributed creativity (Glăveanu, 2014)

V. P. Glăveanu (✉)
Webster University Geneva, Bellevue, Switzerland
e-mail: glaveanu@webster.ch

starts precisely from this premise: that creativity is best understood as a form of action in and on the world, performed in relation to others, and leading to the continuous renewal of culture. While creative action is distributed along several lines, including material and temporal, my focus here will be on its social aspects, above and beyond group creativity (e.g., Sawyer & DeZutter, 2009).

The topic of collective future invites a deeper reflection on the social. By definition, the collective future is "collective" in a double sense. First, and most obvious, it refers to the future of the collective (either a group, community, etc.). Second, future-making always grows out of collective life, of interpersonal and inter-group interactions. While distinct, these are two sides of the same coin (as we are reminded by studies within related areas such as collective memory; de Saint-Laurent, 2014). By placing self–other relations at the core of creativity, imagination, and collective futures, we are not losing sight of the individual that imagines and/or creates, but locating this individual within a broader society. In the end, it is individuals living and acting together that envision and built the future for themselves and for others.

This chapter starts by considering the relation between imagination, creativity, and society. I will argue that creativity and imagination are similar yet distinct phenomena, brought together by their dependence on and, at the same time, contribution to a social environment. Moreover, both processes help us engage with what is possible and, as such, contribute to the future orientation of our thinking and action. Then, I proceed to a discussion of collective futures and elaborate a perspectival approach to this subject. The ways in which creativity and imagination contribute to developing perspectives on society and its future will be discussed here in view of self–other relations. Three ways of building collective futures come out of this analysis: imagining the future for others (monological), with others (dialectical), and towards others (dialogical). In the end, reflections are offered on why the notion of perspectival collective futures matters and why we need to acknowledge the psychological, social, and political dimensions involved in its study.

Creativity, Imagination, and Society

Creativity and imagination are firmly interconnected, yet not synonymous. Despite being often used interchangeably in everyday language and even scientific discussions (see, for example, Vygotsky, 2004), these two notions have different intellectual histories and contribute to different literatures (for more on this, see Glăveanu, Karwowski, Jankowska, & de Saint-Laurent, 2017). In essence, both creativity and imagination designate the human capacity to generate *meaningful novelty* in thought and in action. Both processes express our agency and help us expand our range of mental and cultural resources (e.g., ideas, schemas, images, objects, norms, and so on). The most commonly assumed difference between them is that, while creativity leads to material or materialised outcomes and requires social validation, this is not the case for imagination (Zittoun & Gillespie, 2016). But is this so? When imagining, we might appear to "delve" deeper into the depths of our own minds and away from the gaze of others. And yet, these resources are, at once, psychological and sociocultural, just as the gaze of others can be external as well as internalised. So, then, are we talking about the same process?

In order to answer this question, it might be useful to focus, first of all, on what is essential for imagination and then for creativity. When it comes to the former, the psychological dynamic of "de-coupling", in psychological terms, from the here and now and exploring "spaces" such as the past, future, general, or possible, has been proposed by Zittoun and Gillespie (2015). Indeed, a key characteristic of imagination is the fact that it connects us with *the absent or the not-there* (Jovchelovitch, Priego-Hernandez, & Glăveanu, 2017). This capacity is fundamental for any act of creativity and, from this perspective, imagination becomes a key engine of creative production. However, it is still one of multiple processes involved in creativity. This is because the essential characteristic of creating is *action, doing, or making*, rather than simply "thinking" (despite a long-standing association in creativity research between creativity and divergent thinking; see Runco, 1991). Creative action builds on the relative "freedom" from the here and now provided by the imagination while engaging, as part of its unfolding, a multitude of actors, audiences, and cultural artefacts (Glăveanu, 2013). In other words, creativity is, to a greater degree than imagination, a distributed, action-based process.

Considering the above, constructing collective futures involves an act of imagination *and* creativity; in fact, it illustrates well the deep connections between the two. First of all, engaging with the collective and with the future both require imagination since, in a literal sense, they are both outside of our perceptual horizon. This is clearly the case for the future, defined by what is not-yet-here. It is also the case for our experience of the collective which—even when interacting with others, in large groups, on a daily basis—is still a matter of imaginative construction (see, for this, the notion of imagined communities in Anderson, 1983). Indeed, while there are clear and tangible "traces" of our collective lives—materialised in the presence of others, in public spaces, in institutional settings—imagination is called on to fill the gaps (Pelaprat & Cole, 2011) of our perception and understanding of others and our shared society. At the same time, imagining the collective future is different from imagining a new dish or even imagining one's (personal) future. It is a *political form of imagination* (de Saint-Laurent & Glăveanu, in press; Glăveanu & de Saint-Laurent, 2015) in that it constructs experiences of others and otherness in view of dealing with them, at least symbolically (for an empirical example focused on refugees, see Glăveanu, de Saint-Laurent, & Literat, 2018). No act of imagination escapes the influence of power and ideology and none illustrate this more vividly than the imagination of collective futures.

What does it mean to talk about imagining collective futures as a creative act? First of all, according to the distributed view of creativity, collective futures need to be materialised or expressed in (inter)action; that is, they need to go beyond individual mental constructions and reflect how mind and society—through institutions, technology, mass media, and so on—collaborate in shaping views of self, others, and the future. Second, imaginations of the collective future need to be studied in terms of their social, material, and temporal expression. Who are the actors involved? How are their audiences? What defines their exchanges in shaping a view of the collective future? What kind of cultural artefacts, material and/or symbolic, are used to construct these views? How are new ideas and practices integrated within the existing cultural system? How are old ideas and practices transformed? These are only a few examples of questions raised when approaching the topic collective futures through a creativity lens. More importantly, just as the imagination involved in building collective futures is fundamentally political, the creativity associated with this process is best understood as societal. Elsewhere I elaborated the notion of *societal creativity* (Glăveanu, 2015a) as the creativity involved in addressing collective challenges. These are challenges that go beyond isolated individuals and even isolated communities; they concern entire societies and, oftentimes, have a global dimension (e.g., climate change, terrorism, migration, debates about the political system, etc.). Envisioning collective futures poses similar difficulties. In this sense, creating new and meaningful collective futures has rarely been as urgent as it is today when we are witnessing a global, growing wave of extremism, intolerance, nationalism and populism.

So, when it comes to collective futures, do we imagine, create, or both? The easy answer would be to say that we engage these two processes at once, but this assertion still supports a sharp distinction between the two. A more complex answer, building on the discussion above, points to the *synergy between political imagination and societal creativity in constructing collective futures*. More specifically, what is of interest here is the dynamic between imaginatively constructing images of self and others, while creatively using them to produce change in society. This change can take many forms, from individuals advocating it in conversations or online forums, on issues that concern the collective, to the action of groups such as protesters or social activists reaching out to broader audiences. In all these cases, the intertwined processes of imagination and creativity simultaneously rely on and build networks of sociability (Simmel, 1950), as well as orient individuals and groups towards a shared future. The collective future is, therefore, not merely an end product of the collaboration between political imagination and societal creativity; this future is equally the driving force behind our urge to (re)imagine and (re)create society. Existing views of the collective future (for instance, the utopias and dystopias circulating for centuries in literature and mass culture; see Carriere, Chap. 3, this volume) actively participate in this process. And so do alternative views of the future, coming from less vocal or even marginalised communities within society. To understand how exactly this happens, we need to shift our attention from creativity and imagination to the notion of the collective future itself—or rather, that of collective futures.

Perspectival Collective Futures

It would be wrong to talk about "collective future" in singular, for a number of reasons. To begin with, views of the future are constructed by someone (person or group) in relation to (often opposition to) someone else. They are not static constructions either, but evolve over time in the implicit and explicit collaboration between social actors. Last but not least, as noted above, the mere existence of a perspective on the collective future, particularly a hegemonic view, invites individuals and groups to position themselves towards it, a process resulting again in a multiplicity of perspectives (see also Maarek & Awad, Chap. 10, this volume). It is, in fact, the notion of perspective that comes through in the arguments presented here. Any perspective on the future, and in particular of the collective future, is "produced" from particular positions in dynamic relation to other positions. In other words, collective futures are intrinsically perspectival.

In advocating this understanding, I need to clarify first my use of the notions of position and perspective. Drawing on the pragmatist scholarship of G. H. Mead (1934) and its more recent elaborations (Gillespie, 2005; Martin, 2005), I consider *positions* as the location of the person or group within the physical, psychological, and/or social field, a location that allows the person or group to develop certain views or *perspectives* on him/her/themselves, others, or the field of perspectives itself (in this latter case, we are talking about a meta-perspective). This definition of positions is deliberately broad. A narrower one would associate positions mainly with social and institutional roles. However, identifying positions with roles in society reduces their diversity and dynamic (for a critique, see positioning theory as explained by Davies & Harré, 1990). Indeed, positions "cut across" the material, psychological, and the social and articulate the three in the elaboration of perspectives. Collective futures are a point in case. In constructing perspectives on the future, individuals and groups use their physical presence, social networks, and cultural resources at once. For example, indigenous and rural populations in Colombia might advocate for more just and environment friendly policies (Sierra & Fallon, 2016) not only because they reflect the position of "members of their community", but because they are also occupying a particular space and participating in a certain worldview.

The view of the future as perspectival fits well with the overall perspectival philosophy of Mead and his followers:

> What is perhaps less well known is that Mead's entire thought (...) was grounded in a conception of reality understood as a field of perspectives (...). According to this relational view, perspectives are not the sole possession of individuals, rather 'the perspective is the world in its relationship to the individual and the individual in his relationship to the world' [Mead, 1938, p. 115]. The reality that matters to human beings is not simply 'out there,' independent of individual actions, nor is it something 'in' the individual. Rather, human reality consists of the dynamic, ongoing interrelation of individual and environment that yields perspectives. Perspectives emerge out of 'the relationship between the individual and his environment, and this relationship is that of conduct [i.e., action]' [Mead, 1938, p. 218]. (...) For Mead [1938], sociality itself is understood as a coordination of perspectives, such that participants in interaction are able simultaneously to act within their own and others' perspectives, recalling and anticipating their own and others' conduct. (Martin, Sokol, & Elfers, 2008, pp. 298–299)

A few essential points are made in this passage. First of all, the relational nature of perspectives is clearly highlighted, as well as the fact that they are grounded in action and orient it, rather than simply being cognitive constructions. Second, the social and psychological life of individuals and communities is best understood, from a pragmatist standpoint, as the coordination between perspectives. This equally applies to the ontogenetic development of the person as well as community relations. Third, as an extension of these ideas, imagining and creating collective futures becomes *a matter of coordinating perspectives on the future and articulating different positions over time*. As action orientations, these perspectives do not only create mental or materialised representations of the future (in conversations, narratives, images, etc.), but guide behaviours in more or less subtle ways, from clear expressions of preference in voting to more implicit choices of interacting with some people, rather than others. Importantly, Mead pointed to some concrete processes leading the coordination of perspectives, key among them being the possibility of taking a perspective. Becoming able to think and act from the position of the self as well as that of others is a crucial developmental achievement with significant consequences for society. This ability is cultivated, from early childhood, by position exchanges in play and games, whereby children adopt different roles and shift between them as they interact with present or imagined others (Gillespie, 2006; Gillespie & Martin, 2014). What underpins this process is the possibility of *distantiation* from any one position and perspective, including one's own, and *re-positioning* within the perspective of the other (Martin & Gillespie, 2010). While in play and games this dynamic is physical, with children exchanging places or props, it soon becomes internalised and relies on the work of the imagination.

This last remark helps us bring together our initial discussion of creativity and imagination and the notion of a perspectival collective future. If envisioning and enacting a collective future is a matter of formulating and coordinating perspectives, then imagination and creativity play a central role in this process by precisely enabling acts of distantiation and the emergence of novelty. As discussed earlier, imagination is the main psychological phenomenon relating us to absence and the possible. In turn, creativity exploits this relation in (inter)action and gives it a materialised form. Previously, I have conceptualised the creative process as a dialogue of perspectives (Glăveanu, 2015b), a conception that fits well the analysis of perspectival collective futures. The imaginative construction of perspectives, acts of re-positioning, and position exchanges performed by individuals and groups in relation to the collective future are all essential for our analysis of this phenomenon. They are different from recent proposals of "collective mental time travel" (Merck, Topcu, & Hirst, 2016) and "collective future thought" (Szpunar & Szpunar, 2016), which emphasise the interdependence between past and future (see also de Saint-Laurent, Chap. 4, this volume; Power, Chap. 11, this volume). While zooming in on the temporal aspect of collective futures, these proposals leave the social under-theorised. In contrast, the present discussion of collective futures and their relation to creativity and imagination deliberately starts from society, and more broadly, from self–other positions and relations. The key question it raises is the following: *How are perspectives on the collective future taking into account the position of others and what are their pragmatic consequences for self, others, and society?* In other words, what kinds of (political) imaginations are enacted in building visions of the collective futures and how do they translate into concrete, societal forms of creativity?

In addressing this question, I propose and exemplify below three types of "imagining": for others (within monological relations), with others (within dialectic relations), and towards others (within dialogical relations). This is not meant to be an exhaustive list of mutually exclusive processes. In practice, these ways of imagining the collective future coexist and come to reflect various "struggles" between different groups and communities within society. In what follows, I will try to distinguish them as much as possible using several concrete examples of imagined collective futures.

Imagining for Others

Perhaps one of the most direct ways of building a collective future is to construct them for others. This is the case when, for example, parents imagine the future of their children even before they are born. And, just as this situation illustrates, an imagination of the future projected onto others, who might be too young or weak to respond to it, has important developmental consequences (see the notion of prolepsis in Cole, 1996, and its application to collective memory; Brescó, 2017). Views of the future play the role of catalysts in the life of individuals and communities. They constitute perspectives that need to be answered or engaged with, both when accepted and especially when resisted. In order to understand the dynamic of imagining the future for others we need to start from examining the *power relations* established between the two positions, that is, of those who develop a certain (political) imagination and of those who are subjected to it and defined by it. This process does not always end in the pragmatic consequence of exploiting or marginalising others. In the example of parents, for instance, it is reasonable to assume they would desire the best possible future for their children. However, when it comes to larger groups and the future of the collective, such paternalistic tendencies tend to backfire by, for example, rendering the dominant group stronger and the less powerful one even weaker. A grim reminder of this is offered by Francis's (2011) insightful book, *The imaginary Indian*, and his discussion of Amerindians portrayed in Canada. He writes:

> Ignoble or noble? From the first encounter, Europeans viewed aboriginal Americans through a screen of their own prejudices and preconceptions. Given the wide gulf separating the cultures, Europeans have tended to imagine the Indian rather than to know Native people, thereby to project onto Native people all the fears and hopes they have for the New World. If America was an alien place, then Indians must be seen to be frightful and bloodthirsty. Europeans also projected onto Native peoples all the misgivings they had about the shortcomings of their own civilization: the Imaginary Indian became a stick with which they beat their own society. The Indian became the standard of virtue and manliness against which Europeans measured themselves, and often found themselves wanting. (Francis, 2011, pp. 23–24)

The Natives and the non-Natives, the "Indians" and the Europeans—two dichotomic positions that historically allowed few actual interactions for most people, but actively fuelled the imagination of the colonising nations. The perspective on Amerindians constructed by the latter is fundamental for their own self-understanding and, at the same time, imposed onto the other without dialogue. As in many other colonial projects (see Said's, 1979, discussion of Orientalism), the dialogue between perspectives is *internal to the dominant group*: it is a conversation between the self and the image of the self-resulting from the construction of others. The flexibility of adjusting this construction to serve the dominant group, even allowing some positive features (e.g., closeness to nature, primitive wisdom) is denied to Amerindians who find themselves trapped within the White Canadians' monologue. What were the consequences for the collective future of Amerindians and inter-group relations in the New Word?

> In this view, a modern Indian is a contradiction in terms: Whites could not imagine such a thing. Any Indian was by definition a traditional Indian, a relic of the past. (…) White society was allowed to change, to evolve, without losing its defining cultural, ethnic, and racial characteristics, but Indian society was not. (…) Canadians did not engage in the outright extermination of their Native population. However, they wholeheartedly endorsed the assimilation of the Indian, which in the long run meant the same thing, an end to an identifiable Indian people. In this view of the world, the only good Indians were traditional Indians, who existed only in the past, and assimilated Indians, who were not Indians at all. Any other Indian had vanished. (Francis, 2011, p. 74)

There is no collective future for Amerindians as a group. The imagination of Natives as belonging to the past is highly political precisely because of its pragmatic consequence: "good Indians" are meant to disappear and "assimilated Indians" lose their identity. Francis dedicated a lot of his book to an analysis of how images of (or what we can call here "perspectives" on) Native Americans were created, presented, appropriated and, ultimately, implemented. Many examples of societal creativity are highlighted in his discussion, including the role of policies, literature, and movies in materialising the abovementioned perspectives. As he notes, "images have consequences in the real world" (p. 207), and one of the most direct consequences concerns the absence of a collective future outside of extinction and assimilation. Interestingly, even recent uses of Amerindian culture—for example, at the Vancouver Winter Olympics—are meant to orient our view to the past rather than the future.

Sadly, the history of native populations in Canada is not unique. It illustrates the logic of colonialism that was at work, and continues to function, within large parts of the world. The type of societal creativity this dynamic fosters is exploitative, plundering local communities, and depleting their natural resources (for an expended discussion, see Sierra & Fallon, 2016). The collective future of these marginalised, oppressed communities is *set for them monologically*, excluding dialogue and, with it, the potential for contradiction. It is the same logic that applies within totalitarian states where the party manipulates the imagination of the collective future and "creatively" exploits the population while claiming to represent it (Marková, forthcoming). In both cases, the positions from which the collective future is constructed are rigid and the power of their perspectives to define reality is asymmetrical. Imagining for others, for as benevolent as the ones who imagine are, reduces the agency of those imagined, particularly in what concerns their future within society. Fortunately, even within the most extreme examples of this dynamic, there is always room for resistance—an example we turn to next.

Imagining with Others

People, even within the most oppressed communities, are not passive recipients of the perspectives of others. They do respond to them and attempt, at least, to shape societal discourses in ways that demonstrate their creative agency. However, self–other relations depend on both terms and on the sense of *mutual recognition* that depicts others and their knowledge as valuable. Imagining with others refers, in this context, to the interaction and communication involved in building a more open and perspectival collective future. While power relations do not miraculously vanish, they are accounted for and, in the best scenario, balanced in order to allow the fruitful co-creation of a shared future by multiple social actors. The example of community and grassroots action is powerful in this case (Pilisuk, McAllister, & Rothman, 1996). It illustrates how different groups talk to each other and mobilise their members in order to achieve change. In this process, different perspectives on the collective future are formulated and various voices are heard before reaching a (temporary) consensus about "the way forward". Unlike situations of imagining for others, position exchanges and perspective-taking mark these dialogues with others in an effort to strengthen and promote a shared view of the future.

A good example of imagining with others is offered by rural (campesinos), Afro, and indigenous communities in Colombia who mobilise for the recognition of their rights against abuses from both the national government and multinational companies (Gedicks, 2003). In response to the latter, grassroots forms of resistance emerge with the aim of both resisting the exploitation of local communities and their resources and defining a vision of the collective future. They subscribe to what has been aptly theorised by Catherine Walsh (2012) as *decolonial thought*, which

> finds its base in the particular ways Andean indigenous and Afro-descendant intellectuals and movements understand and use epistemic production as a key component of their political projects, projects aimed not simply at confronting the vestiges of colonialism (decolonialization), but rather at the radical reconstruction of knowledge, power, being, and life itself. Projects aimed at 'decoloniality', understood as the simultaneous and continuous processes of transformation and creation, the construction of radically distinct social imaginaries, conditions, and relations of power, knowledge. (p. 11)

Decolonial thinking, and by extension, decolonial imagination is not assuming the end of colonialism (a critique often addressed to the work on postcolonialism) but aims to understand its present-day transformation and consequences. The completely asymmetrical relations of power between the coloniser and the colonised and the monological relationship established between them (see the previous section) continue to leave their mark on the construction of knowledge about the self. This ongoing colonisation of knowledge translates into a *colonisation of the collective future*, still constructed mainly from the perspective of the coloniser and the logic of neoliberal markets and consumerism. Concretely, this future envisioned by others continues the oppression of rural communities and the exploitation of their natural resources by the government, in cooperation with multinationals. These colonised futures are increasingly challenged by collective acts of creativity based on the mobilisation of community members and the organisation of peaceful protests, artistic acts of resistance combined with taking legal action. I briefly analysed elsewhere (Glăveanu, 2015a) one such instance—the community action in San Luis for the protection of the local river, Rio Dormilón, against the construction of a hydroelectric power station.

What is interesting for our discussion here is the role played by visions of the collective future in building a unitary response from the community. The manifesto published in the local newspaper, *El Arriero* (2014), includes clear evidence of this:

> The river is a fundamental part of our cultural identity and, as such, without it we would lose our connection to the water, the forest and the earth. At the same time, many of our roots and ancestral values like solidarity, peaceful coexistence and dignity, would risk being harmed through ruptures and processes not well understood. We, the inhabitants of San Luis and of this region, who love our river, are bound today by spiritual and cosmic unity, a superior value that has no comparison with what is intended for our river. In addition, today the river Dormilón is a structural axis around which the 'social economy' of San Luis is organized. (…) We see that the river Dormilón moves a great part of our local economy and will do so even more in the future if we keep our dreams clear and act to offer locals and visitors services of rural tourism in accordance to our values. (translated in Glăveanu, 2015a, pp. 196–197)

The use of the future here goes beyond the rhetorical. It demonstrates the dynamic relation between past and future and it is pragmatically employed to defend a specific identity and set of values against the interests of others. In other words, community action builds a position from which the community can speak and formulate its own perspectives on its own future. This process has only intensified in San Luis after the successful campaign for Rio Dormilón. During my last visit, in 2015, one of the local leaders, Luis Evelio Giraldo García informed me about a proposal to strengthen the local community, including a public consultation on the notion of "public goods" and their defence. The small leaflet circulated among the inhabitants of San Luis offered a brief definition of the term ("Public goods are those goods that should belong to us equally and towards the dignity of all"), a few examples (the river, public spaces, the forest, ancient roads, local culture, health and education, etc.), as well as a schema showing the interdependence between "participative society", "public administration", and "the private sector" in promoting more just, equitable, and sustainable forms of development. On the back, members of the community were asked to give their own examples of public goods and reflect on how they participate in their production and maintenance. These initiatives, as well as similar ones, reflect a particular way of imagining the collective future, together with others. I have termed this process dialectical, considering the fact that exchanges between equal participants are meant to generate multiple perspectives, yet ultimately *harmonise them into a shared vision of the future*. This vision can then be used to defend the community members against future abuses of their rights and illegal exploitation of their land. The dialectic move encourages diversity, but it ultimately prioritises consensus (Sennett, 2012).

Imagining Towards Others

The last type of collective future-making is defined by what can be called "imagining towards others". This rather vague formulation is used to point to a fundamental difference between this process and that of imagining with others. As discussed above, an underlying characteristic of imagining with others is its dialectical progression: formulating opposing perspectives and working through them towards a resolution, in iterative steps. In contrast, when imagining towards others we aim first and foremost to engage with the position of the other, rather than his/her or their perspective. This implies a certain degree of openness towards what the other says, thinks, and does that sidesteps the need for consensus. *Polyphony and divergence of perspectives* are placed at the core of this type of imagination, two features that illustrate dialogic self–other relations (Bakhtin, 1981; Marková, 2003). Dialogism is an old philosophy with deep consequences for how we understand imagination, creativity, and society. Applied to the study of collective futures, it emphasises the act of reaching out towards others, trying to understand their position "from within" and, most of all, cultivating difference over uniformity of perspectives (Glăveanu & Beghetto, 2017). In this sense, it is the process that most reveals the perspectival nature of collective futures because it deliberately builds on it, augmenting its strengths and makes us aware of some of its dangers.

A fitting illustration of this dynamic is the culture of public protests that has animated many communities across the world in recent years, from the Arab Spring movements to the most recent anti-Trump protests. While deliberately disruptive and most of times short-lived, manifestations of this kind are unique for bringing different individuals and groups together and fostering diverse perspectives. At the same time, there is little integration between these perspectives and, often, they *coexist* in the juxtaposition between different forms of expression (e.g., slogans, banners, the use of music, street art) and different interests (e.g., to protest a decision, to protest the government, to promote a new candidate, and so on). Nonetheless, demonstrations do also have long-term consequences, as argued by Yalcintas in his analysis of the Gezi protests of 2013 and their importance for the Occupy Turkey movement:

> The Gezi protests inspired musicians, film-makers, novelists, poets, writers, social scientists, and other members of the creative class out of a concern for the aesthetics of the protests, rather than the seizure of political power. The ever-growing variety, amount, and quality of artwork, in the forms of documentary, music, photography, poster, banner, slogan, graffiti, stencil, anthem, novel, short story, poem, and theatre play, in addition to the social research on the forms of artwork produced during and after the Gezi protests, suggest that these protests should be studied and interpreted as well as *action art* [and not only] a social event with political consequences. (Yalcintas, 2015, p. 7)

The use of action, political art in the age of activism captures the dialogical processes behind building collective futures. It reflects the polyphonic nature of collective mobilisation and the multiple voices, interests, and values embedded within it. As I argued elsewhere (Glăveanu, 2017), such episodes cultivate collective wonder by presenting participants and society at large with images of the possible, particularly possible futures. Imagination and creativity both enable and are enabled by social activism precisely because of their orientation towards others and towards the collective future. While the people who participate in demonstrations have a variety of motives for doing so, the process of expressing one's view builds upon a shared sense of sociability and the playfulness and joy of being with others that usually underpins collective life (Jovchelovitch, 2015). More than this, because of the meeting of different people, groups, and perspectives, social action enhances the possibility of becoming *reflexive* and seeing the world, including the future, through the eyes of other people. This is, for researchers working in this area, such as Silas Harrebye, a defining characteristic of creative activism:

> Creative activism can be defined as a kind of meta activism that facilitates the engagement of active citizens in temporary, strategically manufactured, transformative interventions in order to change society for the better by communicating conflicts and/or solutions where no one else can or will in order to provoke reflection (and consequent behavioral changes) in an attempt to revitalize the political imagination. (Harrebye, 2016, p. 25)

Of course, we should not romanticise the study of these movements. Behind the seemingly dialogic exchanges, fostering diversity, and self-expression, often lay the interests of different individuals and groups in society. The apparent lack of leadership also contributes to the failure of such protests to achieve durable social change. The case of Turkey in the aftermath of the Gezi protests is a remainder of this. And yet, as Harrebye and others argue, the value of social activism rests not in finding the (one and only) way forward, but fostering debate about it, including about whether we should all aim towards a single, consensual future. Imagining towards others does not imply imagining towards the same goal, and this is both the great strength and weakness of dialogical forms of social engagement (Sennett, 2012). Their main contribution is to *remind us* of the perspectival nature of the collective future and challenge monological and even dialectic forms of moving towards it.

Final Thoughts and a Critical Agenda

In this chapter, I advanced the notion of perspectival collective futures and used the lenses of creativity and imagination to examine it. These two phenomena are important here since imagination creates the conditions for distancing oneself from a singular position in the world while creativity exploits this potential in action. Concretely, I proposed and illustrated, albeit briefly, three forms of imagining collective futures—for others (monological), with others (dialectical), and towards others (dialogical). Imagining *for others* is characterised by the absence of real dialogue and the imposition of perspectives regarding the collective future. Imagining *with others* is grounded in exchanges of both positions and perspectives with the aim of reaching some form of consensus when it comes to the collective's future. Finally, imagining *towards others* shares the emphasis on dialogue while striving towards diversity and accommodating difference.

Each one of these processes involves a multitude of positions, and yet, their existence is differently recognised and valued. *Monological* forms of future-making implicitly or explicitly deny the position of the other. *Dialectical* forms invite them as a step towards consensus, whereas *dialogical* forms actively maintain plurality and cultivate the tensions specific to it. Important to note, each one of these processes can have negative or positive pragmatic consequences (depending for whom), and they are not mutually exclusive. While, conceptually, it is hard to reconcile monologism with dialectics and especially dialogism, in practice, they may alternate or even coexist, depending again on whose point of view we consider and at what moment in time.

Beyond formulating categories, what else can this framework offer us in times of deep social transformation, times in which the forces of nationalism, xenophobia, and populism threaten the existence and future of liberal democracies in the West and elsewhere? How are we to nurture a different political imagination, one based on tolerance and inclusion, rather than fear and separation? How can creativity help us cope with the post-normal times we are experiencing (Montuori, 2011), and help us build a more promising future for all, instead of the powerful and the wealthy few?

These are important and difficult questions. To properly engage with them, we would need to turn our analytical framework into a practical, intervention tool. We would need, as researchers and practitioners, to recognise our own position in society as one of agency and personal responsibility towards others and towards the future. We should ask ourselves which positions and perspectives are systematically unrecognised or made invisible in our communities. Who do we assume has the least to say about the collective future and why? We should not be afraid of encountering resistance and we should try to cultivate difference for as long as each perspective we engage with recognises the shared humanity between self and others. We must stop constructing false boundaries *between science and politics* and participate in public debates as citizens as well as researchers (Glăveanu, 2017). This is not a call to politicise our research but to recognise the ways in which it is already political.

For Bakhtin (1984, p. 166), "nothing conclusive has yet taken place in the world, the ultimate word of the world and about the world has not yet been spoken, the world is open and free, everything is still in the future and will always be in the future". But if the future, both personal and collective, is always open to change, we have the obligation to try and shape it, even when we feel powerless. As this chapter hopefully shows, whether it is for, with, or towards others, we never imagine or create alone. There is always a future for the collective, but this future is also always measured by *how* the collective came together in shaping it. History teaches us as much.

References

Anderson, B. (1983). *Imagined communities: Reflections on the origin and spread of nationalism.* London: Verso.
Bakhtin, M. M. (1981). *The dialogic imagination: Four essays.* Austin, TX: University of Texas Press.
Bakhtin, M. M. (1984). *Problems of Dostoevsky's Poetics* (C. Emerson, Ed. and Trans.). Minneapolis: University of Minnesota Press.
Brescó, I. (2017). The end into the beginning. Prolepsis and the reconstruction of the collective past. *Culture & Psychology, 23,* 280–294.
Carriere, K. (2018, this volume). Framing the issue: Literature, collective imagination, and fan activism. In C. de Saint-Laurent, S. Obradović, & K. R. Carriere (Eds.), *Imagining collective futures: Perspectives from social, cultural, and political psychology* (pp. 39–58). London: Palgrave Macmillan.
Cole, M. (1996). *Cultural psychology: A once and future discipline.* Cambridge: Belknap Press.
Davies, B., & Harré, R. (1990). Positioning: The discursive production of selves. *Journal for the Theory of Social Behaviour, 20*(1), 43–63.

de Saint-Laurent, C. (2014). "I would rather be hanged than agree with you!": Collective memory and the definition of the nation in parliamentary debates on immigration. *Outlines. Critical Practice Studies, 15*(3), 22–53.

de Saint-Laurent, C. (2018, this volume). Thinking through time: From collective memories to collective futures. In C. de Saint-Laurent, S. Obradović, & K. R. Carriere (Eds.), *Imagining collective futures: Perspectives from social, cultural, and political psychology* (pp. 59–81). London: Palgrave Macmillan.

de Saint-Laurent, C., & Glăveanu, V. P. (in press). Cultural psychology and politics: Otherness, democracy and the refugee crisis. In B. Wagoner, I. Bresco, & V. P. Glăveanu (Eds.), *The road to actualised democracy*. Charlotte, NC: Information Age.

El Arriero. (2014). *Local periodical* (7th ed.). San Luis: Antioquia.

Francis, D. (2011). *The imaginary Indian: The image of the Indian in Canadian culture*. Vancouver, BC: Arsenal Pulp Press.

Gedicks, A. (2003). Resource wars against Native peoples in Colombia. *Capitalism Nature Socialism, 14*(2), 85–111.

Gillespie, A. (2005). G. H. Mead: Theorist of the social act. *Journal for the Theory of Social Behaviour, 35*, 19–39.

Gillespie, A. (2006). Games and the development of perspective taking. *Human Development, 49*, 87–92.

Gillespie, A., & Martin, J. (2014). Position exchange theory: A socio-material basis for discursive and psychological positioning. *New Ideas in Psychology, 32*, 73–79.

Glăveanu, V. P. (2013). Rewriting the language of creativity: The five A's framework. *Review of General Psychology, 17*(1), 69–81.

Glăveanu, V. P. (2014). *Distributed creativity: Thinking outside the box of the creative individual*. Cham: Springer.

Glăveanu, V. P. (2015a). Developing society: Reflections on the notion of societal creativity. In A.-G. Tan & C. Perleth (Eds.), *Creativity, culture, and development* (pp. 183–200). Singapore: Springer.

Glăveanu, V. P. (2015b). Creativity as a sociocultural act. *Journal of Creative Behavior, 49*(3), 165–180.

Glăveanu, V. P. (2017). A culture-inclusive, socially engaged agenda for creativity research. *Journal of Creative Behavior, 51*(4), 338–340.

Glăveanu, V. P., & Beghetto, R. A. (2017). The difference that makes a 'creative' difference in education. In R. A. Beghetto & B. Sriraman (Eds.), *Creative contradictions in education* (pp. 37–54). Cham: Springer.

Glăveanu, V. P., & de Saint-Laurent, C. (2015). Political imagination, otherness and the European crisis. *Europe's Journal of Psychology, 11*(4), 557–564.

Glăveanu, V. P., de Saint-Laurent, C., & Literat, I. (2018). Making sense of refugees online: Perspective taking, political imagination, and Internet memes. *American Behavioral Scientist.* Online first.

Glăveanu, V. P., Karwowski, M., Jankowska, D. M., & de Saint-Laurent, C. (2017). Creative imagination. In T. Zittoun & V. P. Glăveanu (Eds.), *Handbook of Imagination and Culture* (pp. 61–86). New York, NY: Oxford University Press.

Hanchett Hanson, M. (2015). *Worldmaking: Psychology and the ideology of creativity.* London: Palgrave Macmillan.

Harrebye, S. F. (2016). *Social change and creative activism in the 21st century: The mirror effect.* Houndmills: Palgrave Macmillan.

Jovchelovitch, S. (2015). The creativity of the social: Imagination, development and social change in Rio de Janeiro's favelas. In V. P. Glăveanu, A. Gillespie, & J. Valsiner (Eds.), *Rethinking creativity: Contributions from social and cultural psychology* (pp. 76–92). Hove/New York: Routledge.

Jovchelovitch, S., Priego-Hernandez, J., & Glăveanu, V. P. (2017). Imagination in children entering culture. In T. Zittoun & V. P. Glăveanu (Eds.), *Handbook of Imagination and Culture* (pp. 111–136). New York, NY: Oxford University Press.

Maarek, E. A., & Awad, S. H. (2018, this volume). Creating alternative futures: Cooperative initiatives in Egypt. In C. de Saint-Laurent, S. Obradović, & K. R. Carriere (Eds.), *Imagining collective futures: Perspectives from social, cultural, and political psychology* (pp. 199–219). London: Palgrave Macmillan.

Marková, I. (2003). *Dialogicality and social representations: The dynamics of mind.* Cambridge: Cambridge University Press.

Marková, I. (2017). From imagination to well-controlled images: Challenge for the dialogical mind. In T. Zittoun & V. P. Glăveanu (Eds.), *Handbook of Imagination and Culture* (pp. 319–345). New York: Oxford University Press.

Martin, J. (2005). Perspectival selves in interaction with others: Re-reading G. H. Mead's social psychology. *The Journal for the Theory of Social Behaviour, 35,* 231–253.

Martin, J., & Gillespie, A. (2010). A neo-Meadian approach to human agency: Relating the social and the psychological in the ontogenesis of perspective-coordinating persons. *Integrative Psychological and Behavioral Science, 44,* 252–272.

Martin, J., Sokol, B. W., & Elfers, T. (2008). Taking and coordinating perspectives: From pre-reflective interactivity, through reflective intersubjectivity, to meta-reflective sociality. *Human Development, 51,* 294–317.

Mead, G. H. (1934). *Mind, self & society from the standpoint of a social behaviorist.* Chicago: University of Chicago Press.
Merck, C., Topcu, M. N., & Hirst, W. (2016). Collective mental time travel: Creating a shared future through our shared past. *Memory Studies, 9*(3), 284–294.
Montuori, A. (2011). Beyond postnormal times: The future of creativity and the creativity of the future. *Futures, 43*(2), 221–227.
Montuori, A., & Purser, R. (1995). Deconstructing the lone genius myth: Toward a contextual view of creativity. *Journal of Humanistic Psychology, 35*(3), 69–112.
Pelaprat, E., & Cole, M. (2011). "Minding the gap": Imagination, creativity and human cognition. *Integrative Psychological and Behavioral Science, 45*, 397–418.
Pilisuk, M., McAllister, J., & Rothman, J. (1996). Coming together for action: The challenge of contemporary grassroots community organizing. *Journal of Social Issues, 52*(1), 15–37.
Power, S. (2018, this volume). Remembering and imagining in human development: Fairness and social movements in Ireland. In C. de Saint-Laurent, S. Obradović, & K. R. Carriere (Eds.), *Imagining collective futures: Perspectives from social, cultural, and political psychology* (pp. 221–235). London: Palgrave Macmillan.
Runco, M. A. (1991). *Divergent thinking.* Norwood, NJ: Ablex.
Said, E. (1979). *Orientalism.* New York: Vintage Books.
Sawyer, R. K., & DeZutter, S. (2009). Distributed creativity: How collective creations emerge from collaboration. *Psychology of Aesthetics, Creativity, and the Arts, 3*(2), 81–92.
Sennett, R. (2012). *Together: The rituals, pleasures and politics of cooperation.* Haven, CT: Yale University Press.
Sierra, Z., & Fallon, G. (2013). Entretejiendo Comunidades y Universidades: Desafíos Epistemológicos Actuales. [Interweaving communities and universities. Current epistremological challenges]. *Revista Ra Ximhai (México), 9*(2), 235–260.
Sierra, Z., & Fallon, G. (2016). Rethinking creativity from the "South": Alternative horizons toward strengthening community-based well-being. In V. P. Glăveanu (Ed.), *The Palgrave handbook of creativity and culture research* (pp. 355–374). London: Palgrave Macmillan.
Simmel, G. (1950). Sociability. In *The sociology of Georg Simmel* (pp. 40–57). Translated, edited and introduced by Kurt H. Wolff. London: The Free Press.

Szpunar, P. M., & Szpunar, K. K. (2016). Collective future thought: Concept, function, and implications for collective memory studies. *Memory Studies, 9*(4), 376–389.

Vygotsky, L. S. (2004). Imagination and creativity in childhood. *Journal of Russian and East European Psychology, 42*(1), 7–97.

Walsh, C. (2012). "Other" knowledges, "other" critiques: Reflections on the politics and practices of philosophy and decoloniality in the "other" America. *Transmodernity: Journal of Peripheral Cultural Production of the Luso-Hispanic World, 1*(3), 11–27.

Yalcintas, A. (2015). Intellectual disobedience in Turkey. In A. Yalcintas (Ed.), *Creativity and humour in occupy movements* (pp. 6–29). London: Palgrave Macmillan.

Zittoun, T., & Gillespie, A. (2015). *Imagination in human and cultural development*. London: Routledge.

Zittoun, T., & Gillespie, A. (2016). Imagination: Creating alternatives in everyday life. In V. P. Glăveanu (Ed.), *The Palgrave handbook of creativity and culture research* (pp. 225–242). London: Palgrave Macmillan.

Section II

Collective Imaginations

6

Imagining Collective Futures in Time: Prolepsis and the Regimes of Historicity

Ignacio Brescó de Luna

Prolepsis—or the narrative manoeuver consisting of evoking a future event in advance (Genette, 1980)—is a concept borrowed from literary theory[1] that has been used in psychology for studying the contribution of culture and meaning to development. Cole (1996) applies the notion of prolepsis to upbringing insofar as parents' expected goals vis-à-vis their offspring guide their educational childrearing, thus channeling the child's present toward the parents' imagined future. This imagined future is, in turn, culturally mediated, since it is strongly based on the parents' past experiences, including the ways in which they were raised. Prolepsis in developmental contexts implies a rather nonlinear process whereby the expectations envisaged in the imagined future of the child, based on the

---

[1] Contrary to analepsis or flash-back –consisting of bringing the past into the present in the story– prolepsis or flash-forward is a "movement forward in time, so that a future event is related textually before its time, before the presentation of chronologically intermediate events (which end up being narrated later in the text)" (Toolan, 1988, p. 43).

I. B. de Luna (✉)
Aalborg University, Aalborg, Denmark
e-mail: ignacio@hum.aau.dk

parents' past experiences, are brought into the present adult treatment of the baby (Cole, 1996, p.184). In sum, prolepsis can be understood as "the cultural mechanism that brings the end into the beginning" (ibid, p. 183).

In Brescó (2017), I applied the notion of prolepsis to collective memory in order to examine how imagined futures are brought into the present by means of particular ways of reconstructing the past, thus mobilizing collectives toward certain political goals. Such a dynamic relationship between past, present, and future which, as we will see, can be found in certain utopias, nation-building processes and nationalist discourses seeking a nostalgic renewal of the past, poses some problems with respect to the traditional linear concept of time; a concept based on efficient causality, in which events are inevitably pushed from the past into the future (Morselli, 2013). Conversely, in the abovementioned examples, it is an imagined scenario—for example, a classless society—that pulls the present toward the future through a certain way of reconstructing the collective past. Humans do not passively react to stimuli but are constantly constructing other possible worlds (Bruner, 1986) and imagining new futures that can alter our own present and the way we look at the past (Tileaga, Chap. 8, this volume; Zittoun & de Saint-Laurent, 2015). This approach is in line with one of the key assumptions of cultural psychology (Valsiner & Rosa, 2007)—namely, that we are goal-oriented beings and, as such, we use different cultural tools (Wertsch, 2002) to interpret the world and create bridges toward what is not yet given, thus reducing future inherent uncertainty (Abbey & Bastos, 2014).

Along these lines, in Brescó (2017), the notion of prolepsis was discussed vis-à-vis the role of narratives, considered as key meaning-making tools through which past, present, and future can be meaningfully articulated. According to Brockmeier (2009), this narrative standpoint assumes that "our concepts of time are neither universally given entities nor epistemological preconditions of experience but outcomes of symbolic constructions that are by their very nature cultural and historical" (p. 118). In telling stories about ourselves—be it in the first person singular or plural—we dialectically co-construct our past experiences and future expectations through a "self-woven symbolic fabric of temporality" (ibid, p. 118). As Brockmeier (ibid) acknowledges, this view is at odds with the Newtonian ontological assumption according to which time is an absolute and homogenous system; a fixed objective background against which any event can be spatiotemporally localized as a point on a continuous line, regardless of the person who is experiencing, remembering, or imagining it. In fact, as Bevernage and Lorenz (2013) point out, most historians seem to share this standard notion of time by assuming that time is what calendars and clocks mark out. Although history has assumed the existence of "the past" as its object since the advent of modernity, different authors (Hartog, 2003/2015; Koselleck, 1979/2004; Schiffman, 2011) have started questioning how past, present, and future are experienced, distinguished, and articulated throughout history, across cultures, and across classrooms as well (see Carretero, Chap. 13, this volume). This questioning of time categories, previously taken for granted, is gaining momentum in times of crisis, as well as in an increasingly apparent crisis of time. As Lorenz (2014) notes, while the future is losing its promise of progress and seems to hang over us like an imminent threat, the past seems to have lost its fixed place at a safe distance from the present which, in turn, is instantly consumed no sooner than it arrives. In short, the regime of time in which we were comfortably living seems to be called into question (Mudrovcic, 2014).

In taking up this question, this chapter sets out to further explore the notion of prolepsis by looking at how different collectively imagined futures are articulated vis-à-vis various ways of reconstructing the past and understanding the present. Formulated in Koselleck's (1979/2004, pp. 258–9) terms, the main goal is to examine how *horizons of expectations* (the future made present, whether in the form of hope or fear, utopias or dystopias, fatalistic resignation or rational analysis) and *spaces of experience* (the past incorporated into the present through remembering and tradition) dynamically co-construct one another and provide guidance to specific agencies in the course of social or political movement. In Koselleck's own words, there is "no expectation without experience [and] no experience without expectation" (ibid, p. 257). Drawing on Hartog's (2003/2015) notion of *regimes of historicity* and Mannheim's (1936/1979) classical work on changes in the configuration of the utopian mentality, the focus will be placed on the new horizon of expectations generated by modernity in the West, as well as on how the recent crisis of modernity—

and the resulting contraction of such horizon—has impacted the way we reconstruct the past and orient our actions in the present.[2]

Prolepsis and the Regimes of Historicity

According to Hartog (2003/2015), regimes of historicity essentially refer "to how individuals or groups situate themselves and develop in time, that is, the forms taken by their historical condition" (p. xvi). This concept can be conceived as "a heuristic tool [to better understand] the crisis of time, [...] whenever the way in which past, present, and future are articulated no longer seems self-evident" (ibid, p. 16). Regimes of historicity thus imply looking at different dominant orders of time, which eventually go into crisis. According to Koselleck (1979/2004), the advent of modernity at the end of the eighteenth century brought about a gradual estrangement from an order of time dominated by religion, resulting in a new regime of historicity dominated by the idea of progress and an increasing gap between experience and expectation. Hartog (2003/2015) marks out the modern regime of historicity between the French Revolution (1789) and the fall of the Berlin Wall (1989). The expectations of forging a better future having been shattered, the crisis in the modern regime of time seems to be giving way to what Hartog (ibid) calls *presentism*, an experience of time in which the present is omnipresent and the past—present in the form of memory, commemoration, and nostalgia—tends to fulfill an identity function, rather than being a guide for planning the future.

In the next sections, different regimes of historicity will be discussed vis-à-vis different imagined futures and utopias, the latter being understood as "that type of orientation which transcends reality and which at the same time breaks the bonds of the existing order" (Mannheim, 1936/1979, p.173). Commencing prior to the advent of modernity, a discussion on the modern regime of historicity will follow with particular focus on how prolepsis comes into play in mobilizing the past toward an imagined future, especially in the case of the nationalist and socialist

---

[2] As pointed out above, regimes of historicity differ across cultures. However, this is an analysis that lies beyond this chapter.

movements. This will lead us to today's *presentism* and the increasing importance of the past—primarily in the form of nostalgia—in the face of an ever shrinking and threatening future.

Before Modernity: The Future Outside History or the Hereafter as a Promise

What notions of time prevailed in the regime of historicity prior to the birth of modernity in the Western world? If prolepsis is the cultural mechanism that brings the end into the beginning, was there any imagined scenario pulling the present toward—or keeping it away from—the future before the very idea of progress came into being? According to Bevernage and Lorenz (2013), "for Christianity, time was basically biblical time, meaning that it had a clear beginning (God's creation of the Earth) and a fixed end (Judgment Day). Time was basically 'filled in' by the Creation plan of God. There was no time *before*, nor any *after*" (p.41). In that scenario, the present and the past were enclosed within a common historical plane, and future expectations were based on predecessors' past experiences. Future expectations that went beyond all previous experiences were not related to this world; they were outside history, beyond human time. They were directed at the so-called Hereafter, enhanced apocalyptically in terms of the general End of the World (Koselleck, 1979/2004, pp. 264–5). As long as the future was projected in some other-worldly sphere transcending history, the idea of the Hereafter stood as an integral part of medieval order, until utopian movements—for example, millennialism or *chilianism*—started to embody this imagined future into their actual conduct by trying to accelerate the coming of the Millennium, the kingdom of God on Earth before the Last Judgment. Future expectations, hitherto not embedded into any specific goal, took on a mundane complexion as they were felt to be realizable in the here and now. However, as Mannheim (1936/1979) points out, this realization was not based on any real articulation of historical time—namely, a progressive evolution from the present to an imagined future—but on a tense expectation. In Mannheim's (ibid) words, "the promise of the future which was to come [was] a point of orientation, something external to the ordinary course of events from where [the chiliast was] on the lookout ready to take the leap" (p.195).

Modernity: The Future Inside History or Progress as a Promise

With the advent of modernity, people started to differentiate the past—a past already left behind, drenched in superstition, hardship, and darkness—from the present, and the present from the future which, in turn, was brought into human history and time scale in the form of progress. Historical time could be experienced as a linear and irreversible process of growing fulfillment carried out by men themselves. Progress not only provided an ideal to be achieved but also some directionality to history. Whereas the fulfillment of chiliastic expectations may occur at some ecstatic point beyond history, the idea of progress is now embedded into history through a gradual process of becoming (Mannheim, 1936/1979). According to Koselleck (1979/2004), as a result of this process of permanent becoming and change, expectations about the future became increasingly detached from all previous experiences of the past. The future became more open and uncertain as it began to approach the present at an ever-increasing speed.

Interestingly enough, along with this idea of a future based on progress, modernity also brought about modern historiography. As soon as the past started to become differentiated from the present, it became a subject for study in its own right. As Lorenz (2014) points out, "it was the birth of the future that paradoxically gave birth to the past as an object of historical knowledge" (p.48). According to this author (ibid), history as a discipline has gone hand in hand with the modern worldview. On the one hand, this modern worldview is characterized by a rupture "between the past and the present that produces the past as an object of knowledge and simultaneously as an indispensable condition for attaining 'impartial' and 'objective' knowledge of the past" (p. 49). However, on the other hand, "the present is conceived of as both growing and developing out of the past in which it is rooted, which explains [its] continuity" (p. 49). Underlying this notion of distance in time, Leopold von Ranke—considered the father of modern historiography—claimed that it was historians' duty to study the past for itself alone, showing how the past actually was without any ulterior motive other than a desire for the truth (Mudrovcic, 2014). Thus, historians, like antique dealers, were expected to compile the events of the past and bring them into the present by means of historically accurate accounts.

Utopias of Modernity: The Imagined Futures We Must Fight For

However, in the face of the future's increasing uncertainty, the past also gained importance as a tool to orientate the present toward certain imagined futures. As Koselleck (1979/2004) points out, "after 1789 a new space of expectation was constituted whose perspective was traced out by points referring back to different phases of the past revolution. Since then historical instruction enters political life via [various] programs of action legitimated in terms of historical philosophy" (p. 41).

Along these lines, Marxist philosophy of history, built upon the notion of class struggle, served as a guideline for mobilizing and orienting people's actions toward a future imagined in terms of a classless society. According to Mannheim (1936/1979), "historical experience becomes thereby a truly strategic plan," a plan where "it is not only the past but the future as well which has virtual existence in the present" (pp. 221–2). In a different fashion, nationalist movements in the nineteenth century also turned to the past—to a nationalized past (Brescó, 2008)—in order to construct a new future, in this case, the creation of nation-states. To that end, heroic deeds, old grievances, historical claims, heritage, and so on were brought to the present in the form of monuments, poems, and historical narratives (including those taught in schools) with the aim of fostering the nation-building process.[3] Examples of nationalization of the past, as well as nationalization of geographical space abound (López, Carretero, & Rodríguez-Moneo, 2015). "There has always been an Italy," declared Giuseppe Mazzini in the nineteenth century, for whom Italian identity was carved in the topography of the Alps, and in the basins of the Mediterranean and Adriatic seas (Levinger & Lytte, 2001). However,

---

[3] Along these lines, both Gellner's (1983) main argument, according to which nationalism precedes nations, and Hobsbawm and Ranger's (1983) idea concerning the *invention of tradition* point to the uses of the past vis-à-vis the nation-building project.

upon completion of the Italian unification process, the minister Massimo d'Azeglio proclaimed: "we have made Italy, now we have to make Italians" (cited in Hobsbawm, 1990, p.45). These examples show how the alleged permanence of the nation throughout time—the existence of a shared past and a common territory—is discursively constructed by nationalist ideology in order to build the possibility, even the obligation, of a shared future. As Hartog (2003/2015) notes, "the development of national histories in fact went hand in hand with discourses claiming to speak in the name of the future" (p.131). In sum, both Marxism and nationalism—two ideologies typical of modernity—reconstruct the past in light of an already imagined future: the establishment of socialism in one case and the nation-state in the other. This results in a kind of a spiral-shaped relationship between past and future whereby the former appears as a natural path toward the latter.

The notion of prolepsis may help us to better understand this spiral logic. As we can see in Fig. 6.1 below, it is precisely the imagined future (arrow A in the picture) that shapes the way in which the past is reconstructed (arrow B); a past that can be used not only to interpret the present situation, but also as a moral argument for mobilization in order to

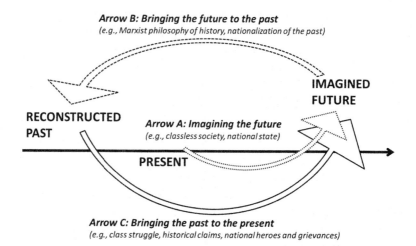

Fig. 6.1 Prolepsis or bringing the future into the present through the reconstruction of the past

attain certain political goals (arrow C). Nation-building processes as well as socialist utopias would be paradigmatic cases of this notion. In both cases, it is the future nation-state—or the classless society, for that matter—that leads the past to be reconstructed in such a way that both political goals become historically justified—namely, whether by reconstructing the past in national terms, or in terms of class struggle. In both cases, the imagined future is presented as a natural consequence of the past, when in fact, the former has been brought into the present by a certain way of reconstructing the latter. Here, just like in Cole's developmental example cited at the beginning, a final cause—the imagined future scenarios, be it of the child or the nation—becomes an efficient one as it acquires pragmatic force for mobilization, thus constraining and guiding present actions. These future scenarios can be understood as *valuational endpoints* (Gergen, 2001) as they set up the criterion from which to endow the past with meaning, as well as to assess the development of events in the present. As Hertog (2003/2015) points out, "the future illuminating the past and giving it meaning constituted a *telos* or vantage point called, by turns, 'the Nation,' 'the People,' 'the Republic,' 'Society,' or 'the Proletariat'" (p.105). This unbearable, and at the same time, alluring, weight of the future turns the present into a transitional period in which different imagined collectives, whether nations or social classes, are called upon to carry the burden of an historical mission. The present then becomes "nothing but the eve of a better if not a radiant tomorrow"; something that could, and indeed should, be sacrificed (ibid, p. 105).

Crisis of Modernity: Stranded in the Present or Haunted by the Past?

What happens when the modern notion of a future based on progress fades away? Weiss and Brown (2013) remark that "the trouble with our times is that the future is not what it used to be" (p. 1). The death of utopias (and their promise of a better world), the threat of climate change, the growth of mass unemployment, the decline of the welfare state (built upon the assumption that tomorrow will be better than today), globalization, the increasing demands of a consumer society based on productivity, mobility, "technological innovation as well as on immediate profit and the rapid obsolescence of things and people" (Mudrovcic, 2014, p. 229)—all these factors, according to Hartog (2003/2015), have been contributing, from the 1970s, to today's crisis of modernity; a crisis in which the future is becoming more and more uncertain, if not threatening, and is thus no longer able to act as a guideline to *proleptically* orient our actions in the present. In such a scenario, we may ask: Does the intelligibility of our world still come from the future?

The answer to this question becomes even more evident in times of crisis—economic, social, political, and institutional. The rupture with the previous state of things, together with the uncertainty that opens up in the future, make past experiences insufficient to interpret the current situation, let alone to create expectations and bridges toward what is not yet given. In such cases, there does not seem to be much of a horizon beyond the present day, as the past becomes of little use in order to plan the future which, in turn, becomes more difficult to envisage. Our historical sense of time seems to squeeze and contract itself, to the point that we may wonder: Where does the future start? Is the future already upon us leaving us with no time to imagine it? Or is the future liquated and consumed no sooner than it becomes present? Looming behind these questions is Hartog's (2003/2015) notion of *presentism*; a feeling of being stranded in the present; a new regime of time which, contrary to the future expectations generated by modernity, is dominated by "the sense that only the present exists, a present characterized at once by the tyranny of the instant and by the treadmill of an unending now" (p. xv).

The Memory Boom: We Cannot Forget …

The articulation between present and future resulting from this new order of time has also led to a change in our notion of the past. Just as the present is no longer steadfastly moving in the path of progress, the past is no longer moving away and lagging behind in the rearview mirror of modernity. On the contrary, it seems that the past—especially the recent past—is still alive and kicking in the present, haunting or consoling us in the form of memory, blame, trauma, nostalgia, debt, mourning, commemoration, and so on. In short, a past that fails to become past and seems to be expanding; a *present past* which is no longer experienced as a *foreign country* (Lowenthal, 1985). As Lorenz (2014) points out, "since around 1990 we have been witnessing the 'shrinking of the future'. This shift of focus from the 'shrinking' future to the 'expanding' past as a consequence of the 'accelerated change' of the present is often seen as explaining the explosive growth of museums in the same period –musealisation of the past" (p.51).

This change in the order of time is an essential factor of the *memory boom* (Winter, 2001) which, for the last decades, has been challenging the ontological notion of "historical past," along with the very role of historiography as a discipline committed to the objective study of a past completely detached from the present. As Mudrovcic (2014) notes, "the temporality of trauma is incompatible with historical temporality, which presupposes an 'historical past' that is irreversible" (p. 235). However, contrary to this classical view of time, some ways of dealing with the past today, such as the politics of regret and reparation, presuppose a limited reversibility of time, or even its imprescriptibility, as is the case of crimes against humanity. As Lorenz (2014) points out, "this limited reversibility is the hallmark of the time of jurisdiction because jurisdiction is based on the presupposition that a sentence and punishment are somehow capable of annulling crime – e.g. in the form or retribution, revenge and rehabilitation" (p.47). Lorenz (2014) concludes that on losing hope of making the future better than the present, the idea that we can somehow improve or repair the past seems to have taken its place.

Nostalgia or Bringing the Past Back to the Future: If Only We Could Go Back to the Good Old Days…

In the face of a threatening future, and an accelerated present beyond our control, we may be tempted to go back in time and try to make the past great again, to take back control, or more bluntly, to bring the past back to the future. As Lorenz (2014) notes, under circumstances of uncertainty and accelerated change, people resort to nostalgia by clinging to an idealized past as if it were a teddy bear. Introduced in the late seventeenth century as a medical concept associated with homesickness, nostalgia has become a catchword today, referring to a longing for the good old days and a mournful sense of loss on both an individual (Wildschut, Sedikides, Arndt, & Routledge, 2006) and collective levels (Smeekes & Verkuyten, 2015). As for the latter, nostalgia may contribute toward preserving the feeling of continuity between the present and the past among the members of a certain group. As Smeekes and Verkuyten (2015) observe in relation to nations, nostalgia can work as an identity management strategy in response to threats to continuity. Here is when different forms of dealing with the past—collectively remembered and re-experienced in the form of memory, heritage, commemorations, and so on—converge into identity (Hartog, 2003/2015).

The foregoing highlights the importance of nostalgia in relation to collective memory (Hakoköngäs, 2016). According to Halbwachs (1950/1980), collective memory constitutes the affective relationship that a particular community has with its past. Contrary to history, considered as dead memory, collective memory refers to the active past inextricably bound to the present identity of a group—for instance, a nation—imagined on the grounds of a shared past (Anderson, 1983). Thus, the past transmitted through collective remembering—no matter how mythical it might be—is never experienced as something detached from the present or as a "foreign country," but rather, as a *present past*, a past lived and felt in the first person plural. That is why nostalgia can play a prominent role in mobilizing people toward the recovery of an idealized national past. Using an ethno-symbolist approach, Muro (2005) shows how nostalgia, materialized in the myth of the Golden Age, has been a key mobilizing element in the radical Basque nationalism, an element used by the Basque pro-independence terrorist group ETA (acronym for *Euzkadi ta Azcatasuna* or Basque Country and Freedom, in English) to justify its arm actions since 1969.[4] Exalted as a means of honoring the fighting spirit of their ancestors, violence was also presented as a way to bring a new political future to that region (see also Brescó, 2016).

---

[4] Since its first armed action in 1969 (at the end of Franco's dictatorship), ETA has caused nearly 900 casualties, including politicians, civilians, and military members. However, after 50 years of violence, ETA has been losing strength in terms of both its operational capacity and social support. In October, 2011, ETA announced the definitive cessation of its armed activity.

According to Muro (2005), "this nostalgic gaze upon the past continually 'reminds' radical Basque nationalists of an imaginary, yet familiar, past which can only be regained by using revolutionary violence" (p. 571).

Along these lines, Levinger and Lytle (2001) propose a model that accounts for the rhetoric of nationalist mobilization. The so-called *nationalist rhetorical triad* features a triadic narrative structure in which (1) an idealized golden age is followed by (2) a period of decadence and loss; a period that would call for (3) an imagined future where the past glory would be recovered. This structure—similar to the traditional *fall* and *rebirth* storyline—constitutes a narrative template (Wertsch, 2002), which can be used to attain different future goals, from the recovery of a supposed lost sovereignty to the restoration of old national values against a backdrop of immigration. As can be noted, prolepsis comes into play here in a way similar to that discussed in the previous section, for the attainment of these goals is what would lead to employ (White, 1986) the past in such a form (in this case, through a tragic genre resulting from a loss) that a moral content can be conveyed to the present; a moral content which would allow the collective to adopt the role of victim, thus making their claims and actions more legitimate.

Nostalgia or Seeking the Future in the Past: If Things Had Been Different, We Could Have…

However, for some authors (Bradbury, 2012), nostalgia would not be "so much a longing for the way things were, as a longing for futures that never came or horizons of possibilities that have been foreclosed by the unfolding of events" (p. 341). Inspired by Freeman's book, *Hindsight* (2010), Bradbury (ibid) conceives nostalgia not as a quest for a lost past, but as a quest for a lost future which was promised and never came; a future which could have happened if things had been different, if we had acted differently. As this author puts it, "perhaps nostalgia is the desire not to be who we once were, but to be, once again, our potential future selves" (ibid, p. 341). In this sense, the "could have" or "should have" of hindsight can move us beyond the confines of an idealized past, felt as something completed and fulfilled, and thus prevent us from experiencing the present as a kind of epilogue (Nietzsche, 1873–76/1957) deprived of any future expectations.

This notion of nostalgia, understood as a kind of backward-looking hope, has a strong parallel with Walter Benjamin's autobiographical quest for the lost future inasmuch as the future was precisely what the Frankfurt school philosopher was seeking in the past (Brockmeier, 2009). Far from conceiving the present as an epilogue in relation to the past, Benjamin's (2006) autobiographical *Berlin Childhood* conceives the past as containing different preludes of possible futures to come. Striving for historical experience and knowledge, Benjamin "is sent back into the past, a past however, which is open, not completed, and which promises the future" (Szondi, 2006, p. 9, cited in Brockmeier, 2009, p. 129). Here, unlike the nostalgic reconstruction of the past discussed in the previous section, prolepsis translates into a critical gaze on the past in light of different future expectations; expectations that were eventually dashed by the course of events. As can be noted, such a critical and imaginative look at the past—in contrast to the reassuring warmth associated with the good old days—reminds us that both the present and the future are always open; something worth remembering, particularly in a current world so enslaved to the present that no other viewpoint is considered admissible (Hartog, 2003/2015).

Conclusion: Prolepsis and Politics of Imagination

Throughout the previous sections we have examined a range of possible ways of imagining and articulating the past, the present and the future. Paraphrasing Karl Mannheim (1936/1979), it might be said that "the innermost structure of the mentality of a group can never be as clearly grasped as when we attempt to understand its conception of time in the light of its hopes, yearnings, and purposes" (p. 188). The future can be imagined as something beyond this world or as a progressive improvement of the present. It might also be imagined as a looming threat inching closer to the present (as environmentalists warn) or as something to be gained and fought for in order to leave behind a past of inequity and social injustice (e.g., in the case of feminist and LGBT movements). Conversely, the past can become "imprescriptible" so that crimes against humanity can be judged in the future. It can also be something to be remembered and not to be repeated (as in the case of the Holocaust) or, by contrast, something to be nostalgically recovered and brought back to the future (e.g., restoration of traditional values). In turn, nostalgia can also involve looking back to the past in search of those futures that never came to pass (e.g., European Union based on solidarity and social justice). Using dynamic systems theory terminology, it could be said that both past and future can potentially act as attractors and/or repulsors (Valsiner, 2005) in different regimes of historicity, thus disclosing and closing off options for imaginable scenarios while implying the possibility or even the imperative of collective action (Straub, 2005). As we have seen, the articulation between past and future—between experience and expectations—adopts different verb tenses (i.e., imperative, subjunctive, indicative, future perfect) and modal verbs (i.e., must, should, can), thus showing different degrees of agency as well as ways of positioning and orienting action within time.[5] This articulation can, in turn, translate into different emotions and states of mind: Hope or fear for the future to come, blame or pride for decisions taken (or not taken) in the past, relief or grief for those times which are finished and gone, or lament for those future promises that never came true.

Yes we can! If only we could go back to the old days, we must fight for our rights, let's make America great again, we shall overcome... as Levinger and Lytle (2001) point out, "action is prefigured in the realm of imagination, and thus it is in the realm of political imagination that an analysis of [political] action must begin" (p. 190). In this respect, prolepsis can be a useful concept to account for how the past is often reconstructed in light of collectively imagined futures and how this might affect the way people orient their actions in the present. As pointed out at the beginning of the chapter, this concept poses some problems with respect to the traditional

---

[5] From a group-based perspective, see Hedetoft (1995) and the imperative, subjective and indicative modalities of nationalism this author proposes, and De Luca Picione and Freda (2016) for an individual-based analysis on oncological patients' positioning within time.

linear concept of time, inasmuch as people's experiences and expectations are dynamically co-constructed and necessarily framed within different regimes of time, which, in turn, change throughout history. As Koselleck (1979/2004) argues, "there is no history which could be constituted independently of the experiences and expectations of active human agents" (p.256). It is no surprise then that today's grim expectations about the future—perceived as a threat, not a promise—together with the experiencing of the present as enclosure, have translated not only into a crisis of time, but also into a crisis regarding the epistemic value of history. At the beginning of the last century, Karl Mannheim (1936/1979) offered his vision on how the lack of future expectations and utopias might impinge upon our historical sense of time:

> Whenever the utopia disappears, history ceases to be a process leading to an ultimate end. The frame of reference according to which we evaluate facts vanishes and we are left with a series of events all equal as far as their inner significance is concerned. The concept of historical time which led to qualitatively different epochs disappears, and history becomes more and more like undifferentiated space. (p. 227–8)

Almost a century has passed since this statement, and some lessons have been learned from the dark side of utopias. And yet, it seems that some form of political imagination (Bottici & Challand, 2011) in relation to the future is needed more than ever. As Glăveanu and de Saint-Laurent (2015) remind us, though utopias have often led to tragic endings, "without imagination, particularly political imagination, human agency would be impossible since the assertion of one's agency is, itself, a political project" (p. 562). According to these authors, along with a "dark" side, there is a "bright" side to political imagination that allows us, both as individuals and collectives, to think of other possible worlds and different future scenarios; futures we can take care of and feel responsible for because, as Morselli (2013) points out, in a no-future society, "the present is the only 'playground' that matters" and "the very concept of responsibility falls" (p. 307). Perhaps, in the face of the world's increasing complexity and unpredictability—characterized by the crisis of progress and new technological risks—it is time to claim back imagination, imagination not at the service of utopias or ultimate ends, but as a tool for us to *think through time* (de Saint-Laurent, Chap. 4, this volume), or more bluntly, to see beyond the ends of our noses; to be able to imagine the future in light of our actions carried out in the present, and to imagine other possible presents in light of those future scenarios we would like to build or avoid. This brings prolepsis to the core of politics of imagination. If, in the context of upbringing, prolepsis implies going from the parent's cultural past to the imagined future of the child and back to the present adult treatment of the child (Cole, 1996), imagining collective futures would imply going from us to future generations, and from future generations back to us.

References

Abbey, E., & Bastos, A. C. (2014). Creating bridges to the future: The poetic dimension through family life. *Culture & Psychology, 20*(2), 232–243.

Anderson, B. (1983). *Imagined communities*. London: Verso.

Benjamin, W. (2006). *Berlin childhood around 1900* (H. Eiland, Trans.). Cambridge, MA: Harvard University Press.

Bevernage, B., & Lorenz, C. (2013). Introduction. In B. Bevernage & C. Lorenz (Eds.), *Breaking up time. Negotiating the borders between present, past, and future* (pp. 7–30). Göttingen: Vandenhoeck & Ruprecht.

Bottici, C., & Challand, B. (Eds.). (2011). *The politics of imagination*. Abingdon, UK: Birkbeck Press.

Bradbury, J. (2012). Narrative possibilities of the past for the future: Nostalgia and hope. *Peace and Conflict: Journal of Peace Psychology, 18*(3), 341–350.

Brescó, I. (2008). Giving national form to the content of the past. A study of the narrative construction of historical events. *Journal of Psychology and Society, 1*(1), 1–14.

Brescó, I. (2016). Conflict, memory and positioning. Studying the dialogical and multivoiced dimension of the Basque conflict. *Peace & Conflict: Journal of Peace Psychology, 22*(1), 36–43.

Brescó, I. (2017). The end into the beginning. Prolepsis and the reconstruction of the collective past. *Culture & Psychology, 23*(2), 280–294.

Brockmeier, J. (2009). Stories to remember: Narrative and the time of memory. *Storyworlds: A Journal of Narrative Studies, 1*, 115–132.

Bruner, J. S. (1986). *Actual minds, possible words*. Cambridge, MA: Harvard University Press.

Carretero, M. (2018, this volume). History education and the (im)possibility of imagining the future. In C. de Saint-Laurent, S. Obradović, & K. R. Carriere (Eds.), *Imagining collective futures: Perspectives from social, cultural, and political psychology* (pp. 255–271). London: Palgrave Macmillan.

Cole, M. (1996). *Cultural psychology: A once and future discipline*. Cambridge, MA: Harvard University Press.

De Luca Picione, R., & Freda, M. F. (2016). Borders and modal articulations. Semiotic constructs of sensemaking processes enabling a fecund dialogue between cultural psychology and clinical psychology. *Integrative Psychological and Behavioral Science, 50*(1), 29–43.

de Saint Laurent, C. (2018, this volume). Thinking through time: From collective memories to collective futures. In C. de Saint-Laurent, S. Obradović, & K. R. Carriere (Eds.), *Imagining collective futures: Perspectives from social, cultural, and political psychology* (pp. 59–81). London: Palgrave Macmillan.

Freeman, M. (2010). *Hindsight: The promise and peril of looking backward*. Oxford, UK: Oxford University Press.

Gellner, E. (1983). *Nations and nationalism*. Ithaca, NY: Cornell University Press.

Genette, G. (1980). *Narrative discourse*. New York: Cornell University Press.

Gergen, K. J. (2001). Self-narration in social life. In M. Wetherell, S. Taylor, & S. J. Yates (Eds.), *Discourse theory and practice* (pp. 247–260). London: Sage.

Glăveanu, V., & de Saint Laurent, C. (2015). Political imagination, otherness and the European crisis. *Europe's Journal of Psychology, 11*(4), 557–564. https://doi.org/10.5964/ejop.v11i4.1085.

Hakoköngäs, E. (2016). Banal nostalgia: Shaping collective memories in advertisements. *Psychology & Society, 8*(1), 39–56.

Halbwachs, M. (1950/1980). *The collective memory* (L. A. Coser, Trans.). Chicago: The University of Chicago Press.

Hartog, F. (2003/2015). *Regimes of historicity: Presentism and experiences of time* (S. Brown, Trans.). New York: Columbia University Press.

Hedetoft, U. (1995). *Signs of nations*. Aldershot: Dartmouth.

Hobsbawm, E. J. (1990). *Nations and nationalism since 1780: Programme, myth, reality*. Cambridge: Cambridge University Press.

Hobsbawm, T., & Ranger, E. (Eds.). (1983). *The invention of tradition*. Cambridge: Cambridge University Press.

Koselleck, R. (1979/2004). *Futures past: On the semantics of historical time* (K. Tribe, Trans.). New York: Columbia University Press.

Levinger, M., & Lytle, P. F. (2001). Myth and mobilisation: The triadic structure of nationalist rhetoric. *Nations and Nationalism, 7*(2), 175–194.

López, C., Carretero, M., & Rodríguez-Moneo, M. (2015). Conquest or reconquest? Students' conceptions of nation embedded in a historical narrative. *Journal of the Learning Sciences, 24*(2), 252–285.

Lorenz, C. (2014). Blurred lines. History, memory and the experience of time. *International Journal for History, Culture and Modernity, 2*(1), 43–63.

Lowenthal, D. (1985). *The past is a foreign country*. New York: Cambridge University Press.

Mannheim, K. (1936/1979). *Ideology and utopia*. London: Routledge & Kegan Paul.

Morselli, D. (2013). The olive tree effect: Future time perspective when the future is uncertain. *Culture & Psychology, 19*(3), 305–322.

Mudrovcic, M. I. (2014). Time, history, and philosophy of history. *Journal of the Philosophy of History, 8*, 217–242.

Muro, D. (2005). Nationalism and nostalgia: The case of radical Basque nationalism. *Nations and Nationalism, 11*(4), 571–589.

Nietzsche, F. (1873–76/1957). *The use and abuse of history*. Indianapolis: Bobbs-Merrill Educational Publishing.

Schiffman, Z. S. (2011). *The birth of the past*. Baltimore, MD: The Johns Hopkins University Press.

Smeekes, A., & Verkuyten, M. (2015). The presence of the past: Identity continuity and group dynamics. *European Review of Social Psychology, 26*, 162–202.

Straub, J. (2005). Telling stories, making history: Toward a narrative psychology of the historical construction of meaning. In J. Straub (Ed.), *Narration, identity, and historical consciousness* (pp. 44–98). New York: Berghahn.

Szondi, P. (1961/2006). *"Hope in the Past." Walter Benjamin's Berlin childhood around 1900* (H. Eiland, Trans.). Cambridge, MA: Harvard University Press.

Tileagă, C. (2018, this volume). Troubled pasts, collective memory, and collective futures. In C. de Saint-Laurent, S. Obradović, & K. R. Carriere (Eds.), *Imagining collective futures: Perspectives from social, cultural, and political psychology* (pp. 153–172). London: Palgrave Macmillan.

Toolan, M. J. (1988). *Narrative: A critical linguistic introduction*. New York: Routledge.

Valsiner, J. (2005). Attractors, repulsors, and directors: Making Dynamic Systems Theory developmental. *Annual Report 2003–2004 of Research and Clinical Center for Child Development, Graduate School of Education, Hokkaido University, Saporo, 27*, 13–25.

Valsiner, J., & Rosa, A. (Eds.). (2007). *The Cambridge handbook of sociocultural psychology*. Cambridge, UK: Cambridge University Press.

Weiss, J., & Brown, R. S. (2013). *Telling tales over time: Calendars, clocks and school effectiveness.* Rotterdam: Sense Publishers.

Wertsch, J. V. (2002). *Voices of collective remembering.* Cambridge: Cambridge University Press.

White, H. (1986). *The content of the form.* Baltimore, MD: The Johns Hopkins University Press.

Wildschut, T., Sedikides, C., Arndt, J., & Routledge, C. (2006). Nostalgia: Content, triggers, functions. *Journal of Personality and Social Psychology, 91*, 975.

Winter, J. (2001). The memory boom in contemporary historical studies. *Raritan, 21*(1), 52–66.

Zittoun, T., & de Saint-Laurent, C. (2015). Life-creativity: Imagining one's life. In V. Glâveanu, A. Gillespie, & J. Valsiner (Eds.), *Rethinking creativity: Contributions from social and cultural psychology* (pp. 58–76). New York: Routledge.

7

Utopias and World-Making: Time, Transformation and the Collective Imagination

Sandra Jovchelovitch and Hana Hawlina

Introduction

Below, Oscar Wilde and Immanuel Wallerstein present two contrasting views that constitute most debates on the value of utopias in transforming society (e.g., Duncombe, 2013; Jacoby, 2005; Wright, 2010).

> A map of the world that does not include Utopia is not worth even glancing at, for it leaves out the one country at which Humanity is always landing. And when Humanity lands there, it looks out, and, seeing a better country, sets sail. Progress is the realisation of Utopias. (Wilde, 1891, p. 247)

> Utopias are breeders of illusions and therefore, inevitably, of disillusions. And utopias can be used, have been used, as justifications for terrible wrongs. The last thing we really need is still more utopian visions. (Wallerstein, 1998, p. 1)

S. Jovchelovitch (✉)
London School of Economics and Political Science, London, UK
e-mail: S.Jovchelovitch@lse.ac.uk

H. Hawlina
University of Neuchâtel, Neuchâtel, Switzerland
e-mail: Hana.Hawlina@unine.ch

© The Author(s) 2018
C. de Saint-Laurent et al. (eds.), *Imagining Collective Futures*, Palgrave Studies in Creativity and Culture, https://doi.org/10.1007/978-3-319-76051-3_7

On the one hand, realising utopias is the essential process through which humanity moves forward; on the other, it is often seen as enabling and justifying totalitarian regimes, repression, wars and genocides. Where both positions intersect is the notion that utopias represent a potent form of collective imagination that is tightly linked with social change and world-making. As such, utopian thinking merits a closer exploration, from the psychosocial processes of constructing utopian visions to the historical processes of their realisation and finally, why so many utopian dreams deteriorate into dystopian realities. The theme of this chapter will be one of temporality and transformation, since a dynamic perspective is necessary to unravel the co-constructive relationship between utopias and societies.

Utopias, by definition, can only exist in the collective imagination. To christen an imagined place or society in which everything is in perfect harmony, Thomas More (1516) forged the word from Greek *ou* (not) and *topos* (place): no place, yet also harkening to *eu* (better) and *topos*: a better place. Thus *utopia* represents a non-existent world superior to our own. While the word was coined in early-sixteenth-century England, utopias have existed for much longer in virtually all cultures across the globe (Sargent, 2010). Imagining better worlds appears to be a universal and essential aspect of humanity (Bauman, 2010), for which More merely provided a (very apt) name.

The reason utopias, as a genre of literature and imagination, have garnered monumental psychological and cultural significance lies beyond their aesthetic or literary value as good stories. Utopias present us with directional fantasy images of possible futures (Elias, 2009), which makes them vital means of orientation in human societies. Among primates, humans are distinguished by imagining better worlds, which implies assessment of the past and present to construct projects for the future. This is an essential function of our future-oriented psychology. Utopias are intrinsic to human thinking both in terms of the representations and symbols they carry and in terms of the temporal and spatial management that their operations enable. It is thus essential to explore the role of utopias within the literature on how humans imagine not only their individual futures, but also the futures of their collectives, social groups, nations, sometimes even the future of the entire world.

We explore utopian collective thinking in two steps. First, we discuss how humans construct utopias and explore imagination as intrinsic to human thinking and social organisation. Imagining better worlds and having a future-oriented psychology is an essential human characteristic. As a prospective organ, the brain shifts temporal linearity by bringing the future into the present and linking it to the past, which roots the human capacity for planning, predicting and projecting. This operates a distanciation from the immediacy of the present environment opening up the possibility for agency and creativity. We will show that people use elements from the past to fill the future with representations of how the social world could be, as opposed to how it is. Second, we will discuss how utopian thinking relates to social change by exploring how communities of imagination build collective futures. We investigate why utopias have earned an unfavourable reputation over the last century and the issues of bringing utopian visions into reality. We will argue that while utopias are built from diverse resources and guide social transformation, they are often composed of collective representations and present the atemporal end point of social development. Traditional utopias tend to be static and monological in their all-encompassing view of a future without tension and contradiction. However, there are utopias that are multivoiced, polemic and contested, fighting their way stepwise through generations.

How Humans Construct Utopias

Humans Have a Future- Oriented Psychology

As individuals, we spend an estimated 20–50% of our waking life engaged in mental activity that is separated from our immediate environment (Kane et al., 2007; Killingsworth & Gilbert, 2010; Mooneyham & Schooler, 2013; Song & Wang, 2012), out of which nearly half is spent in constructing future scenarios (Baird, Smallwood, & Schooler, 2011). Up to a quarter of our waking life is dissociated from the present, experienced in the realms of future possibilities and impossibilities. Schacter, Addis, and Buckner (2007) suggest that we should think of our brain as "a fundamentally prospective organ" that is designed to recombine information from the past and the present to generate simulations of future events (Schacter et al., 2007, p. 660).

The prospective brain's orientation towards the future is not prominent solely on the individual level; societies are constantly dealing with what lies ahead, from the consequences of technological advancement, demographic changes and the long-term effects of global warming, to planning the development of cities and infrastructure or trying to predict the volatile behaviour of the financial markets. A great deal of politics revolve around anticipating which policies would lead to a better society, and during election campaigns candidates aim to convince voters that the future under their government is superior to alternative futures proposed by the other candidates.

Even so, the prospective brain is not proficient in constructing future scenarios at birth; its relationship to time evolves ontogenetically through intersubjective engagement and biological maturation. Classic developmental research shows that temporal reversal, that is, the ability to mentally shift the linearity of time, is enabled by decentration and object conservation (Piaget, 1950; Vygotsky, 1978). Between three and four years of age, children develop the ability to think about the future (Atance & O'Neill, 2001, 2005). From this point forward, humans are no longer constrained by temporal linearity; instead of being bound to a sequential present, they can place the future before the present, draw on the past and reverse the order of action and thinking. Such developmental temporal reversal is the foundation of planning—thinking before acting that guides the present behaviour towards a desired future.

Having a future-oriented psychology offers humans unique evolutionary advantages: first, *prediction*, which allows us to prepare for possible outcomes and thus adapt to future as well as present settings. Second, *creation*, which goes beyond adaptation by recombining experience and material affordances into new forms that are qualitatively different from what has previously existed. Hence humans do not merely adapt to their environment as it is, but also actively change their environment to suit their needs. The link between prediction and creation is *planning*, which allows us to evaluate the predicted possibilities and determine the best course of action to create what has been envisaged.

If the principal function of human future-oriented psychology is to bring into reality what has been imagined, then what is the content of such imagination? To decide how to reshape the physical and social worlds, people rely on visions of a better future that provide blueprints of the ideal state of affairs (Jacoby, 2005; Zittoun & Gillespie, 2016). In this context, utopias can be seen as collective future imagination *par excellence* as they present complete visions of societal and political reorganisation that chart our shared path forward. However, before we can explore how utopias construct future reality, we need to understand how humans construct utopias.

Imagination: Transcending the Present and Engaging the Absent

Cognitive science commonly refers to the imagination as "stimulus independent thought", "decoupled cognition" or "self-generated mental activity" (Petersen & Aarøe, 2013; Schooler et al., 2011; Smallwood, 2013). Common to these definitions is the view that the human capacity for imagination has the function of transcending the immediate environment, generating a form of thought that relies on self and is decoupled or independent from external stimuli. Whereas these formulations aptly capture the potential for independence in human thinking, they offer little to the conceptualisation of how the independence of the imagination is forged. This independence is central to human cognition and is at the basis of representational processes, both individual and collective.

Research on imagination shows the link between imagination, representation (Harris, 2000; Jovchelovitch, Priego-Hernández, & Glăveanu, 2017; Marková, 2017) and the human societal order (Bloch, 2008). To represent is literally to make present something that is actually absent, so that all mental representation relies on imagination. Representation, the basic brick of human cognition, is only possible by means of imagination. Hence, imagination is the foundation of uniquely human cognition, and not one of its properties (Harris, 2000; Jovchelovitch, 2014; Valsiner, 2014; Zittoun & Gillespie, 2016).

At its very core, imagination is representational engagement with the absent. This is achieved by both making the present absent and making the absent present. Thinking beyond the present or current sensory input, the imagination "disrupts the closure of the present" (Levitas, 2004, p. 39) and allows us the freedom to escape from our immediate circumstances. In the absence of the present, imagination turns its functions around and is thus able to make the absent present. Humans recall and create images of what is absent from the immediate environment, to generate their own mental activity via representation. Just as with imagination, representing is neither a perfectly faithful copy of the external world, nor a purely mental construction of an individual; it is rather an extended cognitive process generated by the interrelations between self, other and object-world (Jovchelovitch, 2007). Thus, while "stimulus independent thought" gives the impression of a specific and unusual type of cognition, the imaginative interplay between absence and presence is, in fact, a central aspect of human thinking.

Furthermore, imagination constitutes the basis of human agency by enabling distanciation from immediate experience (Martin & Gillespie, 2010); instead of being trapped in a single perspectival relation to the world, our species is able to distance itself from any one perspective by occupying the intersections of perspectives, which extends our environment in time and space (Mead, 1927). Self-determining choices only become possible in such extended representational environment, which encompasses self, other, object, time and context (Jovchelovitch, 2007, p. 31). This allows humans to act on the basis of what does not (yet) exist and transform social reality in the direction of imagined social possibilities (Zittoun & Gillespie, 2016).

Nevertheless, in order to serve the function of steering sociogenesis, utopias must be perceived as existing in the future of the current reality, not outside of reality altogether. Jovchelovitch et al. (2017) outline a typology of engagement with the absent that can help us illuminate how different relationships between imagination, time and space produce different outcomes. The possible destinations for imagination are: (a) *the nowhere*, a place of the fictional and the fantastic that exists out of our time and space; (b) *the not yet there*, existing in the current location in an anticipated future; (c) and *the elsewhere*, which contains elements that exist in a different location in the present, but are absent from the imaginer's current environment. Within this typology of engagement with the absent, utopias can occupy all three imaginary locations.

The most obvious coordinates of utopia are in the *nowhere*, since that is from where the word derived its name. However, if utopia is completely disconnected from reality and exists outside of time, it fails to exert any transformative influence in the present. This was the traditional location of imagined worlds, since in medieval times, society was conceived of as static and transformable only by divine intervention (Polak, 1973). From the seventeenth century onward, utopias came to be located temporally rather than spatially, in the *not yet there*, as the ideas of progress and evolutionary view of society became widespread (Kilminster, 2014). Utopias henceforth became "directional fantasy images" that paved the way for social transformation (Elias, 2009). Imagining utopias *elsewhere*, on the other hand, is associated with communities that departed from their current societies to build utopian settlements. In this instance, people are brought together by their shared utopian representations and establish actual communities of imagination (which, when realised, often lose resemblance to their utopian template; Sargent, 2010). Some of the first prominent historical instances were communities inspired by Bellamy's *Looking Backward* (1888), and since then, every period has seen groups of people leave their societies to establish alternative social organisations elsewhere (Jacoby, 2005). There is certain allure in constructing utopias from scratch instead of working to perfect increasingly complex and heterogeneous societies, which is evident today in the visions of establishing utopian communities on Mars and other colonialised planets in lieu of improving life on Earth.

Through the interweaving of present and absent, humans spin the fabric of both lived realities and possible worlds—one of the most renowned among which is utopia. While imagining utopias relies on making the present absent and the absent present, there remains the question of *what* is made present and represented when the immediate reality fades. This is the question of content, which we explore next.

Utopias Are Built from the Past

What is the raw material for constructing utopias? Paradoxically, the foundations for building collective futures are mined from the collective past. The process of imagining is supported by memory, especially recollections of one's past experiences (Schacter & Addis, 2007a, 2007b). This link between past, present and future was first elaborated by Vygotsky, who formulated the first law governing the operation of the imagination:

> [...] Imagination depends directly on the richness and variety of a person's previous experience because this experience provides the material from which the products of fantasy are constructed. The richer a person's experience, the richer is the material his imagination has access to. (Vygotsky, 2004, pp. 14–15)

To describe this process, Schacter and Addis (2007a, 2007b) formulated the constructive episodic simulation hypothesis, which posits that simulation of future episodes requires a system that can flexibly recombine details from past experience. It recasts the traditional retrospective role of remembering by emphasising the adaptive value of the prospective brain's future orientation and makes sense of the often fragmentary and error-prone nature of episodic memory (Schacter et al., 2007; Suddendorf & Corballis, 2007). In this light, the central function of remembering past experiences is to obtain a rich assortment of elements that can be subsequently used as the building blocks of elaborate future imaginings.

In composing visions of utopia, people do not start with a blank slate; their imagination is guided by past iterations of utopias, objectified in semiotic artefacts such as books and films, which can act as symbolic resources for envisioning future realities (Carriere, Chap. 3, this volume; Zittoun, 2007). New generations of authors build upon the ideas of their literary ancestors; in the words of China Miéville: "we [contemporary utopian writers] are all More's children" (2016, p. 1). In addition to previously existing utopias, new ones draw from the wealth of past generations' symbolic labour and experiences encapsulated in the form of mythologies, traditions and collective memory. Hence, it is not only individual experiences, but also the wealth of culturally available artefacts that function as resources to expand the scope of the imagination. From the viewpoint of culture, we could reformulate Vygotsky's first law thus:

> Imagination depends on the richness and variety of culturally available artefacts because these provide the material from which the products of fantasy are constructed. The richer a culture's artefacts, the richer is the material that imagination [of individuals within that culture] has access to.

When representations of a better future are objectified in a semiotic artefact (e.g. novel, film, manifesto), they already become a material part of reality and as such, they can be easily reproduced and shared. As they become distributed across a population of minds, utopias bind people together in "communities of imagination" (Zittoun & Gillespie, 2016, p. 111). Hence, many people can participate in the same imaginary scenario, scaffolding their own imagination on other's imaginings encapsulated in cultural artefacts and incrementally build upon them. The semiotic universes of possibility that emerge from collective imagining are usually far too intricate and complex for any single individual to create. Such visions of collective future exert a great emotional charge in the present and galvanise communities of imagination in joint action towards a shared goal (Duncombe, 2013; Jameson, 2005; Zittoun & Gillespie, 2016).

Imagination of the future is thus a dynamic cycle realised in community dialogue and interaction. It is not only fed by the cultural elements provided by the community, but in producing new visions, crystallised and shared as artefacts, it feeds back into the community updating its mythologies and traditions with new narratives for the future. Many utopian imaginings, though initially presenting a break with tradition, become part of the cultural canon and form the tradition that new authors can subsequently build upon (Duncombe, 2013). Individuals use cultural and semiotic artefacts as resources for imagining idealised collective futures, and subsequently, bring their imaginings back into material reality through creating new artefacts. These allow the spread of utopian visions across societies and inspire individuals to build upon them new visions, which feed back into society in a cumulative spiral of transformation.

Utopias Reflect the Present

Cultures enable intricate imaginings and are in turn transformed by them. However, they can also constrain envisioning of collective futures. Utopias, often born out of discontent with the present, are directly informed by the existing state of affairs and respond to issues that their authors find important for bringing about a better society (Sargent, 2010). By examining the themes and contents of utopian works, we can learn about the period in which they originated. While many issues are perennial—economic relations, governance, law and order, religious belief and practice, child-rearing and education—the proposed solutions reflect the values of the time. Each society creates its own utopias, whose "content, form, location and social role […] vary with the conditions in which people live" (Levitas, 1979, p. 19). Though utopian imagination liberates us from the shackles of the present, it is, at the same time, bound to the circumstances out of which it arose.

This is because utopian thinkers of each era are restricted by an "imagination horizon" (Zittoun & Gillespie, 2016, p. 122) that reflects what is possible to think and imagine in each historical juncture. This imaginative horizon sets the limits for the possible reach of imagination, which can relate to anything from the state of technological development (Bacon's *New Atlantis* could benefit from the use of internet) to the social organisation at the time (Plato's *Republic* was hardly utopian for women and slaves). However groundbreaking imaginations are, they cannot fully escape from the common cognitive ground that defines what is representable to a human society. This is the case for individuals as it is for collective thinking. In Jameson's words: "Utopias […] tell us more about our own limits and weaknesses than they do about perfect societies" (2005, p. 35). In addition to their anticipatory function of unveiling potential futures, the content of utopian thinking reveals the present collective identity, the current social reality. Studying utopian imaginings objectified in literature is thus not only an "archaeology of the future" (Jameson, 2005), but even more so, an archaeology of each utopia's present.

How Utopias Construct Societies

Imagining the Collective Present

The collective construction of a path forward requires the sharing of a common present and both are achieved through imagination. Extending their environment beyond immediate time and space, humans are able to build a form of social life described as the transcendental social (Bloch, 2008). The transcendental social, as opposed to the transactional social, refers to an aspect of human social organisation that is unique: the relative stabilisation of roles, interactions and behavioural routines, enabled by abstract rules, institutionalised procedures and constructed statuses and identities that endure in time and transcend moment-to-moment transactions.

Cultural and semiotic artefacts present a key component of the transcendental sociality because they objectify the imagination that establishes roles and relationships between people, spheres and objects (Jovchelovitch, 2014). They anchor imagination in material reality and sustain shared and relatively uniform images by disseminating them through various media. A similar argument was put forward by Benedict Anderson, who conceptualised nations as "imagined communities" because "the members of even the smallest nation will never know most of their fellow-members, meet them, or even hear of them, yet in the minds of each lives the image of their communion" (Anderson, 1991, p. 6). This image of communion only emerged because the printing press allowed for the dissemination of information that enabled people to vividly imagine those others living within the state's territory. The materialised artefacts make the imagined community seem empirically grounded and provide a concrete referent for a sense of simultaneity in nations. This enables "all peoples on earth [to] have a common present" (Arendt, 1968, p. 83) and collectively build a common future. We thus arrive at a recursive relationship in which communities construct imaginations and these, in turn, construct communities (McBride, 2005). While this section explored how societies are created and enabled by imagination, the next will focus on how they are transformed by it.

Utopias Relativise the Present and Open It to Change

A common trigger for the imaginative flight is dissatisfaction with present circumstances (Kane et al., 2007; Sargent, 2010). Dissatisfaction, or critical reflexivity on the present, kindles the desire to make it absent, to imagine alternatives, to bring forward a not-yet reality. In the first instance, imagination offers a break from the present and cushions its discontents. However, merely escapist reveries rarely have a transformative effect on the real world (Wright, 2010). For example, an alienated office worker might periodically drift away into daydreams of spending time with his family. On the other hand, he might imagine a reality without unpaid overtime and altogether improved working conditions, new legislation and political bodies, or even an economic system that avoids exploitation. In the second scenario, he imaginatively constructs an alternative, which relativises the present situation and reveals it as amenable to change. Nevertheless, he cannot engender change in the direction of the fantasy by himself—he needs to communicate the vision to mobilise collective agency in order to transform the imperfect present.

This is one of the core functions of utopias—to provide desired alternatives that can galvanise collective action to change the status quo. Dreams of an alternative world inevitably expose the flaws of the present one. By default, a better alternative represents a critique and a reflection of the current state of affairs (Elias, 2009; McBride, 2005). It lifts us from a single perspectival relation to the world by introducing a new perspective, an alternative representation from the vantage point of which we can reflect on the self and society. This moment of distanciation from the present can be destabilising (Duncombe, 2013) or cause a rupture (Zittoun, 2007) in which what was taken for granted becomes questionable. Once another option has been shown, one "cannot safely return to the assurances of their own present, as the naturalness of their world has been disrupted"

(Duncombe, 2013, p. xli). The mere existence of an imagined alternative makes the current state of affairs a matter of choice; not only does it introduce the possibility of change, but continuing without change also becomes an option that demands attention and justification.

Utopian imaginings present a sociopolitical thought experiment that allows people to explore the potential consequences of imagined alternatives. This makes them an indispensable component of societal development. While Vygotsky conceptualised how the use of technological and psychological tools contributes to human mental organisation (Vygotsky, 1978, 1981), we can conceive of utopias as societal tools that are used to shape human social organisation and propel societal development. Analogous to how people utilise psychological tools to act on themselves to alter the internal flow and structure of mental functions ("semiotic mediation", Hasan, 1992), societies use utopias as "collective semiotic guidance" (Valsiner, 1998) to reassess and alter existing social structures and functioning.

The Eternal Present of Utopia

Utopias tend to portray an ideal architecture of human society, the final accomplishment of historical progress and social change. As such, utopias themselves are paradoxically static and present a timeless, fixed state in which their inhabitants live perfect, agreeable lives in complete consensus; as Dahrendorf (1958) asserted, "all utopias from Plato's Republic to George Orwell's brave new world of 1984 have had one element of construction in common: they are all societies from which change is absent" (p. 122).

Herein lies a paradoxical issue that inheres even the most zealous attempts to bring utopias into the present: they call for change and yet they are themselves devoid of change. Most traditional utopias are monophasic, relying on a vision that is collectively shared. Classic utopias provide blueprints of an ideal future down to every last detail, from the eating arrangements to the subjects of conversation (Jacoby, 2005). They operate on the fictitious premise that the same ideals are shared by all members of society and "often betray more a will for domination than for freedom; they prescribe how free men and women should act and live and talk, as though they could not figure this out for themselves" (Jacoby, 2005, p. xv). Paradoxically, within a blueprint utopia, an imagined alternative to the current reality does not tolerate alternative representations. Moreover, if a utopia would ever be achieved, utopian imagination would be rendered obsolete, as there would be no further horizon of societal becoming. There are no new utopias within a utopia, no need for a psychology oriented towards imagining collective futures.

The utopian end state is suggestive of a social psychological process whereby social thinking is homogenous and constraining; all social groups partake the same vision and sociocognitive horizon. This suggests a society of collective representations, where "habitual, taken-for-granted and homogeneously shared beliefs, sentiments and ideas" (Jovchelovitch, 2007, p. 44) are held by a group or a society as a whole (Pickering, 1999). This high level of sharedness and lack of alternative representations sustains collective reality and guarantees strong social cohesion (Durkheim, 1898/1959, 1912/2008). However, human societies are rarely monological and free from alternative representations. Actual social realities are much more pluralistic and characterised by cognitive polyphasia, which denotes the coexistence of diversified and at times conflicting representations within the same society or even the same individual (Jovchelovitch & Priego-Hernández, 2015; Moscovici, 1961/2008, 1988). In this sense, utopias contain a human and a post-human component: striving for a better world is an essentially human endeavour, but living in a timeless, consensual, perfect society is no longer a human dream, but rather suggests a post-human world. Living in such a world reaches beyond our polyphasic, future-oriented psychology.

The Perils of Proclaiming Utopias in the Present

Paradoxically, static and unchanging utopias fuel the dynamism that propels social change and historical progress. The problem is that while utopias portray the desired state of affairs, an ideal end point of social progress, they do not show the path to achieving it. Should people aim to advance towards utopia step by step through incremental improvements? Alternatively, should they try to bring utopia into being through a sudden and violent revolution? Furthermore, there is no guarantee that when realised, utopia will usher in a harmonious and idyllic society; as the previous section showed, that would necessitate a fundamental transformation of human psychology. No one can predict what utopia will actually become and it is often argued that a logical fulfilment of utopia is dystopia, a quintessentially flawed society (*dys*- derived from a Greek root meaning diseased or faulty; Jacoby, 2005). Finally, the issue is not just the difficulty of bringing an ideal future into the present, but whether we are even capable of imagining such a future. Building on Marx and Morris, Jameson (1982) argued that our envisioning the future always falls short of a true utopia, which is literally unimaginable. However, the gaps and design flaws in our imagination did not always halt the construction of utopias in reality, often to disastrous consequences.

Especially in the twentieth century, utopias have garnered a bad reputation because realising centrally planned, homogenous and rigid visions of the future invariably resulted in totalitarianism and oppression (Kilminster, 2014). The most often cited examples of degenerated utopias are Stalin's Soviet Union, Nazi Germany, Maoist China, Khmer Rouge in Cambodia, Milošević's Serbia—a lion's share of twentieth century horrors is commonly attributed to utopianism (e.g., Arendt, 1951; Dahrendorf, 1958; Malia, 1996; Popper, 1945; Weitz, 2006). Each of these cases presented a radical break with the present and an uncompromising march towards an imagined future, which resulted in immeasurable human cost. Each started as a small group's imagination of an alternative future that became law, a programme for everyone to follow and uphold (Duncombe, 2013; Weitz, 2006). Lasky argued that utopias tend to fail because they are based upon a "triple error: utopias conceived as a sterile monolithic harmony; revolution as a dogmatic commitment to total change and violent reconstruction; principles of hope and belief transmogrified into an orthodoxy incompatible with heretical dissent or critical opposition" (1976, p. xx).

Such orthodoxy is hardly compatible with the previously described functions of utopias—to relativise the current reality, to keep us from being complacent and open up alternatives that liberate us from an unsatisfactory present. Manheim (1936) proposed that functionally, utopia is the opposite of ideology since "utopias are those ideas which are incongruous with and transcendent of reality and oriented toward changing society, whereas ideologies, though also transcendent, are oriented toward maintaining it" (p. 23). In this vein, utopian visions disintegrate the hegemony of totalitarian regimes and threaten their continued existence. In Zamyatin's famed anti-utopia *We* (1924/1993), the culmination of the totalitarian One State's pursuit of utopia is the invention of the "Great Operation" that surgically removes the nodule for imagination, promising people that they will become perfect, free of anxiety and dissatisfaction. Zamyatin, who was inspired (and subsequently exiled) by the Soviet regime, provides us with an evocative literary demonstration of the socially subversive potential of imaginations. So, do utopias institute totalitarianism or threaten it?

As we posited when examining the location of utopias, they can only guide social progress when situated in the future. In the moment that utopias are proclaimed as accomplished, they lose their transformative potential. As empirical reality, they rely on a social psychological dynamic of homogeneity and hegemony, and as such, take on the reverse function of maintaining the status quo. As Levitas (1979) warned, utopias can become an integral and legitimising aspect of ideology. In a supposedly achieved utopia, imagining alternatives becomes threatening. Since the imagination is an essential aspect of human cognition and cannot be suppressed, imaginary thinking is subjected to control, either by being systematically channelled through engineered semiotic artefacts or by limiting access to those that do not obtain official approval (Marková, 2017). If we return to our reformulation of Vygotsky's first law, it follows that restricting the access to cultural artefacts diminishes the richness and diversity of materials a culture can use for imagining. This serves to constrain the multiplicity and diversity of cultural imaginations. Imagination is thus yoked in the service of glamorising the present and dreaming away its flaws instead of seeking transformative alternatives.

Conclusion: The Future of Utopias

We conclude returning to the beginning: Can we determine which sentiment rings closer to the truth, Wilde's praise of utopias' potential to evolve societies or Wallerstein's rejection of utopias as justification for political atrocities? Historically, Wallerstein's view seems to prevail. Bringing utopias into being has been a very tempestuous endeavour that invariably ended in disappointment. Utopian visions have been associated with brutal regimes, ethnic cleansing, systemic violence and terrorism (Jacoby, 2005; Kilminster, 2014; Wallerstein, 1998). This begs the question: Would humanity fare better by discarding utopias?

One way to progress without the trajectory of utopian vision is through negation of the flawed aspects of the present, as Adorno advocated; "the true thing determines itself via the false thing" (1988, p. 12). This is manifested in all negatively framed political messages: No to war, No to corruption, No to dictators, No to racism, No to inequality and so forth. However, Duncombe (2013) cautions that such expressions of widespread dissatisfaction with present circumstances, albeit pervasive in contemporary societies, often fail to engender significant social change precisely because they lack a utopian vision of what the alternative would look like. For example, the most persistent critique of the Occupy movement was that it failed to articulate a viable programme for restructuring society and its evident flaws (Stekelenburg, 2012).

Importantly, it is difficult to engender positive change without altering the surrounding context as well. For instance, achieving a sustainable protection of the environment calls for a thorough restructuring of the current economic system, with its accompanying ideologies and people's value systems and lifestyles. Arguably, it demands urban redevelopment, new energy infrastructure, a shift in international relations towards greater political cooperation, and so on—an altogether changed world. What appears as isolated improvements often necessitate comprehensive visions of transforming the world, which takes us back to utopias. These positive fantasies of a wholly improved reality often carry a potent motivational charge and mobilise a greater number of people than mere expressions of discontent or dreams of the future that focus on a single issue. In his comprehensive analyses of utopias, Bloch (1988, 1995) concluded that humans never tire of wanting things to improve, and thus, they will always need utopias to set the trajectory of improvement.

If we rely on utopias to guide sociogenesis, then what kind of utopias do we need? We have identified the problematic issue at the heart of most utopian projects: their visions of the future built a static and out-of-time single perspective, which contain a post-human dystopia of a totalising consensus. When realised, they become hegemonic and potentially oppressive. As all monological cognition, they tend to be enforced in a top-down manner precluding tolerance for alternatives, diversity, or indeed, subversive imagination. However, discarding utopias altogether is equally problematic, as they are an expression of our future-oriented psychology and play a central role in propelling human development.

We suggest that a shift in utopian thought towards less determined, more ambiguous and decentralised utopias could better accommodate human thinking about the future and our need to continue imagining better worlds. This shift can be felt in repeated calls for processual and communicative utopias (Habermas, 1989), relative utopias (Camus, 2008), realistic utopias (Rawls, 2003), real utopias (Wright, 2010), little utopias (Unger, 2007) and iconoclastic utopias (Jacoby, 2005). Wallerstein himself proposes to trade utopianism in favour of utopistics (1998). With different emphases and nuances, these authors stress the importance of more polyphonic and permissive utopias based on a careful analysis of the present and appraisal of realistic possibilities of improvement. They caution against unilateral "utopian social engineering" (Popper, 1945, 1957), instead advocating for more bottom-up utopian projects championed by different groups within a society, a more organic growth from "manywheres" (Schweder, 2003) that relies on a distributed collective imagination (Zittoun & Gillespie, Chap. 2, this volume) and is initiated by active minorities. In Glăveanu's terms (Chap. 5, this volume), utopias imagined *with others* and *towards others* should replace traditional imaginings of utopias *for others*. In this view, utopias are not hegemonic, characterised by collective representations and suppression, but composed of diverse, polemic representations that compete and are contested in the public sphere.

Through generations, dreams of a better future steer social change and are, in turn, transformed by it, always marching two steps ahead and maintaining their position in the unreachable no-place. Each new envisioning of alternative realities pushes the imagination horizon outwards and provides a resource on which the following dreamers will be able to scaffold their own imagination. Thus, as Wilde wrote over a century ago, humanity is always sailing towards utopias, but its progress should not be steered by any one single actor.

References

Adorno, T. W. (1988). Something's missing: A discussion between Ernst Bloch and Theodor W. Adorno on the contradictions of utopian longing. In E. Bloch (Ed.), *The utopian function of art and literature: Selected essays* (pp. 1–17). Cambridge, MA: MIT Press.

Anderson, B. (1991). *Imagined communities: Reflections on the origin and spread of nationalism*. London: Verso Books.

Arendt, H. (1951). *The origins of totalitarianism* (Vol. 244). New York: Houghton Mifflin Harcourt.

Arendt, H. (1968). *Men in dark times*. New York: Harcourt Brace.

Atance, C. M., & O'Neill, D. K. (2001). Episodic future thinking. *Trends in Cognitive Sciences, 5*(12), 533–539. https://doi.org/10.1016/S1364-6613(00)01804-0.

Atance, C. M., & O'Neill, D. K. (2005). The emergence of episodic future thinking in humans. *Learning and Motivation, 36*(2), 126–144. https://doi.org/10.1016/j.lmot.2005.02.003.

Baird, B., Smallwood, J., & Schooler, J. W. (2011). Back to the future: Autobiographical planning and the functionality of mind-wandering. *Consciousness and Cognition, 20*(4), 1604–1611. https://doi.org/10.1016/j.concog.2011.08.007.

Bauman, Z. (2010). *Socialism: The active utopia*. London: Routledge.

Bloch, E. (1988). *The utopian function of art and literature: Selected essays*. Cambridge: MIT Press.

Bloch, E. (1995). *The principle of hope*. (N. Plaice, Trans.) (1. MIT paperback ed). Cambridge, MA: MIT Press.

Bloch, M. (2008). Why religion is nothing special but is central. *Philosophical Transactions of the Royal Society of London B: Biological Sciences, 363*(1499), 2055–2061. https://doi.org/10.1098/rstb.2008.0007.

Camus, A. (2008). *Neither victims nor executioners: An ethic superior to murder*. Eugene: Wipf and Stock.

Carriere, K. (2018, this volume). Framing the issue: Literature, collective imagination, and fan activism. In C. de Saint-Laurent, S. Obradović, & K. R. Carriere (Eds.), *Imagining collective futures: Perspectives from social, cultural, and political psychology* (pp. 39–58). London: Palgrave Macmillan.

Dahrendorf, R. (1958). Out of utopia: Toward a reorientation of sociological analysis. *American Journal of Sociology, 64*(2), 115–127.

Duncombe, S. (2013). Open utopia: Introduction. In T. More & S. Duncombe (Eds.), *Open utopia* (pp. ix–lv). Brooklyn, NY: Minor Compositions.

Durkheim, É. (1898). Individual representations and collective representations. In *Sociology and philosophy* (pp. 1–34). London: Cohen and West.
Durkheim, É. (1912). *The elementary forms of the religious life*. Mineola, NY: Dover Publications, Inc.
Elias, N. (2009). *Essays I: On the sociology of knowledge and the sciences* (R. Kilminster & S. Mennell, Eds.). Dublin, Ireland: UCD Press. http://www.ucdpress.ie/display.asp?isbn=9781906359010&
Glăveanu, V. P. (2018, this volume). Perspectival collective futures: Creativity and imagination in society. In C. de Saint-Laurent, S. Obradović, & K. R. Carriere (Eds.), *Imagining collective futures: Perspectives from social, cultural, and political psychology* (pp. 83–105). London: Palgrave Macmillan
Habermas, J. (1989). *The structural transformation of the public sphere: An inquiry into a category of bourgeois society*. Cambridge, MA: MIT Press.
Harris, P. L. (2000). *The work of the imagination* (Vol. xii). Malden: Blackwell Publishing.
Hasan, R. (1992). Speech genre, semiotic mediation and the development of higher mental functions. *Language Sciences, 14*(4), 489–528. https://doi.org/10.1016/0388-0001(92)90027-C.
Jacoby, R. (2005). *Picture imperfect: Utopian thought for an anti-utopian age*. New York: Columbia University Press.
Jameson, F. (1982). Progress versus utopia; or, can we imagine the future? *Science Fiction Studies, 9*(2), 147–158.
Jameson, F. (2005). *Archaeologies of the future: The desire called utopia and other science fictions*. New York: Verso.
Jovchelovitch, S. (2007). *Knowledge in context: Representations, community, and culture*. New York: Routledge.
Jovchelovitch, S. (2014). The creativity of the social: Imagination, development and social change in Rio de Janeiro's favelas. In V. P. Glăveanu, A. Gillespie, & J. Valsiner (Eds.), *Rethinking creativity: Contributions from cultural psychology* (pp. 76–92). New York: Routledge.
Jovchelovitch, S., & Priego-Hernández, J. (2015). Cognitive polyphasia, knowledge encounters and public spheres. In G. Sammut, E. Andreouli, G. Gaskell, & J. Valsiner (Eds.), *The Cambridge handbook of social representations* (pp. 163–178). Cambridge: Cambridge University Press.
Jovchelovitch, S., Priego-Hernández, J., & Glăveanu, V. P. (2017). Imagination in children entering culture. In T. Zittoun & V. P. Glăveanu (Eds.), *Handbook of imagination and culture*. Oxford: Oxford University Press.
Kane, M. J., Brown, L. H., McVay, J. C., Silvia, P. J., Myin-Germeys, I., & Kwapil, T. R. (2007). For whom the mind wanders, and when: An experience-

sampling study of working memory and executive control in daily life. *Psychological Science, 18*(7), 614–621. https://doi.org/10.1111/j.1467-9280.2007.01948.x.

Killingsworth, M. A., & Gilbert, D. T. (2010). A wandering mind is an unhappy mind. *Science, 330*(6006), 932–932. https://doi.org/10.1126/science.1192439.

Kilminster, R. (2014). The debate about utopias from a sociological perspective. *Human Figurations, 3*(2). https://quod.lib.umich.edu/h/humfig/11217607.0003.203/--debate-about-utopias-from-a-sociological-perspective?rgn=main;view=fulltext

Lasky, M. J. (1976). *Utopia and revolution*. Chicago: University of Chicago Press.

Levitas, R. (1979). Sociology and utopia. *Sociology, 13*(1), 19–33. https://doi.org/10.1177/003803857901300102

Levitas, R. (2004). For utopia: The (limits of the) utopian function in late capitalist society. In B. Goodwin (Ed.), *The philosophy of utopia*. London: Routledge.

Malia, M. E. (1996). *The Soviet tragedy: A history of socialism in Russia, 1917–1991* (1st Free Press pbk. Ed.). New York: Free Press.

Manheim, K. (1936). *Ideology and utopia*. London: Routledge/Kegan Paul.

Marková, I. (2017). From imagination to well-controlled images: Challenge for the dialogical mind. In T. Zittoun & V. P. Glăveanu (Eds.), *Oxford handbook of culture and imagination*. Oxford: Oxford University Press.

Martin, J., & Gillespie, A. (2010). A neo-Meadian approach to human agency: Relating the social and the psychological in the ontogenesis of perspective-coordinating persons. *Integrative Psychological and Behavioral Science, 44*(3), 252–272. https://doi.org/10.1007/s12124-010-9126-7.

McBride, K. (2005). *Collective dreams: Political imagination and community*. University Park: The Pennsylvania State University Press.

Mead, G. H. (1927). The objective reality of perspectives. In E. S. Brightman (Ed.), *Proceedings of the Sixth International Congress of Philosophy* (pp. 75–85). New York: Longmans, Green and Co. https://doi.org/10.5840/wcp6192726.

Miéville, C. (2016, November 4). 'We are all Thomas More's children' —500 years of Utopia. *The Guardian*, sec. Books. https://www.theguardian.com/books/2016/nov/04/thomas-more-utopia-500-years-china-mieville-ursulale-guin.

Mooneyham, B. W., & Schooler, J. W. (2013). The costs and benefits of mind-wandering: A review. *Canadian Journal of Experimental Psychology/Revue*

Canadienne de Psychologie Expérimentale, 67(1), 11–18. https://doi.org/10.1037/a0031569.

More, T. (1516). *Utopia*. Mineola, NY: Dover Publications.

Moscovici, S. (1961). *Psychoanalysis: Its image and its public*. Cambridge: Polity.

Moscovici, S. (1988). Notes towards a description of social representations. *European Journal of Social Psychology, 18*(3), 211–250. https://doi.org/10.1002/ejsp.2420180303.

Petersen, M. B., & Aarøe, L. (2013). Politics in the mind's eye: Imagination as a link between social and political cognition. *American Political Science Review, 107*(2), 275–293. https://doi.org/10.1017/S0003055413000026.

Piaget, J. (1950). *The psychology of intelligence*. New York: Routledge.

Pickering, W. S. F. (1999). Representations as understood by Durkheim. In W. S. F. Pickering (Ed.), *Durkheim & representations* (pp. 11–23). Hoboken: Taylor & Francis Ltd.

Polak, F. (1973). *The image of the future*. Amsterdam: Elsevier Scientific Publishing.

Popper, K. R. (1945). *The open society and its enemies*. Princeton: Princeton University Press.

Popper, K. R. (1957). *The poverty of historicism* (repr). London: Routledge.

Rawls, J. (2003). *The law of peoples* (5. pr). Cambridge, MA: Harvard University Press.

Sargent, L. T. (2010). *Utopianism: A very short introduction*. Oxford: Oxford University Press.

Schacter, D. L., & Addis, D. R. (2007a). Constructive memory: The ghosts of past and future. *Nature, 445*(7123), 27–27. https://doi.org/10.1038/445027a.

Schacter, D. L., & Addis, D. R. (2007b). The cognitive neuroscience of constructive memory: Remembering the past and imagining the future. *Philosophical Transactions of the Royal Society of London B: Biological Sciences, 362*(1481), 773–786. https://doi.org/10.1098/rstb.2007.2087.

Schacter, D. L., Addis, D. R., & Buckner, R. L. (2007). Remembering the past to imagine the future: The prospective brain. *Nature Reviews Neuroscience, 8*(9), 657–661. https://doi.org/10.1038/nrn2213.

Schooler, J. W., Smallwood, J., Christoff, K., Handy, T. C., Reichle, E. D., & Sayette, M. A. (2011). Meta-awareness, perceptual decoupling and the wandering mind. *Trends in Cognitive Sciences, 15*(7), 319–326. https://doi.org/10.1016/j.tics.2011.05.006.

Shweder, R. (2003). *Why do men barbecue?* Cambridge, MA: Harvard University Press.

Smallwood, J. (2013). Distinguishing how from why the mind wanders: A process–occurrence framework for self-generated mental activity. *Psychological Bulletin, 139*(3), 519–535. https://doi.org/10.1037/a0030010.
Song, X., & Wang, X. (2012). Mind wandering in Chinese daily lives—An experience sampling study. *PloS One, 7*(9), e44423.
Stekelenburg, J. v. (2012). The occupy movement: Product of this time. *Development, 55*(2), 224–231. https://doi.org/10.1057/dev.2012.6.
Suddendorf, T., & Corballis, M. C. (2007). The evolution of foresight: What is mental time travel, and is it unique to humans? *Behavioral and Brain Sciences, 30*(03), 299–313. https://doi.org/10.1017/S0140525X07001975.
Unger, R. M. (2007). *The self awakened: Pragmatism unbound.* Cambridge, MA: Harvard University Press.
Valsiner, J. (1998). *The guided mind.* Cambridge, MA: Harvard University Press.
Valsiner, J. (2014). *An invitation to cultural psychology.* Los Angeles: Sage.
Vygotsky, L. S. (1978). *Mind in society: The development of higher psychological processes.* Cambridge, MA: Harvard University Press.
Vygotsky, L. S. (1981). The genesis of higher mental functions. In J. V. Wertsch (Ed.), *The concept of activity in Soviet psychology* (pp. 37–72). Armonk: M. E. Sharp.
Vygotsky, L. S. (2004). Imagination and creativity in childhood. *Journal of Russian and East European Psychology, 42*(1), 7–97.
Wallerstein, I. M. (1998). *Utopistics: Or historical choices of the twenty-first century.* New York: New Press.
Weitz, E. D. (2006). *A century of genocide: Utopias of race and nation* (3. print., and 1. paperback print). Princeton: Princeton University Press.
Wilde, O. (1891). The soul of man under socialism. *The Fortnightly Review, 49*(290), 292–319.
Wright, E. O. (2010). *Envisioning real utopias.* London: Verso.
Zamyatin, Y. (1924). *We.* New York: Penguin Books.
Zittoun, T. (2007). The role of symbolic resources in human lives. In J. Valsiner & A. Rosa (Eds.), *The Cambridge handbook of sociocultural psychology* (pp. 343–361). Cambridge: Cambridge University Press.
Zittoun, T., & Gillespie, A. (2016). *Imagination in human and cultural development.* London: Routledge. https://doi.org/10.4324/9780203073360.
Zittoun, T., & Gillespie, A. (2018, this volume). Imagining the collective future: A sociocultural perspective. In C. de Saint-Laurent, S. Obradović, & K. R. Carriere (Eds.), *Imagining collective futures: Perspectives from social, cultural, and political psychology* (pp. 15–37). London: Palgrave Macmillan.

8

Troubled Pasts, Collective Memory, and Collective Futures

Cristian Tileagă

This is a chapter about how nations imagine possible futures in the context of transitional justice and coming to terms with the communist past in Eastern Europe. For post-communist countries engaged in democratic development, the most significant question was that "of the relation of the treatment of the state's past to its future" (Teitel, 2000, p. 3). This chapter focuses on the condemnation of communism in Romania in the Tismăneanu Report and on how the Report is constructing the image of a collective future around the issue of how to represent the communist era in public consciousness.

Transitional Justice and Prefiguring the Future

Two conceptions of justice have been key to approaching and appraising the relation of the management of the state's past to its future: on the one hand, a universalist conception of justice underpinned by the ideal of

C. Tileagă (✉)
Loughborough University, Loughborough, UK
e-mail: c.tileaga@lboro.ac.uk

comprehensive corrective justice as a *sine qua non* for full democratic and liberal transformation. On the other hand, a realist conception of justice premised on the close interdependence between law and politics. The idea of full, uncompromising, corrective justice has been perhaps the most influential in fuelling and sustaining strong efforts at reimagining a national collective future firmly grounded in the development of a distinct social imaginary around an unambiguous representation of communism as an enemy of human rights. Romania has been the country that advocated this model of corrective justice through the condemnation of communism in the Tismăneanu Report. In doing so, it reimagined a *future* ethics of memory based on new democratic values strengthened by the condemnation of communism.

However, I want to argue that this collective reimagining of communism (and rhetorical construction of a collective future around the idea of transitional, corrective, justice) is not devoid of ambivalence; it is not immune to the operations of repression and resistance, especially when related to representing communism as Other, that is, as not reflecting national values and national interests. In this chapter, I contend that any cultural and political analysis of imagining of collective post-communist future(s) needs to be able to describe, and engage with, the nature of this ambivalence.

One key aspect of the reimagining of communism in post-communist countries was centred around the theme of "how we *ought* to live together in society" (Taylor, 2003, p. 3, my emphasis). The "ought" points to what is yet-to-be, to a yet-to-be-imagined future based on reinterpreting the nature of the communist social order. It is this process of reinterpretation that has been described by historians and political scientists of communism as the greatest challenge post-communist societies have had to face (Stan, 2006). The various theoretical and practical concerns with lustration, decommunization, restitution of property, retroactive justice, and more generally, with the new political vocabulary of transition, have arisen out of—and received their significance from—the struggles of institutional and individual memory against the background of living with troubled, painful, and difficult pasts. As Stan (2006, p. 383) argues, nations have designed various policy tools to sift the historical truth from the official lie about the communist past, to identify the mechanisms of repression employed to quash dissent and opposition, to establish the link between the communist party and the political police, to catalogue the manifold crimes of the outgoing regime, and to sort the villains (the communist torturers) from the angels (the victims of the communist regime).

Active, retrospective, revealing acts of remembering have supported policy tools as key means through which injustices can be redressed, victimization and responsibilities recognized, and suffering acknowledged (cf. Tismăneanu, 2008).[1]

Although these practices have arisen out of demands to engage with troubled and difficult pasts, they were also about imagining collective futures. National collective memory is retrospective as well as prospective (it is about what has been, but also about what has not been yet realized). In imagining collective futures, forging the national collective memory was fuelled by the tension between, on the one hand, the optimism of betterment brought about by democratic changes and on the other hand, the pessimism of some at seeing the disappearance of familiar social landmarks.

As other contributors to this volume have shown (see de Saint-Laurent, Chap. 4, this volume, Brescó de Luna, Chap. 6, this volume) past, present, and future are put in circular dialogue by individuals, groups, communities, and nations. Whilst post-communist nations were driven irresistibly into the future, their face was, arguably, still turned towards the past. Benjamin's image of the angel of history neatly captures this impossible quandary:

> his face is turned toward the past. Where a chain of events appears before *us*, *he* sees one single catastrophe, which keeps piling wreckage upon wreckage and hurls it at his feet. The angel would like to stay, awaken the dead, and make whole what has been smashed. But a storm is blowing from

---

[1] Historians and political scientists also emphasize the role of socio-structural and political factors that have hindered or limited the reach and significance of these acts of remembering—see, for instance, for the case of Romania, Grosescu and Fijalkowski (2017) on the influence of legal culture, and Gussi (2017) on the role of the timing of transitional justice measures.

Paradise and has got caught in his wings; it is so strong that the angel can no longer close them. This storm drives him irresistibly into the future to which his back is turned, while the pile of debris before him grows toward the sky. What we call progress is *this* storm. (Eiland and Jennings, 2003, p. 392, emphasis in original)

Troubled Pasts, Collective Futures, and Mnemonic Imagination

One cannot fully understand how past, present, and future are put in circular dialogue by individuals, groups, communities, and nations without engaging with the relationship between imagination and memory. As Zittoun & Gillespie (Chap. 2, this volume) argue, from a sociocultural perspective, imagination is "a deeply sociocultural phenomenon, in its origin, mediation and consequences." That is very much true for memory, as it is for other psychological phenomena. Memory manifests itself and takes various forms at different levels of social and political organization, in public and in private, in elite discourse and in lay meanings, in the guise of personal as well as societal remembering.

As Keightley and Pickering (2012) note, imagination and memory are intertwined resources for making sense of experience: "imagination is vital in reactivating memory, and memory is vital in stimulating imagination" (p. 51). Keightley and Pickering use the notion of "mnemonic imagination" to refer to the relationship between remembering that "draws upon certain symbolic resources … and is in itself intrinsic to cultural processes of one kind or another" (p. 82), and imagination through which we "develop a sense of the temporal relations between different experiences, different episodes and different stages in our lives" (p. 51).

Keightley and Pickering describe the workings of individual memory and individual imagination. I argue that their argument can be extended when engaging with collective memory and collective imagination. Remembering communities (in this specific case, post-communist nations) engage in numerous "temporal transactions" and imaginative reconstructions in order to produce a nationally relevant collective story. In the context of transitional justice, nations connect memory and imagination through socially and politically organized practices (lustration, decommunization, truth and reconciliation, etc.). The emerging mnemonic imagination (and the emerging narrative) is seen as providing "the conditions for transformative action in the present oriented towards an anticipated future" (Keightley & Pickering, 2012, p. 75). It can be argued that imagination, and not only memory, is multidirectional (cf. Rothberg, 2009). Imagination, as does memory, points in different directions, serves different functions, and operates beyond concerns with truthfulness of perspectives.

One relevant example comes from the troubled history of reconciliation in South Africa. The main purpose of the Truth and Reconciliation Committee was to imagine the collective future of interethnic relations based on a collective narrative. However, as Andrews (2007) shows in the context of testimonies and responses to the Truth and Reconciliation Commission (TRC) there was no unique or collective narrative model that was used by all of the social actors. Although citizens recounting tales of suffering represented a unique (and successful) model of rebuilding a "broken" nation, it was far from being a uniform one, with different stories being told, sometimes as the result of pressures on victims to tell certain kinds of stories while testifying, or as the outcome of different experiences and perspectives of victims and perpetrators, and various other individuals and groups challenging official versions of the past and demanding redress. As Andrews argues, the concern of the TRC focused on the creation of acceptable, believable, pragmatic versions of memory more than on the truthful collective memory, and therefore, on developing realistic and usable images of the past history of race relations rather than truthful ones.

It can be argued that the diversity of these acceptable, believable, pragmatic, accounts testifies to an active interrelationship between memory and imagination. We know that memories that are articulated out of living with a difficult and sometimes contested past (Brown & Reavey, 2015; Byford & Tileaga, 2017) should not be seen simply as truthful accounts, but instead, involving imaginative reconstructions in "terms of what is being recollected and its significance for ongoing identification with self and others." (Brown & Reavey, 2013, p. 55). Moreover, another key role of imaginative reconstructions is to symbolically align past, present, and future, and create a sense of collective continuity.

Case Background

In the majority of former communist states, reckoning with a troubled and painful communist past has presupposed a strong dimension of recuperation and reassessment of communist memory and history through empowering the victims, identifying the victimizers, and revealing the nature and the extent of crimes and abuses perpetrated by the defunct communist regime (Tismăneanu, 2008). The official condemnation of the communist regime in Romania in the so-called Tismăneanu Report, that is, the final report of the Presidential Committee for the Analysis of the Communist Dictatorship in Romania, chaired by Professor Vladimir Tismăneanu, was a peculiar case in point. As an initiative unmatched by any other Central and Eastern European country except Germany, which constituted two history commissions in 1992 and 1994, the Committee set out to give a definitive account of the crimes and abuses of communism in that country (1945–1989).[2] The avowed ambition of the Tismăneanu Report was to provide a synthetic and rational account of the history of communism and, in doing so, to facilitate the creation of a unified collective memory of communism capable of overriding any competing individual or community experiences or perspectives (Tismăneanu, 2007a).

The leading author of the Report was Vladimir Tismăneanu, an internationally renowned expert (political scientist and historian) of communism. The Report consisted largely of an account of communism's political methods and institutions. It aimed at documenting the repressive and criminal nature of the totalitarian society and giving an exhaus-

---

[2] For more details on the structure, scope and reactions to the Tismaneanu Report, see Ciobanu (2009), Cesereanu (2008) and Tismăneanu (2007a).

tive account of communism as a self-perpetuating political system. In December 2006, in front of the Romanian Parliament, the then president Traian Băsescu officially condemned the crimes and abuses of the communist regime, declaring communism as "illegitimate" and "criminal." This is demonstrated by the following three excerpts from the Report:

Excerpt 1
"Condemning communism is today, more than ever, a moral, intellectual, political, and social duty/obligation. The democratic and pluralist Romanian state can and ought to do it. Also, knowing these dark and saddening pages of 20th century Romanian history is indispensable for the younger generations who have the right to know the world their parents lived in."

Excerpt 2
"Against the facts presented in this report, it is certain that genocide acts have been committed during 1945–1989, and thus the communist regime can be qualified as criminal against its own people."

Excerpt 3
"Taking act of this Report, the President can say with his hand on the heart: the Communist regime in Romania was illegitimate and criminal."[3]

As I show elsewhere (Tileagă, 2009), by emphasizing the criminality and illegitimacy of the communist regime, the Report creates, affirms, and legitimates a narrative for a normative ethics of memory that transmits moral responsibilities to new generations. In doing so, it projects, and imagines, a *future* ethics of memory based on the values underpinned by the condemnation of communism. The act of condemnation itself is offered as a foundational moment for an alternative ethics of memory and justice.

---

[3] Report, pp. 35–36, 211, and 776, respectively.

Pre-empting the Future: Time and National Identity

The Report and the president's address clearly mark the boundaries of the "event," that is, "state of affairs" under scrutiny. There is a clear temporal delineation of the period: 1945–1989. The period is described in different ways: in the Report, it is referred to as "four decades and a half of obsessive following in the construction of an impossible utopia"; in the president's address, it is described as "a grim chapter in our country's past."

Yet, the Report does not solely rely on the temporal delineation of its "object of inquiry." As some authors have argued, the politics of coming to terms with the past "consists first and foremost in structuring time" (Santiso, 1998, p. 26). The focus on the present, the past, and the future is said to frame and establish the boundaries of moral and political courses of action. In political discourse (as in ordinary talk), "time is a resource … to be drawn on … in order present an identity, establish a truth or defend an interest" (Taylor & Wetherell, 1999, p. 39). In this particular case, the structuring of time is achieved by joining a political agenda (of condemnation and reconciliation) and pre-empting the future of the nation. This is a feature of both the Report and president's address:

Excerpt 4
"The moment has finally come for this methodically maintained state of amnesia to end. The recuperation of memory, as well as the identification of responsibilities is indispensable to the workings of a democratic political community." (Report, p. 10)

Excerpt 5
"The moment has come to identify the nature and the legacies of the communist regime." (Report, p. 626)

Excerpt 6
"17 years after the December 1989 revolution, the moment has fully arrived for all the communist archives to be made public and accessible." (Report, p. 640)

Excerpt 7

"The imported communism we experienced in our own lives for five decades is an open wound in the history of Romania whose time to heal has come once and for all." (President's address)

Excerpt 8

"We believed that we could forget communism, but it did not want to forget us. Therefore, the condemnation of this past arises as a priority for the present, without which we shall behave in the future too in a way which resembles the burden of an unhealed illness." (President's address)

The pragmatic actions identified by the Report and the president are presented as actions stemming from an authoritative collective time summon (cf. Leeuwen, 2005). As Billig (1998) has argued, "the construal of time is crucial to ideology" (p. 209). The time *for* coming to terms with the past points reflexively to a political agenda that is rhetorically structured to work against the "ambivalence" of previous political positions, such as *avoiding* or *refusing* to come to terms with the past.

Moreover, closing a chapter in the nation's history entails a "healing" process: the closing of an "open wound" and alleviating "the burden of an unhealed illness". The message of both the Report and president's address seems uncontroversial: the future (of the nation) depends on a clean, and immediate, break with the communist past. Together with the other features identified in the Report and president's address (see Tileaga, 2009), it provides the ethical *grounds* for the implementation of moral/political/legal courses of action.

Condemnation and reconciliation are constituted as activities that embody the values and goals that the Romanian nation aspires to. Condemnation and reconciliation are presented as an integral part of the political *project* of the nation. As other examples show, they are constitutive of both "future action and future reality" (Dunmire, 2005, p. 484):

Excerpt 9

"The future of Romania is dependent upon assuming its past, that is upon condemning the communist regime as enemy of the human race. Not doing it, here and now, will forever burden us with the guilt of complicity, be it only through silence, with the totalitarian Evil." (Report, p. 19)

Excerpt 10
"This symbolic moment represents the balance sheet of what we have lived through and the day in which we all ask ourselves how we want to live henceforward." (President's address)

There are two significant ideological aspects in all these excerpts. On the one hand, there is a clear progressive *promise* of national change and transformation clearly tied to a repertoire of national progress.[4] It would seem that a close adherence to this political agenda would give the "assurance" that moral transformation is irreversible, and that it would be "no longer possible … to fall back into the past" (Habermas & Michnik, 1994, p. 11). In conjunction with the other characteristics of communism ("illegitimate" and "criminal"), the Report reflexively positions communism as an "evil" political ideology. On the other hand, communism is described as an "evil" outsider—it is distanced from the national self. There is an active resistance in engaging with collective imagining of the contested space of the popular memory of communism. The Report's own resistance to, and avoidance of, an alternative, collective imagining of communism privileges "a particular future … over alternative futures" (Dunmire, 2005, p. 486).

Communism as the Other

In the remainder of this chapter, I want to argue that this ambivalence in the Report stems from an unresolved tension between wishing to express the uniqueness of a troubled and painful past and wishing to repress unwanted and shameful experiences that may point in the direction of perceiving communism as a genuine national experience. The Report's attitude towards communism (as not "us": "foreign import", "illegitimate", and ultimately, "criminal") can be seen as part and parcel of a broader set of social practices that, I argue, are relevant to understanding

---

[4] 'In narratives of national progress in which time is constructed as a forward movement or flow, there is an implied determinism, or, more colloquially, the notion of fate or destiny' (Taylor & Wetherell, 1999, p. 51).

the official appraisal of communism in public consciousness. Drawing upon Billig's (1999) work on "social repression" and Frosh's (2010) notion of "resistance", I call these practices "social practices of avoidance" (cf. also Tileagă, 2017). Billig's account of repression stresses the importance of social practices of "avoidance" that are part and parcel of conversational practices of society around topics or feelings that are too "difficult" to discuss. Resistance refers to "something to be overcome"; analysis is a process of understanding the mind that is "at war with itself, blocking the path to its own freedom." (Rose, 2007, p. 21 *apud* Frosh, 2010, p. 166).

As I intimated elsewhere (Tileagă, 2017) the Report fails to resolve the foundational problem that is facing any historical inquiry into troubling and difficult pasts. This idea is expressed by LaCapra (1994) who writes about the need to reconcile "the relation between the requirements of scientific expertise and the less easily definable demands placed on the use of language by the difficult attempt to work through transferential relations in a dialogue with the past having implications for the present and future." (p. 66)

LaCapra (1994, p. 4) distinguishes between "constative" historical reconstruction and "performative" dialogic exchange with the past. As he argues, this latter "performative" dialogic exchange relies on certain unconscious memory activities. The process of canonization of a single, and all-encompassing, collective narrative around the nature of communism in Romania has been, predominantly, a constative historical reconstruction based on the archival, factual, reconstruction of experiences. However, as I showed elsewhere (see Tileagă, 2017), this constative historical reconstruction encapsulates distinctive practices of avoidance.

Perhaps the most striking illustration of avoidance is tied to the imaging of communism as the Other in the Report. As I have also shown elsewhere (see Tileagă, 2009, 2012), communism is described in general terms throughout the Report as a "regime" and an "ideology," a "utopian conception," an "enemy of the human race" that instituted "the physical and moral assassinate," and survived "through repression." However, communism is also described in national terms: a "(foreign) occupation regime," "criminal towards its own people," and "antinational," among others. In doing so, the Report proposes a specific method of reasoning about Romanian history and memory that constitutes communism as the Other, not quite "us." Interestingly, the narrative of communism is not self-condemnatory or self-blaming, but rather, communism is distanced from (the national) self. This is demonstrated by the following excerpts:

Excerpt 11
"The total Sovietisation, through force, of Romania, especially during the period 1948–1956, and the imposition under the name 'dictatorship of the proletariat' of a despotic political system ruled by a profiteering caste (nomenklatura), tightly united around its supreme leader."

Excerpt 12
"Pretending to fulfill the goals of Marxism, the regime has treated an entire population as a masse of lab mice part of a nightmarish social engineering experiment."

Excerpt 13
"…the imposition of a dictatorial regime totally surrendered to Moscow and hostile to national political and cultural values."

Excerpt 14
"The Romanian Popular Republic, who has come into being through diktat, or more exactly, through a coup d'état, symbolizes a triple imposture: it wasn't even a Republic (in the full sense of the phrase), it wasn't popular, and, most certainly, it wasn't Romanian."[5]

Moreover, the communist regime is also found "responsible" for crimes "against the biological makeup of the nation." Through references to physical and psychological effects (for example, "psychological weakening and disheartenment of the population," and "decreased capacity for physical and intellectual effort"),[6] communism is externalized and objectivized (Leeuwen, 1995) as a *sui generis* political ideology designed to undermine the Romanian ethos. The Report describes communism as

---

[5] Report, pp. 774, 775, 774, 765, respectively.
[6] Report, pp. 461–462.

"antipatriotic," whereas the Romanian communist leaders are portrayed as lacking "patriotic sentiments," and Romanian communist politics are described as not representing the affirmation of a "patriotic spirit/will."[7]

Paradoxically, the basic premise for the condemnation of Romanian communism is to construe communism as the Other; in other words, as not reflecting Romanian values and national interests. This position can be said to reflect an active avoidance of the implication that communism may have been in any way a "criminal" ideology that reflected, and furthered, national interests. The textual construction of the negative qualities of communism in the Tismăneanu Report ("enemy of human rights," "illegitimate," and "criminal") opens the way for the operation of social repression, the suppression of the socially inappropriate thought that communism may have been historically part and parcel of national identity. The negative attributes of communism are distanced from the (national) self. The Report actively resists alternative ideological implications, especially those that closely reflect nationalist representations of communism in popular culture. As Frosh notes, resistance is a useful notion to understanding the subtleties of ambivalence. "Resistance," Frosh points out, "has general significance as a way of indicating how a person might want something but not want it at the same time." (2010, p. 167)

The Romanian post-communist transition has developed its own complex social conventions and discursive codes that resist and repress the issue of collective involvement in the perpetuation of the communist system. By constructing communism as the Other, paradoxically, even progressive texts such as the Tismăneanu Report are engaging in collective avoidance of this very sensitive issue at the heart of successful transitional justice. By positioning communism on the *outside*, the Report actively represses a performative dialogic exchange with the past and collective imagining of the contested space of the popular memory of communism.

The basis of a performative dialogic exchange with the past, as LaCapra argues, is rooted in the notion of "working-through" taken-for-granted

---

[7] Report, p. 765, 773, 30, respectively. cf. also Tileagă, 2009.

ethical and political considerations.[8] By stifling mnemonic imagination the Report is resisting the forging of (new) transactional relationships between past and present that fall outside the tried-and-tested interpretive schemas of the professional historian and political scientist of communism. As Keightley and Pickering remind us, "forging transactional relationships between past and present necessitates the past being available for new uses in an ever-changing present, and this involves not only reflexively considering the past from our own perspective but also imaginatively engaging with the relations which others might have with particular pasts, or how they might view our own relations to the past" (2012, p. 178).

As new generations of young people participate in the public debate on the nature of communism, they acquire specific routines of thought, and in addition, they learn the accepted and acceptable social conventions and discursive codes that present communism, and its legacy, as the Other (not "us"!). Building a mnemonic community implies a process of formal, as well as informal, mnemonic socialization. According to the Report, the idea that "we" (Romanians) may have had anything to do with the perpetuation of the communist regime must be suppressed from national consciousness. It can be argued that the Report fails as a tool of mnemonic (political) socialization. Unlike other instruments of political socialization (e.g., national museums dedicated to the legacy of communism in eastern Europe—House of Terror (Budapest) or Memorialul Sighet (Sighet)), explicitly designed to accomplish the goals of mnemonic socialization, that is, socialization into particular images (of genocide), memories (of victimhood), and narratives (of redemption) about the past, present, and future of the nation, the Report engages with the communist past in the absence of mnemonic imagination.

By making official narratives more accessible, and by bringing vernacular narratives to the surface, museums become sites where both consensus, as well as contestation and resistance, around national and local history can take shape. In contrast, the Report seems to downplay social

---

[8] As LaCapra continues, "working-through implies the possibility of judgment that is not apodictic or ad hominem but argumentative, self-questioning, and related in mediated ways to action." (1994, p. 210).

factors, social frameworks, and social relations that make social remembering and social imagination possible by prioritizing disciplinary allegiance and expert knowledge. The Report champions the perspective of the professional historian/political scientist to understand and interpret a troubled and difficult recent past. It champions a privileged, closed system for describing the world. In the Report, the contingent, context-related, and context-dependent emergence of social memory is contrasted with the (presumed) stability and permanence of historical archives.[9] "Self-sufficient" professional research endeavours, to use LaCapra's (2001) term, are usually extremely effective in shielding canonical ideologies and images from the impact, contradictions, and unforeseen consequences brought about by mnemonic imagination.

Conclusion

The fall of communism has propelled nations forward, into an exciting, yet uncertain future; however, nations are still finding it very difficult to "move on," to leave the past behind. "One wants to get free of the past," Adorno observed, "one cannot live in its shadow," but the "past one wishes to evade is still so intensely alive." (Adorno, 1986, p. 115).

Prefiguring the future of post-communist nations has entailed a strong dimension of, and engagement with, retrospective and transitional justice. The conventional approach, that of "telling the truth" about the past and making it public, is believed to enlighten people and change perceptions. "Telling the truth" about the past is also seen as a progressive attempt to stifle and "control" returns of "negative currents" (for example, revisionist accounts and nostalgia), to bring the "repressed" oppressive ideology and effects of communism into public consciousness, and thus, to banish the risk (and fear) of repetition. Yet, at the same time, as I

---

[9] As Tismăneanu himself acknowledges: "For me, as historian and political scientist, the verdict of such a commission was not needed in order to argue that 'communism has been an aberrant system, criminal, inhuman'" (Tismăneanu, 2007b). For the professional historian, like Tismaneanu, communism is both an object of loathing and desire. A process of "canonization" of a unique representation of recent history requires that alternative experiences, perspectives, and interpretations are actively suppressed.

attempted to demonstrate in this chapter, the same, progressive, conventional approach based on "telling the truth" can mask and repress an insufficiently worked-through transferential relation with a controversial past by turning it into an obstacle to fulfilling the avowed goals of social justice. In this chapter, I have shown how the Tismăneanu Report, condemning communism in Romania, feeds the illusion that transitional justice can be "fixed for all time" (Teitel, 2000). Thus, it obscures, masks, and suppresses as much as it reveals key ideological aspects of the appraisal of communism in public consciousness.

This position should not be seen as denying the significance and overall social value of the conventional ways in which historians or political scientists approach the issue of coming to terms with the recent communist past. Historical knowledge of the objective (ideological) makeup of political regimes and other social formations should be continually sought as a remedy for half-truths, political manipulation, or simply ignorance. Yet, such knowledge, when used and reproduced as a "matter of fact," is arguably inadequate with regard to the handling of dilemmas and ambiguities of collective memory or to the development of broader social scientific frameworks of analysis. One needs to strive to find the meaning of the collective memory of communism in the sometimes contradictory, paradoxical attitudes and meanings that members of society uphold and negotiate, and not only in and through official representations of recent history "compressed into generalities." (Veyne, 1984, p. 63).

LaCapra rightly argues, "the after effects ... of traumatic events are not fully owned by anyone and, in various ways, affect everyone" (2001, p. xi). The fixation on a single, unique, all-or-nothing description of the nature of (Romanian) communism in the Tismăneanu Report has led, perhaps not surprisingly, to resistance. Political scientists have shown that transitional justice policies based on an all-or-nothing description of the nature of (Romanian) communism have only offered "partial justice, and therefore constituted a politically feasible and morally defensible solution that was, nevertheless, far from being perfect." (Stan, 2006, p. 385). One could go even further and claim that any hope of full mastery of historical events, of the "last word", is a regressive step.

As Billig (1997) argues, when one engages in ideological analysis, one shifts the focus from the individual unconscious to the social and collective constitution of the unconscious. Romania has sustained a strong, unfailing commitment to meaningful, official, and unofficial memory and identity projects of coming to terms with the communist past. It has overcome numerous barriers, and over the years, it has created a "vigilant critical culture" (Nussbaum, 2013, p. 124) that has supported transitional justice, and the continuation of liberal and democratic values. This vigilant critical culture, however, is not devoid of ambivalence; it is not immune to the operations of repression and resistance. One key foundation of this ambivalence is an active resistance in engaging with a collective reimagining of the contested space of the popular memory of communism (by distancing communism from the national self) set against a progressive promise of social justice.

There is a need to excavate the nature of this ambivalence, to unearth more of the nature of repression and resistance that may stand in the way of a full understanding of social and transitional justice. Without exploring the nature of this ambivalence fully, there is the risk that this progressive, vigilant critical culture will be at odds and greatly out of synch with other active, progressive, social imaginary currents in society. This progressive, vigilant critical culture cannot hope to fulfil both a formative, as well as normative, mnemonic socialization function (cf. Connerton, 1989) without engaging directly with the mnemonic imagination that feeds the collective imagining of the contested space of the popular memory of communism. Moreover, without exploring the nature of this ambivalence fully, this vigilant critical culture will find it very difficult to fight some of the most enduring and pernicious myths of, and obstacles to, transitional justice—namely, that "political justice is political vendetta" and that "justice is unnecessary" (cf. Stan, 2006).

The question of how to take communism into public consciousness remains the greatest political, epistemological, and ethical challenge facing post-communist states. One other important challenge is finding appropriate responses to ambivalence by fostering a renewed mnemonic imagination of communism. If, as Keightley and Pickering argue, imagination and memory are to be conceived as intertwined resources for making sense of experience, then one must ensure that the two are brought into close contact, that they are used to explore the (communist) past through the lens of possible or alternative futures.

The imperative of a "shared memory" entails the "integration" and "calibration" of different perspectives and stances (Margalit, 2002). This means, primarily, the integration and calibration of what is not yet worked-through, of ambivalent and suppressed meanings. It also means the integration and calibration of mnemonic imagination that envisages alternative possible collective futures. Imaginative and performative reconstructions of a troubled and contested past can enable individuals, as well as communities and nations, to "turn around" on their schemata, to "reshuffle their constituent elements" (Keightley & Pickering, 2012, p. 57) in order to reposition themselves differently within the circular cycle of past, present, and future.

Acknowledgements I am grateful to John Wiley & Sons for permitting me to reproduce and adapt here material published elsewhere.

References

Adorno, T. (1986). What does coming to terms with the past mean? (T. Bahti & G. Hartman, Trans.). In G. Hartman (Ed.) *Bitburg in moral and political perspective* (pp. 114–129). Bloomington: Indiana University Press.
Andrews, M. (2007). *Shaping history: Narratives of political change*. Cambridge: Cambridge University Press.
Billig, M. (1997). Discursive, rhetorical and ideological messages. In C. McGarty & S. A. Haslam (Eds.), *The message of social psychology* (pp. 36–53). Oxford: Blackwell.
Billig, M. (1998). *Talking of the royal family* (2nd ed.). London: Routledge.
Billig, M. (1999). *Freudian repression*. Cambridge: Cambridge University Press.
Brescó de Luna, I. (2018, this volume). Imagining collective futures in time: Prolepsis and the regimes of historicity. In C. de Saint Laurent, S. Obradović, & K. R. Carriere (Eds.), *Imagining collective futures: Perspectives from social, cultural, and political psychology* (pp. 109–128). London: Palgrave Macmillan.
Brown, S. D., & Reavey, P. (2013). Experience and memory. In E. Keightley & M. Pickering (Eds.), *Research methods for memory studies* (pp. 45–59). Edinburgh: Edinburgh University Press.

Brown, S. D., & Reavey, P. (2015). *Vital memory and affect: Living with a difficult past*. London: Routledge.

Byford, J., & Tileagă, C. (2017). Accounts of a troubled past: Psychology, history, and texts of experience. *Qualitative Psychology, 4*, 101–117.

Cesereanu, R. (2008). The final report on the holocaust and the final report on the communist dictatorship in Romania. *East European Politics and Societies, 22*, 270–228.

Ciobanu, M. (2009). Criminalising the past and reconstructing collective memory: The Romanian Truth Commission. *Europe-Asia Studies, 61*, 313–336.

Connerton, P. (1989). *How societies remember*. Cambridge: Cambridge University Press.

de Saint-Laurent, C. (2018, this volume). Thinking through time: From collective memories to collective futures. In C. de Saint Laurent, S. Obradović, & K. R. Carriere (Eds.), *Imagining collective futures: Perspectives from social, cultural, and political psychology* (pp. 59–81). London: Palgrave Macmillan.

Dunmire, P. (2005). Preempting the future: Rhetoric and ideology of the future in political discourse. *Discourse & Society, 16*, 481–513.

Eiland, H., & Jennings, M. (Eds.). (2003). *Walter Benjamin: Selected writings* (volume 4: 1938–1940; translated by Edmund Jephcott and others). Cambridge, MA: Harvard University Press.

Frosh, S. (2010). *Psychoanalysis outside the clinic: Interventions in psychosocial studies*. Basingstoke: Palgrave Macmillan.

Grosescu, R., & Fijalkowski, A. (2017). Retrospective justice and legal culture. In L. Stan & L. Turcescu (Eds.), *Justice, memory and redress in Romania: New insights* (pp. 100–123). Cambridge: Cambridge Scholars Publishing.

Gussi, A. (2017). Paradoxes of delayed transitional justice. In L. Stan & L. Turcescu (Eds.), *Justice, memory and redress in Romania: New insights* (pp. 76–99). Cambridge: Cambridge Scholars Publishing.

Habermas, J., & Michnik, A. (1994). Overcoming the past. *New Left Review, I/203*, 3–16.

Keightley, E., & Pickering, M. (2012). *The mnemonic imagination: Remembering as creative practice*. Basingstoke: Palgrave Macmillan.

LaCapra, D. (1994). *Representing the Holocaust: History, theory, trauma*. Ithaca: Cornell University Press.

LaCapra, D. (2001). *Writing history, writing trauma*. Baltimore, MD: Johns Hopkins University Press.

Margalit, A. (2002). *The ethics of memory*. Cambridge, MA: Harvard University Press.

Nussbaum, M. (2013). *Political emotions: Why love matters for justice*. Cambridge, MA: Harvard University Press.

Rose, J. (2007). *The last resistance*. London: Verso.
Rothberg, M. (2009). *Multidirectional memory: Remembering the Holocaust in the age of decolonization*. Stanford: Stanford University Press.
Santiso, J. (1998). The fall into the present: The emergence of limited political temporalities in Latin America. *Time & Society, 7*, 25–54.
Stan, L. (2006). The vanishing truth: Politics and memory in post-communist Europe. *East European Quarterly, 40*, 383–340.
Taylor, C. (2003). *Modern social imaginaries*. Durham: Duke University Press.
Taylor, S., & Wetherell, M. (1999). A suitable time and place: Speakers' use of 'time' to do discursive work in narratives of nation and personal life. *Time & Society, 8*, 39–58.
Teitel, R. (2000). *Transitional justice*. Oxford: Oxford University Press.
Tileagă, C. (2009). The social organization of representations of history: The textual accomplishment of coming to terms with the past. *British Journal of Social Psychology, 48*, 337–355.
Tileagă, C. (2012). Communism in retrospect: The rhetoric of historical representation and writing the collective memory of recent past. *Memory Studies, 5*, 462–478.
Tileagă, C. (2017). Conceptions of memory and historical redress. In L. Stan & L. Turcescu (Eds.), *Justice, memory and redress in Romania: New insights* (pp. 2–23). Cambridge: Cambridge Scholars Publishing.
Tismăneanu, V. (2007a). Confronting Romania's past: A response to Charles King. *Slavic Review, 66*, 724–727.
Tismăneanu, V. (2007b). *Refuzul de a uita: articole și comentarii politice (2006–2007)*. Bucharest: Curtea Veche.
Tismăneanu, V. (2008). Democracy and memory: Romania confronts its communist past. *Annals of the American Academy of Political and Social Science, 617*, 166–180.
van Leeuwen, T. (1995). Representing social action. *Discourse & Society, 6*, 81–106.
van Leeuwen, T. (2005). Time in discourse. *Linguistics and the human. Sciences, 1*, 127–145.
Veyne, P. (1984). *Writing history: Essay on epistemology* (M. Moore-Rinvolucri, Trans.). Middletown, CT: Wesleyan University Press.
Zittoun, T., & Gillespie, A. (2018, this volume). Imagining the Collective Future: A Sociocultural Perspective. In C. de Saint-Laurent, S. Obradović, & K. R. Carriere (Eds.), *Imagining collective futures: Perspectives from social, cultural, and political psychology* (pp. 15–37). London: Palgrave Macmillan.

9

Imagining Collective Identities Beyond Intergroup Conflict

Cathy Nicholson and Caroline Howarth

Central to the construction of imagined futures are collective identities that characterise and define a situated and imagined place in a world of other groups. In this chapter, we aim to explore how collective identities are constructed in the context of intergroup conflict, and discuss the processes that steer and support that development. What was imagined in the past remains central to any discussion of imagined futures for both groups, as past hopes and dreams can and do remain unfulfilled. In addition, we cannot discuss the construction of a collective identity of one group without discussing the other, as they each remain interrelated to one another as co-partners in conflict. We use the Israeli-Palestinian conflict as an example of continued protracted conflict, where collective identities, based on in-group righteousness and out-group hostility, have tended to become entrenched within their respective societies. However, an in-group/out-group binary positioning between the groups is not the only way of understanding the conflict. We aim to demonstrate the

---

C. Nicholson (✉) • C. Howarth
London School of Economics and Political Science, London, UK
e-mail: C.G.Nicholson@lse.ac.uk; C.S.Howarth@lse.ac.uk

© The Author(s) 2018
C. de Saint-Laurent et al. (eds.), *Imagining Collective Futures*, Palgrave Studies in Creativity and Culture, https://doi.org/10.1007/978-3-319-76051-3_9

complexity of intergroup relationships in contexts of conflict, which can be challenging to define, yet demand exploration and careful analysis.

First, we discuss the roles of the cultural and political context in the shaping of constructions of the future and collective identities resulting in the perceived impermeability of group boundaries. Second, we suggest how the theory of social representations is useful to discuss the dialogical nature of intergroup conflict, particularly in terms of the relationship between collective identities and social representations. This leads to an examination of narratives as the architecture of social representations and an exploration of such narratives from those enmeshed in the conflict. From these narratives, it becomes possible to explore and define deep-seated themata. Themata can be conceptualised as tightly held kernels of social knowledge that remain embedded in cultural, social and personal lives, over extended periods of time. Third, and finally, we discuss how futures can either be imagined as a continuation of the conflict, or as one where the ending of hostilities can be envisaged as alternative social representations become more prominent. What this has revealed is the complex interdependent relationship between context, collective identities, narratives and themata in discussions of intergroup conflict and the importance of unravelling and defining the relationship between these concepts, as we attempt to do in this chapter.

Cultural and Geopolitical Context: Imagining Futures from the Past

From the outset of the Israeli-Palestinian conflict, both groups constructed their collective identities along nationalist lines, rooted in ideological ideas of sovereignty and independence (Rouhana, 2007; Sand, 2012). The expansion of pan-Arab nationalism, during the British Mandate in Palestine (1922–1948) following World War 1 (1914–1918), related to a cultural and national revival within the non-Jewish Palestinian population and connected to a wider movement from Lebanon and Egypt, leading to the development of a pan-Arab ideology

(Abu-Ghazaleh, 1972). The mix of Arab history and culture, alongside European education policies under British (and French influence in Lebanon), resulted in new imagined alternative futures of independence and sovereignty (Said, 2003). Under this growing Arab nationalism, the development of organisations such as the Arab League entered the political arena as a motivational movement to legitimise the growing resentment of perceived Jewish hegemony and increasing immigration.

The imagined futures of Jewish nationalism began almost 200 years before the nation of Israel became a reality:

> All nations, from the humblest to the most exalted possess a peculiar and irreplaceable way of life and unique national destiny. Let us follow our own way. (Von Herder 1744–1803 quoted by Goldberg (1996, p. 5))

By the middle of the nineteenth century, an acceleration of this development led by the founder of the Zionist movement, Theodore Herzl (1860–1904), created an opportunity to secure a safe haven as a nation for the Jewish people:

> No one can deny the gravity of the situation of the Jews. Wherever they live in perceptible numbers, they are more or less persecuted .... according to the countries in social circles in which they occur. (Herzl, 1934, p. 23)

Britain, influenced by Zionist idealism, discussed the establishment of 'a national home in Palestine' under the Balfour Declaration of 1917 (Smith, 2013) as long as the rights of the indigenous Palestinian population were upheld. The mass genocide of six million Jews during the Holocaust (1933–1945), 30 years after the death of Herzl, could only serve to strengthen the argument for a safe homeland. With the rise in the number of Jewish immigrants to Palestine outnumbering the quota set by the British to appease the indigenous population, there followed a deterioration in the already tense relationship between the Jews and the indigenous Arab population (Muslim, Christian, Druze and Bedouin) over territory that both groups claimed as their own (Barr, 2011). The United Nations recommended the partitioning of the land between the

Jewish and the Arab populations, with Jerusalem placed under an international protectorate. Although the subsequent international vote accepted the resolution (33 votes to 13, with 10 abstentions), the Arab contingencies were among those who voted against. A request to the International Court of Justice to revoke the vote failed, leaving the plan to proceed formally towards partition when the terms of the British Mandate of Palestine was due to expire. Although Britain accepted the result of the vote, it refused to enforce it, stating it was unacceptable to both sides (Barr, 2011). As Britain formally left Palestine on 14 May 1948, independence was declared by the leaders who represented the Jewish residents, leading to the birth of the national state of Israel, civil war and ensuing political intractability. The Palestinians mark this day as the 'Nakba,' translated as the catastrophe.

Bar-Tal (2011, 2014) defines intractability as a state of being where the two parties remain locked in opposition, unable to compromise as the psychological and national investment becomes too entrenched to leave aside. This further exacerbates the conflict as both sides are unable to extricate themselves, as they may perceive that the cost of retracting is greater than the cost of remaining in the situation. A stalemate position ensues, prolonging the conflict, reflecting national aspirations based on the 'us' and 'we' and 'them', where outsiders remain foreigners "who do not belong to the state in which we are" (Kristeva, 1993, p. 96). This positioning becomes indispensable to individuals and collective life as "routinisation contributes to the intractability of the conflict because participants do not feel an urgency to terminate it" (Bar-Tal, 2014, p. 46). This routinisation reflects an 'ethos of conflict' (Bar-Tal, 2007), where groups remain locked in their own political ideologies that become embedded in all aspects of social and cultural life. Education of history, both as a formal and informal institutional process has shown how the relationship between the past, present and future (Carretero, Chap. 13, this volume) remains a significant cultural artefact where the past can be both idealised and romanticised. Thus, there can remain an unwillingness to seek a compromise that might lead to a sustainable peace agreement leading to the conflict becoming a categorised entity, rather than an organic (negotiated and so changeable) process of intractability. The resulting victory for one group in 1948 and the defeat of the weaker group has led to an asymmetric conflict, where each has become intertwined with the other's positioning.

The intersubjective base of any dialogical relationship (Gillespie & Cornish, 2010) reflects the groups' mutual awareness of the conflict as each group competes with the other through a domain of power relations and states of tension (Jovchelovitch, 2007). The interdependent relationship between groups in conflict is paramount, as collective identities do not develop in isolation, but do so as partners in conflict. This codependency of one group towards the other remains a dialogical one even when dismissing the other group's positioning (Linell, 2009; Marková, 2003). Following a dialogical approach, we can explore complex cultural representational fields through multiplicities of knowledge systems (de Saint-Laurent, 2014) that inform collective identities as they evolve or remain frozen over time.

Characteristics of Shifting Collective Identities

Individuals subscribe to many identities in their daily lives, which both define their place in the world and relationship towards others. The relationship across personal, social and collective identities is one that can be considered in the context of conflict, where violent and threatening life experiences will have a direct effect on personal and group development. Harré (1998) describes the personal self as "having a sense of self, to be disposed to express oneself in particular ways," (p. 56) and as a "site from which a person perceives his world and a place from which to act" (p. 3). At the same time, the self pertains to the way in which others see them, the way they seem to other people. The boundaries between the personal and social become blurred as they remain intimately entwined, as individuals belong to many social groups and their allegiance to them may shift over time, dependent on personal and sociocultural contexts (Northrup, 1989).

Social identity theorists (Brewer, 2001; Reicher, 2004; Tajfel, 1981; Tajfel & Turner, 1979) illuminate the interaction between the individual and social groups to explore and explain comparative positions in relation to others. Such work has been significant in helping us understand intergroup processes—looking at how different groups relate to one another, how group relations define in-group identities and behaviours as well as out-group interactions. This is particularly pertinent in the context of conflict, where an individual derives a sense of the positive benefits of belonging to his or her group, to build self and group esteem against adversaries. For example, a perceived social identity is central to Jewish Israelis' and Palestinians' sense of belonging to the land, their culture, their history and their citizenship, (Bar-Tal, 2011). In effect, social identities provide a perceptual prism through which the world is experienced, as well as a means of coping with and challenging threat and disadvantage (Reicher & Haslam, 2012). Theories of social identity highlight the significance of minority group identification as a precursor to identity politics by ascribing identities and stereotypes to oppressed groups to challenging more powerful ones (Billig, 2002). Reicher (2004) discusses identities as projects that allow the possibility of collective action where the nature of these identities becomes determined by those who act collectively, and so, open possibilities of ultimately shaping their social world. The idea of a collective identity, rather than a social identity, represents a change in theoretical focus from the relationship between the self and a defined, often singular, social group, to one that incorporates the wider society. This has been well illustrated by Power (Chap. 11, this volume), who discusses how a social movement in Ireland was formed to protest about a change in national water status, based on moral appraisals that impacted their motivations and justifications for collective action. The sense of coming together and developing a collective identity, in the context of economic recovery, reflected the significance of civil engagement in asserting a voice against the status quo.

Various definitions of collective identity have been discussed in the literature, for example, as a shared space linked to collective agency and located in action and interaction rather than in individual self-conceptions (Snow, 2001). Melucci (1989, 1996) emphasises the significance of the Other when discussing collective identities, defining it as a process, rather than a product, where action is given voice through a common language, developed through rituals, practices and cultural artefacts as a reflexive network of relationships distinguishing oneself from the other. Through identification with others, we can clarify our understanding of who we are (Howarth, 2002), or who we think we are, in an ongoing process of sharing goals, practices, and values, as Flesher Fominaya (2010) has highlighted:

> Although collective identity can be understood as (potentially) encompassing shared interests, ideologies, subcultures, goals, rituals, practices, values, worldview, commitment, solidarity, tactics, strategies, definitions of the enemy or the opposition and framing of issues, it is not synonymous and cannot be reduced to any of these things. (p. 398)

Rather than reduce collective identity to a set of shared characteristics, we can discuss collective identity in terms of dialogicality, heterogeneity, diversity and inclusivity, where contradictions across them are inherent (McDonald, 2002). As Gillespie, Howarth, and Cornish (2012) have pointed out, by categorising groups as solid entities, we close down a discussion that may highlight the nuances of collective identities that would allow a deeper understanding of identity positioning within a given spatial and temporal field. In contexts of personal and collective threat, however, in-group homogeneity can become more salient with the hardening of group boundaries representing exclusivity of one group over another. This can give legitimacy to a self/group positioning, and at the same time, may necessitate a certain group conformity within that boundary. Individual identification is dependent on relations to an outer world, and group identifications are meaningless without individual identifications (Strömbom, 2013) as they remain entangled with each other, as all identifications are irrevocably social and relational. Collective identities contain the historical contexts of their own and perceptions of the others' imagined pasts and power relations (Strömbom, 2013), whether through the construction of national identities (Reicher & Hopkins, 2001) or those relating to any group positioning when imagining a future. Obradović (Chap. 12, this volume), for example, discusses the processes by which citizens frame their culturally rooted national identities through times of national upheaval that reflects their sense of history when contemplating an imagined future. How these collective identities are constructed can be discussed through a filter of a foundational base of social knowledge embedded in the cultural, social and political life of group members, as social representations. By exploring these representations, we can interpret how groups in conflict identify with their positioning from past disappointments and present orientation towards imagined futures.

The Role of Social Representations in Forming, Maintaining and Transforming Collective Identities

By exploring the social representations of those enmeshed within conflicts, we can begin to unravel intractability, not only through identity positions, but also through the social psychological processes that influence them. Social representation theory, developed from the work of Moscovici (1961/2008), is discussed as a network of epistemological ideas that explores how social knowledge is developed and communicated across the social world to construct social realities. Since its inception, the theory has been interpreted in a variety of ways dependant on the theoretical trajectory followed, such as dialogicality (Marková, 2003), identity (Howarth, 2002), narratives (Jovchelovitch, 2012; Nicholson, 2016), historical representations (Bar-Tal, 2014; Liu & Hilton, 2005), semantic barriers (Gillespie, 2008), amongst others. However, paramount to the core of the theory is the relationship between the three basic components of self/other/object, which reflects the relational and dialogical nature between them, whether applied to individuals, groups or societies (Marková, 2000). The exploration of intergroup interaction is central to social psychological enquiry. When the groups represent a majority or minority in the context of asymmetry, the relationship between them entails a mutual interdependency of social influences (Moscovici & Marková, 2000). A social thinking system can be explored where ideas and belief systems are communicated across social worlds;

> through the social, psychological and ideological dynamics of the production and re-production of knowledge, particularly knowledge that relates to the social categorisation, differentiation and identification of social groups and communities. (Howarth, 2011)

Social representations are thus simultaneously both receivers and creators of social knowledge, developed through communication, acting as mediators of knowledge between the individual and a plethora of collectives. Social representations are neither solely a cognitive nor a social process, but simultaneously both, where a social object is not simply reproduced in the mind of an individual, but is embedded within a social construction of knowledge systems within the public sphere (Moscovici, 2000). By constituting knowledge systems, social representations reflect common sense through language, embedded within a particular community: "Representation, communication and language are the only path to knowledge that we have" (Jovchelovitch, 2007, p. 99), and so, they act as containers of the complexities and contradictions of social life. Social representations work to continually maintain social structures and institutions or to reflect resistance to the status quo. Hence, they can be defined as being hegemonic and support systems of ideology, or emancipatory and provoking systems of change (Howarth, 2011). We can begin to discuss the possibilities of how knowledge systems are framed from the past, but are not completely determined by it, and so, change becomes a possibility (Howarth, Andreouli, & Kessi, 2015). By exploring social representations across groups in conflict, we can reflect the fundamentally dynamic and collective ongoing re-productions of meaning and social relations in daily life.

As we discuss the significance of developing and fluid collective identities, we can elaborate on how social representations can inform, influence and transform identities. Social representations are shaped and communicated through dialogue with others, both as affirming and /or transformative processes. This dynamic relationship between collective identities and social representations can be discussed in this context as one where one feeds into the other, which can both stabilise and destabilise a status quo. Both concepts may appear as fixed entities when examined at any given point in time, but over time, they both fluctuate and/or transform in response to the conflict environment where group boundaries are tightened, loosened or remain in ambiguous flux. In contexts of intergroup conflict, the process of imagining the future is often tied to current identity politics and projects, both of which become shaped by—and are given meaning through—shared social representations. As the next sections will illustrate, the dynamic relationship between identities and representations can be discussed through the development of group narratives that link the past with the present and which, in turn, can limit how we might imagine the future.

Narratives as the Architecture of Social Representations

The experiences and stories about the past and how it relates to the present by individuals embedded in geopolitical areas bounded by conflict can appear as narratives related to the development and communication of social representations within each community. Bar-Tal (2014) suggests that central to social representations of intractable conflict is a collective master narrative that "focuses on its entirety … provides a complete and meaningful picture of the conflict" (p. 5.4). By exploring the social representations of those living in conflicts, we can begin to address intractability, not solely through identity positions, but through the processes that influence them.

Bruner (1990), an early pioneer of using narratives as stories, discusses how we extrapolate meaning from the multitude of conversations around us that directs how we see and understand our worlds. Other scholars have found this approach fruitful when exploring collective memories; for example, Wertsch (2008) discusses schematic narrative templates as foundations to present social communication and László (1997), talks of frozen historical stories communicated through culture that live on in some way. We argue that collective narratives provide social understandings based on the relationship between the interpreted past and current events. Bar-Tal and Antebi (1992) suggest these collective narratives lie at the base of belief systems that serve to represent a constructed shared collective identity. Hammack (2011) explored stories given by Israeli and Palestinian youth when talking about the conflict, finding that a tragic master narrative was found to account for the Palestinian experience, centred on dispossession and loss, complicated further by a lived experience of Israeli military occupation. By contrast, the metanarratives of

Israeli youth were based on a perceived, rather than a realistic, threat from the Palestinians relating to recent national experiences of suicide bombings and social representations of the Holocaust as an eternal threat. As Hammack (2011) suggests, such studies demonstrate the utility of exploring narratives of those enmeshed in intractable conflict to shed light on these underlying themes of shared experiences. Furthermore, narratives can reflect a current political and ideological position as "narratives provide an ideal paradigmatic lens through which to consider thoughts, feelings and action in a political context" (Hammack & Pilecki, 2012, p. 76).

Narratives as the architecture of social representations exemplify an imagined construction of the past to express how a group perceives and deals with their past (Jovchelovitch, 2012). This remains distinct from any given objective descriptions of the past in terms of facts of past actions. Historical narratives "tend to be considered as part of the stable core of a representational field, and yet they are neither homogenous nor consensual but open platforms for the construction of alternative, often contradictory representations." (Ibid., p. 441). As well as understanding the imagined past as a conduit for an imagined future, these representations demonstrate layers of perceptions and belief systems that relate to the building of collective identities, building and breaking group solidarity and social cohesion. Collective memories can undergo major revisions over time to construct historical narratives that accommodate and reflect a particular political climate. The referencing of these constructions can construct and further develop collective identities (Howarth, 2002). In times of intergroup tension, a tendency towards a more collective homogenous positioning that tightens boundaries can come into effect as group solidarity takes on a significant meaning (Nicholson, 2016). This shared sense of an imagined collective is continually accompanied by a range of mediated representations, supported by institutional meta narratives through education, official commemorations and other cultural artefacts such as museums (Weiser, 2015). We can discuss the past as an imagined trajectory where historical representations serve to develop a group solidarity in the present, which looks to imagined futures for the realisation of their dreams (Liu & Hilton, 2005). By exploring the very foundations of a given set of social representations to highlight a nucleus of an imagined past, we can begin to discuss how imagined futures might be formulated that connects the individual to the collective sense of who we were and who we want to be.

Themata as the Foundation of Social Representations and Collective Identities

As discussed above, narratives form the architectural foundations of social representations that feed into the construction of collective identities. The construct of themata can serve to highlight these foundations, as kernels of knowledge to explore past and future imagined trajectories. Moscovici and Vignaux (2000) discuss how a semantic kernel of knowledge reflects a foundational aspect of a social representation that develops dynamically through ideas and language. Such a construct was identified using the concept of themata. Holton (1975) first coined the term in this context, as a process of social thinking in the form of opposites or antinomies, between which lies interdependence and tension. For example, when discussing social representations of democracy, themata[1] of justice/injustice, free/not free would be manifest in the conversation (Marková, 2000). Themata differ from themes identified in a given data set, due to the significance of the foundational and antinomic nature of a particular context. Not that themes are considered unimportant. The identification of themes can map out pathways that lead to the discovery of underlying themata where these representations emerge and re-emerge within the context under investigation (Marková, 2000). The inclusion of themata in the discussion of imagined futures of groups in conflict can illuminate foundational semantic kernels that have, over time, played a part in developing narratives that form the social representations which continually construct emerging, evolving and dynamic collective identities in two ways. First, exploring themata across groups in conflict, we can try and illuminate the differences of emergent dialogical themata across the groups, rather than discussing one group in isolation. By doing so, we can explore the foundational representations of the conflict and how that

---

[1] Themata denotes the plural where more than one pair of antinomies is discussed, and thema, the singular.

has become part of social knowledge in the present, that affects how the futures might be imagined. Second, by exploring the interdependence of the antinomies, it is possible to discuss their interdependence, not as bipolar either/or processes, but as relational processes that open up possibilities of reflecting change and transformation.

Drawing on empirical work using a sample of Jewish Israeli and Palestinian participants to explore narratives of an imagined past and future, Nicholson (2017) showed how each group perceived and defined themselves in a dialogical relationship to the other when discussing the conflict. The inclusion of themata here shows its usefulness in exploring the cultural and identification processes that can serve to stand as boundary markers between and across the groups. Through a systematic thematic analysis of the qualitative data (Attride-Stirling, 2001), followed by a further coding of the data exploring underlying constructs for each group, a total of four antinomy pairs were identified, two for each group. For the Jewish Israeli participants, themata of exclusivity-inclusivity juxtaposed with threat-security was interpreted as representing these positions in relation to the other group. For the Palestinian participants, themata of unrecognition-recognition and oppression-freedom reflected their positions as shown in Fig. 9.1 below:

Not only did this analysis and identification of themata demonstrate the asymmetry across the groups, it also highlighted how each group's narratives charted a trajectory leading from a foundational kernel as a base of their social representations of the conflict, to the development

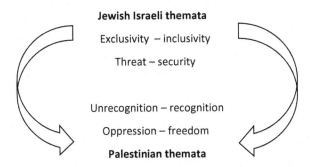

Fig. 9.1 Themata to denote kernels of embedded social representations

and construction of their collective identities. For the Jewish participants, the longed for utopian ideal of an imagined future of a Jewish homeland, following generations of anti-Semitism culminating in the Holocaust, became more than an imagined future to a present reality. However, the extent to which exclusivity of the sovereignty of the Jewish people over the non-Jewish people remained foundational to the conflict, as the existing inhabitants found their own imagined future of sovereignty dashed through civil war illustrated by the thema of unrecognition of the Palestinian group. Crucially, rather than interpreting these themata as solely in terms of exclusivity and unrecognition, we can acknowledge how inclusivity and recognition were also present in the representational field of the participants who took part in the study. When participants discussed their imagined futures, some Jewish Israeli participants also talked of bridging narratives where the future was imagined as moving towards inclusivity, where Palestinians might be more equally recognised as equal citizens. In the Palestinian narratives, the recognition of the state of Israel as a more inclusive future for both groups, whether as an imagined future of sharing a sovereign state, or being separated as two independent entities, was evident. But this is only one part of the story. The thema of threat-security lay close to the surface of the Israeli Jewish narratives, giving rise to social representations around the significance of fear that infiltrated their lives on personal, collective and institutional levels, contributing to their sense of collective identity. These were built around an imagined secure future through measures of security to reduce their fear of perceived threat from the Palestinians. One of the properties of this thema is related to that of oppression-freedom in the Palestinian representational field. They discussed their narratives of oppression as a result of the security measures of the Israeli Jewish, leading to loss of freedom and rights of sovereignty through living within the confines of a military occupation. Their imagined future was often discussed in terms of the desire to regain some dignity for their perceived loss of collective agency. Yet, the cycle of violence can continue when a minority from the weaker group use violent resistance to combat such oppression, only to be met with collective military and civilian punishment by the stronger group, dashing any hopes of any dignified imagined future.

Themata that include both groups' social representations of collective memories and meta narratives as a conduit for their imagined futures can be useful as a starting point from whence to discuss a move away from conflict, rather than being permanently immersed within the confines of intractability. The construction of collective identities in relation to the identified themata establishes the part played by past imagined futures and how they might be played out in the future. At the level of the individual, there have been shifts to reflect a plethora of groups who do not fit into collective representations of two opposing hostile groups or the narratives of intractability that have often been assigned to them (Nicholson, 2017). Heterogeneity and dialogue across and within groups, as well as within individuals themselves, reflect the complexity of trying to define collective identities that fit into neatly defined entities. It is within these complexities that social representations of social recognition of the other across imagined boundaries can—and should—be explored.

Directions of an Imagined Future

The complexity of factors motivating groups to explore imagined futures away from conflict or remain within its confines, makes it problematic to discuss particular influences that initiate change. Of significance is the relationship between the political elites and the people, mediated through institutions and cultural norms and beliefs and communicated as social representations. The perceived intractability of the Israeli-Palestinian conflict (Bar-Tal, 2011, 2014) can be discussed both as a political positioning as well as a cultural one, creating top-down collective identities through hegemonic social representations, leading to the maintenance of tightly held group boundaries. Added to this, the community's social representations of the imagined near and long past, intermixed with present-day positioning, have created barriers that limit alternative social representations from circulating within society (Gillespie, 2008). The relevance of identifying intergroup themata in this context is a good starting point for a discussion of imagined futures. We can reflect on both the barriers as well as alternative imagined futures that build intergroup bridges away from conflict. Examples of those who have followed this latter trajectory include those who have developed collective identities through belonging to social movements that hold the possibility of veering away from the status quo. This has allowed for these individuals to explore alternative paths, either within their own group or across intergroup relationships, resulting in changing and transformed collective identities.

Israeli peace movements have adopted versions of Palestinian narratives entrenched in themata of oppression–freedom and unrecognition–recognition relating to their own theme of exclusivity-inclusivity, to explore intractability away from the mainstream. For example, SISO (Save Israel—Stop the Occupation) encourages collective action within Israel to encourage responsibility to deal with a situation that is perceived as departing from collective moral codes and norms of both Jewish and international communities (Schnell & Bar-Tal, 2016). Collective identities that include this moral dimension reflect the intergroup relationship from base themata, communicated through social representations of the conflict and expressed in narratives that resist the status quo. The idea of 'peace gaps' (Aggestam & Strömbom, 2013) that encourage local initiatives to influence local, nation and international communities to embrace alternative imagined futures can also be discussed within the framework of themata. Israeli and Palestinian NGOs work both separately and together within their communities, to address structural barriers by highlighting human rights abuses and international law responsibilities, both at home and internationally. Israeli organisations such as Machsom Watch (machsomwatch.org) and the Israeli B'Tselem, collect and document material related to human rights abuses towards Palestinians living under military occupation that directly address the Palestinian thema of oppression—freedom relating to that of Israeli threat—security:

> From day to day, civilians living in the West Bank and Gaza are faced with the real implications of ongoing military occupation. The resulting violations of human rights erode the dignity of the Palestinian people and the integrity of Israeli democracy. B'Tselem aims to protect the human rights of those living under occupation, and in doing so, ensure the future of Israelis and Palestinians to live in freedom and security. (btselem.org)

All Jewish Israelis undertake military training and a minimum of two years' duty. Breaking the Silence (2012), an organisation made up of veterans of the Israeli Defence Force (IDF), has documented their challenging experiences that run counter to the preferred version of a moral army serving to protect its citizens, in order to communicate to the Israeli public about everyday life situations when serving in the Occupied Territories. This aligns itself to the theme of unrecognition–recognition of the Palestinian predicament related to a need for security due to threat that has remained foundational to Israeli nationhood. The objective to expose a perceived reality to mainstream citizens to challenge the status quo is a common feature of these NGOs. These projects aim to challenge hegemonic social representations circulating in society that lie at the base of constructing collective identities, to imagine a shift in the intractability of the conflict towards an alternative future that steers away from conflict. The Israeli NGO Zochrat, translated from Hebrew as 'remembering,' challenges how the past is presently represented through institutions to inform the Jewish Israeli public of the ongoing injustices of the Nakba, the term given for the Palestinian catastrophe in 1948. Their long-term objective to fight for the right of the return of those refugees and their descendants, who made up the 80% of the Palestinian population displaced during that time, remains politically contentious. The Israeli theme of exclusivity–inclusivity is activated in this context to address the Palestinian theme of unrecognition–recognition as a foundation of an imagined future, where the two groups might find the opportunity to reconcile the past:

> Zochrot will act to challenge the Israeli Jewish public's preconceptions and promote awareness, political and cultural change within it to create the conditions for the Return of Palestinian Refugees and a shared life in this country. To do so, Zochrot will generate processes in which Israeli Jews will reflect on and review their identity, history, future and the resulting discourse through which they conceive of their lives in this country. (www.zochrat.org)

The challenging of collective identities through such organisations demonstrates the possibility of transformation to acknowledge the other's position as the politically weaker minority group, as those who become involved in such organisations have already done so.

Palestinian narratives of foundational themata also correspond to the construction of collective identities of local activists and the formation of organisations who imagine a future based on freedom and recognition of their lack of sovereign status. A period of violent resistance to perceived oppression and unrecognition of their status throughout two intifadas (1987–1993, 2001–2005), suicide bombings (1989–2008) and continued sporadic terrorist attacks, can be discussed in relation to Israeli narratives around thema of threat-security exemplifying the dialogical relationship across the two groups. The subsequent non-violent resistance national protocol echoes how Palestinian NGOs operate from a different anchoring due to their weakened status. By addressing themata of unrecognition–recognition related to oppression–freedom, the objective of communicating a perceived reality to outside parties is paramount. Al-Haq is one such NGO that promotes human rights within the rule of international law by documenting violations of rights in the Occupied Territories, regardless of the identity of the perpetrator, to undertake advocacy across local, national and international bodies (www.alhaq.org). This is particularly relevant to ongoing global relationships through a consultative status with the United Nations Economic and Social Council. The Palestinian-led Boycott, Divestment, Sanctions (www.bdsmovement.net) rests on the premise that its people are entitled to the same human rights as defined by the United Nations. The South African anti-apartheid movement was the inspiration behind the movement as a call for action to pressure Israel to comply with international law for an imagined future of freedom, rather than oppression for the Palestinian people. Its status is perceived as contentious by pro-Israeli groups due to the perceived politicised narratives (Hallward, 2013), and yet, reaches out to international audiences to spread awareness of the plight of the Palestinian people, yet at the same time, accord the recognition of the state of Israel and its people. Other small-scale local projects centre on imagining a more peaceful and sustaining future. For example, a project based in Gaza that discussed and encouraged young people to engage in imagined projects of tourism in the future surpassing their present predicament (McIntosh, 2015) illustrates the extent to which NGOs attempt to address the present in relation to imagined futures.

We have discussed how each group has initiated movements to imagine a future based on foundational themata away from conflict that resonates with a present positioning. Movements that embrace both Israeli and Palestinian narratives have also developed, where collective identities of reconciliation relate to an imagined future of collective social recognition and co-existence with the other. Organisations such as Combatants for Peace and The Parents Circle focus on intergroup loss and suffering to initiate conciliatory dialogue across the groups. Members of the The Parents Circle—Families Forum (www.theparentscircle.com) include 600 families, both Jewish Israeli and Palestinian, who have lost a close family member due to the conflict. Their insight into the relevance of joint activities as a prerequisite to tolerance, peace and reconciliation has led to public meetings at home and abroad. Member of Combatants for Peace include veterans of the Israeli Defence Force and ex-Palestinian combatants who have also initiated dialogue to create a non-violent strategy towards a joint peaceful and sustainable future (Perry, 2011). These NGOs have used their experience of suffering to develop social representations of reconciliation, as a way forward in imagining a sustainable, more peaceful future (Kis-Lev, 2015).

The development of these collective identities that reflect a shift in the relationship between the self and other in relation to protracted conflict suggest that alternative social representations related to foundational themata, driven by new social experiences, can become more prominent as futures are imagined away from conflict. Bar-Tal (2004) argues that all intergroup relations incorporate a variety of concepts such as tolerance, peace and reconciliation which can be perceived as being insufficient to change a direction of protracted conflict, as the overall negativity remains too deeply entrenched. Yet, Bar-Tal (2004) also argues that any movement where the acceptance of the other, and the collective recognition of the other's legitimate right to exist, is a position that can act as an intermediary stage, towards a more sustained movement away from conflict.

The Imagined Future of Research

This chapter has explored how collective identities of those bound by conflict are shaped by local, social, cultural and political contexts and can remain static through social representations of intractability or become more fluid to reflect some local and societal change. Long-held beliefs and positions that reflect themata, underlying the foundations of the conflict, remain in the present representational field and will necessarily impact on any future imagined social reality. By exploring narratives from those embedded in conflict, our role as researchers can allow us to identify relevant social representations that relate to the formation of collective identities in the context of conflict. These collective identities may further entrench the ongoing conflict, or allow a space for another future to be imagined, or more often, a little of both. The political context is central in determining these identities and representational processes as a major sphere of social influence. It is at the level of the community where we can explore grassroot systems that remain meaningful to the population that allows further insights, rather than solely discussing the role of political discourse as a measure of intractability. By examining the complexity of themata for each group, dialogically related to the other, yet set within a power asymmetry, this approach can take into account the symbolic value of such a process, as well as the role of including the voices of those integral to the conflict being heard (Obradović & Howarth, 2017).

In examining intergroup conflict in today's world, it is imperative that we develop a nuanced understanding of the social psychological processes that not only sustain conflict, but also hold the possibilities and imaginations of a different future, of recognition, freedom and peace. While such imaginings may seem fleeting in the contexts we have discussed here, to do otherwise may only help sustain the relations of conflict, unrecognition and hostility that mark many parts of the globe today.

References

Abu-Ghazaleh, A. (1972). Arab cultural nationalism in Palestine during the British mandate. *Journal of Palestine Studies, 1*(3), 37–63.

Aggestam, K., & Strömbom, L. (2013). Disempowerment and marginalisation of peace NGOs: Exposing peace gaps in Israel and Palestine. *Peacebuilding, 1*(1), 109–124.

Attride-Stirling, J. (2001). Thematic networks: An analytical tool for qualitative research. *Qualitative Research, 1*(3), 385–405.

Bar-Tal, D. (2004). The necessity of observing real life situations: Palestinian-Israeli violence as a laboratory for learning about social behaviour. *European Journal of Social Psychology, 34*(6), 677–701.

Bar-Tal, D. (2007). Socio-psychological foundations of intractable conflicts. *American Behavioural Scientist, 50*(11), 1430–1453.

Bar-Tal, D. (2011). *Intergroup conflicts and their resolution.* London/New York: Psychology Press.

Bar-Tal, D. (2014). Collective memory as social representations. *Papers on Social Representations, 23,* 5.1–5.26.

Bar-Tal, D., & Antebi, D. (1992). Siege mentality in Israel. *Papers on Social Representations, 1*(1), 49–67.

Barr, J. (2011). *A line in the sand: Britain, France and the struggle that shaped the Middle East.* London: Simon & Schuster.

Billig, M. (2002). Henri Tajfel's 'cognitive aspects of prejudice' and the psychology of bigotry. *British Journal of Social Psychology, 41*(2), 171–188.

Breaking the Silence. (2012). *Our harsh logic. Israeli's soldiers' testimonies from the occupied territories, 2000–2010.* New York: Metropolitan Books.

Brewer, M. (2001). Intergroup identification and intergroup conflict. In R. Asmore, L. Jussim, & D. Wilder (Eds.), *Social identity and intergroup conflict reduction.* Oxford: Oxford University Press.

Bruner, J. (1990). *Acts of meaning.* Cambridge, MA: Harvard University Press.

Carretero, M. (2018, this volume). History education and the (im)possibility of imagining the future. In C. de Saint-Laurent, S. Obradović, & K. R. Carriere (Eds.), *Imagining collective futures: Perspectives from social, cultural, and political psychology* (pp. 255–271). London: Palgrave Macmillan.

De Saint-Laurent, C. (2014). "I would rather be hanged than agree with you!": Collective memory and the definition of the nation in parliamentary debates on immigration. *Outlines, 15*(3), 22–53.

Flesher Fominaya, C. (2010). Collective identity in social movements: Central concepts and debates. *Sociology Compass, 4*(6), 393–404.

Gillespie, A. (2008). Social representations, alternative representations and semantic barriers. *Journal for the Theory of Social Behaviour, 38*(4), 375–391.

Gillespie, A., & Cornish, F. (2010). Intersubjectivity: Towards a dialogical analysis. *Journal of the Theory of Social Behaviour, 40*(1), 19–46.

Gillespie, A., Howarth, C., & Cornish, F. (2012). Four problems for researchers using social categories. *Culture and Psychology, 18*(3), 391–402.

Goldberg, D. J. (1996). *To the promised land: A history of Zionist thought.* London: Penguin.

Hallward, M. C. (2013). *Transnational activism and the Israeli-Palestinian conflict*. New York: Palgrave Macmillan.

Hammack, P. (2011). *Narrative and the politics of identity: The cultural psychology of Israeli and Palestinian youth, culture and identity*. New York/Oxford: Oxford University Press.

Hammack, P., & Pilecki, A. (2012). Narrative as a root metaphor for political psychology. *Political Psychology, 33*(1), 75–103.

Harré, R. (1998). *The singular self: An introduction to the psychology of personhood*. London: Sage.

Herzl, T. (1934). *The Jewish State: An attempt at a modern solution of the Jewish question* (2nd ed.). London: Central Office of the Zionist Organisation.

Holton, G. (1975). On the role of themata in scientific thought. *Science, 188*, 328–334.

Howarth, C. (2002). Identity in whose eyes? The role of representations in identity construction. *Journal for the Theory of Social Behaviour, 32*(2), 145–162.

Howarth, C. (2011). Representations, identity, and resistance in communication. In D. Hook, B. Franks, & M. Bauer (Eds.), *The social psychology of communication* (pp. 153–168). Basingstoke: Palgrave Macmillan.

Howarth, C., Andreouli, C., & Kessi, S. (2015). Social representations and the politics of participation. In P. Nesbitt-Larking, C. Kinnvall, & T. Capelos (Eds.), *The Palgrave handbook of global political psychology*. London: Palgrave Macmillan.

Jovchelovitch, S. (2007). *Knowledge in context: Representations, community and culture*. London/New York: Routledge.

Jovchelovitch, S. (2012). Narrative, memory and social representations: A conversation between history and social psychology. *Integrative Psychological and Behavioural Science, 46*(4), 440–456.

Kis-Lev, J. (2015). *My quest for peace: One Israeli's journey from hatred to peacemaking*. Chicago: Goldsmith.

Kristeva, J. (1993). *Nations without nationalism*. New York: Columbia University Press.

Lázló, J. (1997). Narrative organisations of social representations. *Papers on Social Representations, 6*(2), 155–172.

Linell, P. (2009). *Rethinking language, mind and world dialogically: Interactional and contextual theories of human sense-making*. Greenwich, CT: Information Age Publishing.

Liu, J. H., & Hilton, D. J. (2005). How the past weighs on the present: Social representations of history and their role in identity politics. *British Journal of Social Psychology, 44*(4), 537–556.

Marková, I. (2000). Amédéé or how to get rid of it: Social representations from a dialogical perspective. *Culture & Psychology, 6*(4), 419–460.

Marková, I. (2003). *Dialogicality and social representations*. Cambridge: Cambridge University Press.

McDonald, K. (2002). From solidarity to fluidarity: Social movements beyond "collective identity"—the case of globalization conflicts. *Social Movement Studies, 1*(2), 109–128.

McIntosh, I. (2015). Gaza: Visioning peace in a place like hell. *Palestine-Israel Journal of Politics, Economics and Culture, 20*(2), 154–159.

Melucci, A. (1989). The symbolic challenge of contemporary movements. *Social Research, 52*, 781–816.

Melucci, A. (1996). *Challenging codes: Collective action in the information age*. Cambridge: Cambridge University Press.

Moscovici, S. (1961/2008). Psychoanalysis: Its image and its public (D. Macey, Trans.). Cambridge: Polity Press. *La psychoanalyse, son image et son public* (2nd rev. ed.). Paris: PUF (first edition 1961).

Moscovici, S. (2000). *Social representations: Explorations in social psychology* (G. Duveen, Ed.). Cambridge: Polity Press.

Moscovici, S., & Marková, I. (2000). Ideas and development. In G. Duveen (Ed.), *Social representations: Explorations in social psychology* (pp. 224–287). Cambridge: Polity Press.

Moscovici, S., & Vignaux, G. (2000). The concept of themata. In S. Moscovici (Ed.), *Social representations: Explorations in social psychology*. Cambridge: Polity Press.

Nicholson, C. (2016). The role of historical representations in Israeli-Palestinian relations: Narratives from abroad. *Peace and Conflict. Journal of Peace Psychology, 22*(1), 5–11.

Nicholson, C. (2017). The role of collective memory in protracted conflict. *Culture and Psychology, 23*(2), 217–233.

Northrup, T. A. (1989). The dynamic of the identity in personal and social conflict. In L. Kiesburg, T. A. Northrup, & S. J. Thorson (Eds.), *Intractable conflicts and their transformation*. Syracuse, NY: Syracuse University Press.

Obradović, S. (2018, this volume). Creating integration: A case study from Serbia and the EU. In C. de Saint-Laurent, S. Obradović, & K. R. Carriere (Eds.), *Imagining collective futures: Perspectives from social, cultural, and political psychology* (pp. 237–254). London: Palgrave Macmillan.

Obradović, S., & Howarth, C. (2017). Everyday reconciliation. In C. Howarth & E. Andreouli (Eds.), *Everyday politics*. London: Routledge.

Perry, D. (2011). *The Israeli-Palestinian peace movement: Combatants for peace*. New York: Palgrave Macmillan.

Power, S. (2018, this volume). Remembering and imagining in human development: Fairness and social movements in Ireland. In C. de Saint-Laurent, S. Obradović, & K. R. Carriere (Eds.), *Imagining collective futures: Perspectives from social, cultural, and political psychology* (pp. 221–235). London: Palgrave Macmillan.

Reicher, S. (2004). The context of social identity: Domination, resistance, and change. *Political Psychology, 25*(6), 921–945.

Reicher, S., & Haslam, A. (2012). Change we can believe in; the role of social identity, cognitive alternatives, and leadership in group mobilization and transformation. In B. Wagoner, E. Jensen, & J. A. Oldmeadow (Eds.), *Culture and social change: Transforming society through the power of ideas*. Charlotte, NC: Information Age Publishing.

Reicher, S., & Hopkins, N. (2001). *Self and nation*. London: Sage.

Rouhana, N. M. (2007). *Palestinian citizens in an ethnic Jewish State: Identities in conflict*. New Haven/London: Yale University Press.

Said, E. (2003). *Culture and resistance: Conversations with Edward W. Said* (D. Barsamian, Ed.). London: Pluto.

Sand, S. (2012). *The invention of the land of Israel: From Holy land to homeland*. London: Verso.

Schnell, I., & Bar-Tal, D. (2016). After 50 years: Save Israel: Stop the occupation. *Palestine-Israel Journal of Politics, Economics & Culture, 21*(3), 72–80.

Smith, C. D. (2013). *Palestine and the Arab-Israeli conflict: A history with documents*. Boston: Bedford/St. Martins.

Snow, D. (2001). *Collective identity and expressive forms*. University of California, Irvine eScholarship Repository. http://repositories.cdlib.org/csd/01-07

Strömbom, S. (2013). *Israeli identity, thick recognition and conflict transformation*. Basingstoke: Palgrave Macmillan.

Tajfel, H. (1981). *Human groups and social categories: Studies in social psychology*. Cambridge: Cambridge University Press.

Tajfel, H., & Turner, J. C. (1979). An integrative theory of intergroup conflict. In W. G. Austin & S. Worschel (Eds.), *The social psychology of intergroup relations*. Monterey: Brooks/Cole.

Weiser, M. (2015). National identity within the national museum: Subjectification with socialization. *Studies in Philosophy and Education, 34*(4), 385–402.

Wertsch, J. V. (2008). Blank spots in collective memory: A case study of Russia. *Annals of the American Academy of Political and Social Science, 617*, 58–71.

Section III

Creating Socio-Political Change

10

Creating Alternative Futures: Cooperative Initiatives in Egypt

Eman A. Maarek and Sarah H. Awad

Triggered by the dissatisfaction with the present, we imagine alternative futures of how the world could be for better or worse. And while power dynamics within the status quo in many parts of the world do not inspire an optimistic vision of the future, certain events disrupt the norm and open up the possibilities that were once thought impossible.

The Egyptian uprising in 2011 was one such event: after only 18 days of protests, crowds of people were able to topple a 30-year authoritarian regime and reclaim their denied collective agency. This uprising was not only manifested in the protests in squares, but was also followed by a burst in grassroots initiatives. The revolution inspired different groups to imagine a better future for the country and actualize this imagination through many youth-led initiatives that included cooperatives, nongovernmental organizations, political parties, and art and media projects.

E. A. Maarek (✉)
Independent Researcher, Cairo, Egypt

S. H. Awad
Aalborg University, Aalborg, Denmark
e-mail: awads@hum.aau.dk

© The Author(s) 2018
C. de Saint-Laurent et al. (eds.), *Imagining Collective Futures*, Palgrave Studies in Creativity and Culture, https://doi.org/10.1007/978-3-319-76051-3_10

For a brief time after January 2011, those initiatives flourished as the power dynamics between individuals in the society and those in power juggled, and visions of a more equal society with freedom and social justice were seen as an achievable target. This window of opportunity for change gradually tightened as different powers with goals different from those of the revolution took charge. After the toppling of the Mubarak regime, the military took the lead in the transition period, followed by the Muslim Brotherhood presidency for a year and then a coup d'état that led to the current military-backed regime. Six years after the uprising, the current government exercises tight security control over different forms of assembly and freedom of expression, silencing any counter voice or action that could provoke another upheaval. This repression is supported by many who suffered from the turbulence of the uprising and who see these measures as necessary responses to terrorism threats in the region. The above-mentioned progression of events has put those who were and still are holding on to the revolutionary cause through a personal as well as a social rupture. The future imagination they had during the uprising and heightened sense of hope for a better future were quickly met by political powers that worked against those imagined collective futures. This inflicted a sense of despair and loss.

In parallel to this timeline of social and political changes, we will look in this chapter at three cooperative initiatives that developed out of the uprising and follow their progression over the past six years. Cooperatives are "autonomous association of persons united voluntarily to meet their common economic, social and cultural needs and aspirations through a jointly owned and democratically controlled enterprise" (see International Labor law, R. 193, 2002; www.ica.coop). The case studies are looked at as tangible projects through which groups of people actualized their future imagination into action in present time, choosing to embody change rather than wait for it to happen in a distant future. The selected cooperative initiatives were all initiated by young people who engaged with the revolution as a utopian vision of a possible future after the suppressive regime was removed. We will look at how, when this utopian vision was faced with the constraints of reality, each group reacted differently to realize their objectives.

The focus will be on the experience of individual social actors involved in these collective initiatives, their motives, opportunities as well as constraints, and how they make sense of social change now and their agency throughout the different political changes. We will first discuss the close connection between imagining alternative futures and engaging in prefigurative politics; then we will discuss the history of cooperatives internationally and in Egypt, leading to the analysis of three cases from Egypt. In conclusion, we argue that imagination was a key process in going beyond the momentum of the revolution to collaborative action that materialized what people aspired for as a collective future as well as what they believed they were capable of amidst the uprising. The case studies are also used to highlight the potential of cooperatives in opening up venues for decentralized everyday forms of resistance and change as opposed to mass revolution and violent seizure of state power.

From Imagination to Prefigurative Politics to Sustainable Change

Imagining the future takes us into an arena of possibilities, an alternative from our current reality. Imagining a better future has been, in many instances, the motive as well as the outcome of uprisings and social change. Revolutions are times of idealized imagination of the collective future, as individuals experience a heightened sense of agency, and collectively reimagine and reconstruct their social identity (Reicher & Haslam, 2012). In those "troubled times, utopian impulses flourish because the impossible seems more reasonable than the realistic" (Leonard, 2014). The seemingly stable societal structures then seem less immune to change, and agency takes prime over status quo.

Imagination here is seen from a social psychological perspective as a higher mental as well as emotional function that enables individuals to fully feel and understand their worlds (Cornejo, 2017). Imagining an alternative future, thus, involves a process of distancing oneself from the here-and-now situation (Vygotsky, 1987) and engaging in a dynamic semiotic process that is not bound to the constraints of the current socially shared reality. This distancing does not imply impassiveness with the present, but rather a reflexive engagement with the here and now, which triggers an anticipation or exploration of possible next moves (Zittoun & Gillespie, 2016). It is thus a mistake to assume that because imagination is "not real," it cannot have "real" consequences (Zittoun & Gillespie, Chap. 2, this volume). When we distance ourselves from the constraints of the present time and engage in a reflexive process of imagining alternative future outcomes, we are able to come back to the present with new possibilities.

The interest of this chapter is in the actions individuals partake within their present time to conceive a collective imagined future, when people mobilize collaboratively in the present to put their imagined future of the community into action, looking at the dynamics as well as the constraints between imagined collective futures and actual attempts to realize those dreams.

Cooperatives initiatives are one example of putting an imagined picture of society into experimentation through the principles of the collective. It is based on the idea that communities understand best their social and economic needs, and are capable of developing collective projects to serve those needs independent of the established system; it thus provides an alternative way to centralized systems managed by government and big companies. Looking at cooperative initiatives in times of social change highlights two important aspects: first, the perception of past, present, and future, where cooperatives can be viewed as individuals' realization of past problems, search for resolutions through future imagination, and the translation of those into present action. Second, we can examine the connection between the individual and the collective agency. In a state of collective agency, people collaborate and put their resources together to influence change (Bandura, 2006).

Cooperatives that come out of the context of protests could be seen as examples of new institutions that transform a temporary prefiguration to a more sustainable social change. Protests and uprisings are times of prefiguration, where the taken-for-granted structures are shaken. Prefigurative politics refers to the process by which individuals create alternative social relations to their surroundings and work with others to create grassroots social changes challenging the established dominant economic, political, and social systems (Yates, 2015). To prefigure here is to anticipate or enact some feature of an "alternative world" in the present, as though it has already been achieved (ibid.).

Although prefiguration is regularly described as a new form of doing political action, and it is increasingly used for analyzing contemporary movements, the term has been in use for several decades. It was first defined by Boggs (1977) as "the embodiment within the ongoing political practice of a movement, of those forms of social relations, decision-making, culture, and human experience that are the ultimate goal." Prefiguration is said to create utopic alternatives, though on a limited scale, in the present (Yates, 2015). Prefigurative politics has thus been aligned closely with anarchism, and notions of nonviolent direct action that sees authoritarianism and coercion as fundamentally unjustifiable (Epstein, 1991).

While prefiguration in protests open up new ways of conceptualizing the social order and new potentials for transformative frameworks (Graeber, 2002), it is limited in its impact, as it is bound by the place and time of the protest (Agustín, 2015). This raises the question how this prefiguration can lead to societal alternative and future change, if it only imagines the future through spatialized practices—created in a geographically limited democratic space and a specific time—without contesting domination in other spheres of society (ibid.). Social change requires a set of sustainable activities and practices in addition to political mobilization (Epstein, 1991). It requires social actions that create counter-institutions, a transformation of relationships, and the construction of community (Yates, 2015). Through those counter-institutions, temporary uprising prefiguration becomes more sustainable social change, and the alternatives created form a "dual power" in opposition to established order (Maeckelbergh, 2011).

To elaborate more on the concept of cooperatives as a step beyond prefigurative politics that create alternative institutions with potential power, we need to further define what we mean by institutions and power. By institutions, we wish to adopt a general conception of it that involves practices (social, economic, political, ideological, and practices), norms, as well as more concrete and material institutions (Agustín, 2015). Power is not seen as a top-down control from established institutions, but as a dependent factor that requires collective acceptance. Institutions only get to have power by acceptance of the public, so in this understanding, power originates from below. This explains how social movements could have power, and can implement social change by collective rejection of existing power structures and by challenging dominant institutions through creating alternative ones (Agustín, 2015).

In what follows, we will demonstrate how the chosen cooperative initiatives were implemented as a kind of laboratory trials experimenting with how the desired future could look like and operate in comparison to the resisted present social order, and how cooperatives move beyond dissatisfaction and temporary assembly into practical long-term plans. Historically, this is also how cooperatives were initiated, as will be discussed in the next section.

Historical Background of Cooperatives

The global history of cooperatives reflects how they were initiatives triggered by the desire to create social change through imaging different settings of the society. Robert Owen—who is known to be the founder/inspirer of the cooperative movement—believed that if the working individuals ever were to achieve equality, then they must change first their attitude. This requires them to know, believe in, and be equipped to fight for a collective cause, which creates an autonomous "internally-sufficient" system that serves their communities. An internally sufficient system is attained when cooperative activities achieve surplus that can cover all its duties and liabilities toward its members and the community, and thus guarantee its independence (Aboud, 2015).

The cooperative movement developed in Europe in the nineteenth century, primarily in Britain and France. The first documented consumer cooperative was founded in 1769. By 1830, there were several hundred cooperatives. Some were initially successful, but most cooperatives founded in the early nineteenth century had failed by 1840. The real development and growth happened when the Rochdale Society of Equitable Pioneers established the "Rochdale Principles," which are cooperative guidelines that better established the idea of cooperatives in 1844 (ibid.).

In 1895, the global body of the International Cooperatives Alliance was founded, which created unified criteria for cooperatives. According to ICA, a cooperative is an autonomous association of persons united voluntarily to meet their common economic, social, and cultural needs and aspirations through a jointly owned and democratically controlled enterprise. According to ICA, cooperatives are based on the values of self-help, self-responsibility, democracy, equality, equity, and solidarity. In the tradition of their founders, cooperative members believe in a collective cooperatives identity that values principles of honesty, openness, social responsibility, and caring for others.

This background about the initiation and growth of the idea of cooperatives is informing of certain aspects in its potential of social and economic change. First, part of the nature of change is passing through a continuous process of success and failure. The initial idea of a collective, autonomous, internally sufficient group kept going up and down since the nineteenth century until cooperatives crystallized in the twenty-first century as an alternative social and economic structure. Second, cooperatives proved their effectiveness by offering a practical solution in response to the dissatisfaction with the system, and materialized the values they called for through specific projects that the community could benefit from. Third, the ideals of cooperatives went beyond their application to specific projects, to their advocacy of those ideals to the wider society. The success of specific projects in providing services to communities helped to mainstream the changes to make them more acquirable and sustainable in other societal structures and influenced a change in the principles governing those structures. For example, cooperatives' ideals promote a collective shared financial body that equally supports services to all individuals within a society; this ideal goes against systems that promote competitiveness and individual benefits that do not serve the wider community.

Cooperative Movements in Egypt

Cooperatives started in Egypt in the beginning of the twentieth century (1908) due to a social mobilization led by several intellectuals. Omar Lotfy, who studied agricultural cooperatives in Italy, established the first cooperative for peasants under his supervision. The initiative was successful and popular in a sense because its main actors were the peasants who responded to the call and took part in the grassroots organizations to meet their needs. This movement happened prior to any legislative or state action; it was not until 1923 when the first Egyptian cooperative law was issued (Barakat & Maarek, in press).

The concept of cooperatives continued to grow in Egypt. By 1930, there were about 297 documented cooperatives (Aboud, 2015). The turning point in this growth was in 1952 during President Nasser's era, when a series of legislative reforms changed the framework of cooperatives to be supervised and controlled by the state, thus serving solely the implementation of the government socioeconomic plans.

Since then, the legal framework governing the cooperatives has influenced the nature of existing cooperatives to be more of a governmental instrument controlled by the regime, not by the cooperative members. Such laws isolated cooperatives completely from the global cooperative movement that promotes independence. The present legal framework turned cooperatives into an illusive body, where basic cooperative principles such as voluntary membership and independence in taking decisions are violated (e.g. law 122, 1980 for agricultural cooperatives, forced any land owner to be a member in the prior established coop in their geographical zone) (Barakat & Maarek, in press). Laws also created hierarchical power relations since they gave rights to the concerned state representative to interfere in the internal decisions of cooperatives.

After the 2011 revolution, there were many calls to create a unified code for cooperatives that is independent of this constraining law and that allows cooperatives to work freely away from the controlling hand of the government. Given the postrevolution complicated political scene, such calls did not realize any concrete changes, and the formal legal path of cooperative resurrection failed. This led some activists to act outside the parochial legal framework, creating cooperatives with no legal documentation, and starting their activities without waiting for the long routine process to get approved, as will be illustrated in the case studies later.

Beyond Protest: Different Cooperative Trials After Revolution

The early days of the Egyptian revolution in 2011 uncovered the power of collective imagination and its inevitability, as well as the inability of any regime to suppress it. In 2011, the fear of regime broke as one of the dominative taboos among Egyptians and the protesters became aware of how powerful it was to unite together as they celebrated the success of the 18 days of protest in toppling the regime. This was coupled with the awareness of the temporal nature of this collective assembly, and that after the protests were over, activists would need more sustainable collectives to keep the momentum of change. That is where the idea of cooperatives came as an option to sustain the revolutionary goals.

The collective vision of future social life has been clearly materialized in Tahrir Square and other squares all over the country through building up a simulation for a desired society. Protestors created many committees in charge of safety, nutrition, cleaning, media, and mobilization. The togetherness in the square showed how close the demands and values of both the street vendor and the university professor were; this similarity highlighted the fact that the regime and current structures were the obstacles that stood against communities working together for their own good.

To keep this invaluable gain, scenarios of what could happen after the protests were discussed among activists as well as speculations of what would happen if the revolution failed to topple the regime. There was a strong motive to find a way to stay connected with this community through a sustainable target. This motive remained with many protestors who went back to their local communities with potential projects for development.

The data discussed next will look at some of those trials and how, in their success as well as in their failures, they helped actors see in a tangible form what exactly needs to be changed to make their picture of a more just humane future possible.

Three Case Studies

Data from these three case studies is part of a bigger fieldwork project carried out by the first author. The research project involved an in-depth study of the history and development of cooperatives in Egypt (Barakat & Maarek, in press). It included field visits, historical archives, and interviews with activists and members of cooperatives. The focus of this chapter will be on cooperatives that emerged after the 2011 revolution, how the revolution changed the vision and future imagination of those initiatives, and how the development of those cooperatives progressed as the revolution took a counter turn. Data for these case studies include six interviews with their founders and members in the years 2012 to 2014, in addition to follow-up interviews in 2016. Follow-up interviews were mainly concerned with the development of the initiatives and the participant's thoughts and emotions with regards to the counter-revolution situation and how they reflect back on the initial revolution success and the initial stage of founding the cooperative.

The interviews were conducted, transcribed, and analyzed in Arabic, and then quotes for the chapter were translated by the authors into English. Consent was acquired from participants. Names of participants and cooperatives are omitted for anonymity.

Transportation Cooperative in Fayoum

MN is the founder of a transportation cooperative in the city of Fayoum (Fayoum is one of the poorest governorates in Upper Egypt). He actively took part in the 2011 revolution, and was motivated to advocate for the collective good of the revolution after he went back to his village in Fayoum. He organized local meetings to discuss the social and economic problems people suffer from in the village. One of the major problems was the lack of decent transportation means for village inhabitants to commute to the city or surrounding areas. The monopoly of transportation was in the hands of the private sector, and the failure of the state to provide such basic services opened the door for exploitation in terms of deciding the routes and tariffs. MN suffered from this issue himself since he was a school student and grew up with pent-up anger toward the inability to have decent affordable services. He mentioned how his school peers from the adjacent villages made fun of his transportation options.

The outcome of his meetings was to create a transportation cooperative owned by village residents to have a sustainable solution. "I look forward to declare my village the first cooperative village in Egypt," he stated proudly in an interview in 2014. The establishment of the cooperative struggled with the legal framework for almost two years to get formally registered. In spite of the delay, the initiative already succeeded in implementing change on the ground. It not only provided an alternative community-owned means of transportation, but it also partly broke the monopoly of the private sector. Once the private transportation company owners heard about the initiative, they adhered to the people's demand to provide decent vans at affordable prices.

Recycling Cooperative in Helwan

AM, the founder and board director of an environmental cooperative in Helwan (Helwan is a city south of Cairo, considered part of greater Cairo), was also highly driven by the slogans of the revolution: bread, freedom, human dignity, and social justice. After the protests, he decided to start reading cooperatives' laws and think about the different mechanisms that could help put the revolution slogans into action projects. For years his neighborhood suffered terribly from excess garbage that was not regularly collected. He envisioned a cooperative project that would not only solve the garbage problem but also generate income. The cooperative idea of putting the revolution slogans into action was not through the technical core of the recycling activity, but through acquiring the right to live in a clean environment and the ability to replace the unfulfilled role of the state services with citizens' systemic collaboration.

He stated: "The problem of garbage collection and clean streets was irritating me since long and after the 18 days of protest I wanted, like others, to build on the collective spirit of the square by action, so this cause was the first to come to mind." AM used the political platform and network that was created through the protests to advocate for his idea of creating a cooperative for recycling. He was very pragmatic and aware that the first step was to build awareness in his neighborhood on the idea of cooperatives. He took concrete steps and printed a simple introductory page about the idea of cooperatives in the form of a Q&A leaflet. He approached people who he had already been in contact with through the protests, and directly advocated his idea of a recycling cooperative. He then proceeded to invite others to become members of the cooperative: "I was telling everyone I briefed: if you are convinced, sign as a founding member immediately."

Cooperative members were aware of the constraining legal framework imposed on cooperative establishments. They decided to be practical and postpone the bureaucratic process and confrontation with the system until they obtained concrete results and proved successful in their initiatives. After the project was initiated, they started doing the paperwork and planned to work around the imposed rules, AM explains: "On paper, we abide by the governing laws of cooperatives which contradict with our autonomy and independence, but in reality we apply and follow the values of cooperatives (…) we are always ahead of the local authority's requests and meetings, providing them with all paperwork needed, in return we manage it internally in a different way… That's why we succeed."

A Cooperative for Cooperatives in Fayoum

This case is different from the previous two in that the founder MH faced the reality in a more revolutionary manner. He and his group rejected the system and filed a constitutional case against the governing laws of cooperatives, while establishing their group under the laws of nongovernmental organizations (NGOs). This reflects their different perception of power relations, as MH states: "It is us and the revolution against the deep state structures."

It commenced at the end of the 18 days of protest, triggered by the same motive of continuing the dream of change that seemed possible. MH and other young university students in his city of Al Fayoum decided to establish a cooperative to incubate cooperatives for disadvantaged working women: "We saw those women already running their own projects independently, they were selling fresh pre-prepared vegetables. So we thought of bringing them together and help them work as a group to cut down the expenses they bear individually, hence maximize their profit and independence."

Faced by the complicated and corrupt public service system, MH and his group found no sense in faking their new emerging institution as being under cooperative law: "Not worth wasting our time and resources to be registered as a cooperative, the required conditions were meant to discourage people from establishing cooperatives." The decision was to comply with the law of NGOs;: "It is easier to deal with only one government authority (that of NGOs) rather than tens in the case of cooperative registration (…) in the end of the day, we know that all these legal structures are artificial and not meant to empower the masses," said MH.

The cooperative expanded as an incubator of other smaller initiatives. It currently provides technical support to other potential groups in several traditional crafts such as pottery and textile. The cooperative groups that had been formed under this initiative have succeeded in working and applying the cooperatives' principles according to their interviewed members. They continue to achieve a sufficient surplus to sustain and are able to meet their needs to work and secure a regular income. Yet they are not legally registered till now. In the follow-up interview, MH still expresses the same ideas communicated since the first interview, four years back; "We will keep going for our dream with the same spirit and enthusiasm, no matter the failures, because when we fail we will get the chance to know what needs correction." MH always speaks of "We," not "I," which is also indicative of his wider principles in relation to cooperatives.

Analysis and Discussion: Collective Imagination and Social Change

Looking at the three case studies and analyzing the interview data using thematic network analysis (Attride-Stirling, 2001), we found the recurring themes to be centered on two key forces: on the one hand, social and structural constraints, and on the other, agency and opportunities for action, presented in Fig. 10.1. Interviewees perceived those two factors in a variety of ways, and expressed different resistance strategies and tactics to mediate between them.

In the first cooperative, MN succeeded in liberating the village from the private sector transportation monopoly as a social constraint, but did not attempt a second step of liberating himself from the constraints of state structural power. He still saw state power as the only kind of possible structure that guarantees "protection" from the monopoly and threat of private sector. He repeated in many instances in the interview: "The fact is I hate the state and would never like to attach myself to any governmental or official work, however, being part of the state as a cooperative grant me the protection I need to challenge the power of the private companies."

MN and some other village residents, mainly students, used radical tactics and strategies certain times, which followed the revolution practices directly. For example, they circulated a petition and called for action throughout the entire village. They were aware of and utilized the government officials' fear of emerging protests, especially after the revolution, and thus used the opportunity of the public dissatisfaction to protest against the transportation situation and create pressure on government officials through collective action. Such strategies show the heightened sense of agency and realization of collective action power that came after the revolution and motivated this cooperative's members to implement their future ideas at the village level.

They also resorted to different tactics in the different stages of their cooperative. In the early stage of advocacy, they relied on the revolution momentum and the high hopes of their community. In certain instances, they were confrontational with government employees, and in others,

Fig. 10.1 Recurring themes in the data

negotiated with them to pass their documents. They had to work around the excessive routine by different means that did not always abide by their principles: "My strategies varied in dealing with the official constraints. In some cases, I had to threaten them that if they do not do their job, the residents of the village will protest in front of the governorates, in other instances we had to give gifts as bribes," MN explains.

The significant motivation and action relating to the first case study was mainly in the time right after the revolution in 2011. During this initial stage, MN managed to transmit the collective revolution dream to a local one in his village. However, this motivation was short-lived; as the revolution momentum and its popularity suffered, he also struggled with the ideals that motivated him in the first place. In a follow-up interview with him in 2016, MN said: "After the revolution failed, I regretted every moment I spent with people or for people. I reached nowhere compared to my non-activist peers who never cared about their community or country and moved ahead with their careers."

This case highlights the heightened sense of imagination that gets transformed into action in times of rapid social change after revolutions, while not necessarily being sustainable. When the context allowed for radical change, MN and members of the cooperative took radical steps toward change and were able to establish their own structure. After the counter-revolution, they still feel the dissatisfaction with present reality and even more, but their imagination of possible change is unable to drive them as before to take actions and expand their cooperative. This has led to a current static state of the transportation cooperative; it is not progressing beyond the initial outcome and not expanding to include more vehicles or more sustainable solutions for the transportation problem.

This first case also highlights the connection between the individual and collective imagination. The collective imagination was the motivator for the individual to be inspired and it facilitated a supportive context to visualize different alternatives for the present difficulties. However, as the collective spirit of the revolution suffered with the succeeding regimes and as the risks associated with collective action increased, the motives and hopes of individuals suffered.

In the second case, one of the main constraints mentioned was related to lack of awareness. They faced lack of awareness from people wanting to join for the profits, seeing it as a business opportunity, and lack of awareness from government officials who would not know the difference between a cooperative and an NGO. AM explains how he tried to take a nonconfrontational approach to maneuver this through convincing the local government employees of the national benefit coming out of his cooperative idea.

AM utilized different tactics and strategies to deal with the undesired present and impose his own imagined tomorrow: "I focused on finishing the registration process as soon as possible because time matters much to keep members motivated and mobilized for change. In less than one year, the cooperative was officially established and registered," he proudly said. AM and his group also utilized every way that could help in advocating for their cooperative: "We were 83 members at the time of registration and we reached 157 members plus the advisory board through campaigning the cooperative on Facebook."

This case shows the influence of individual imagination over the collective one. Because AM had not faced a direct personal issue with garbage collection (contrary to MN in the first case), he was able to distance himself from the immediate problem and plan practical ways for a solution. This distancing was also reflected in how this cooperative applied the concept of collectiveness in a highly selective way. They chose the members of the board from a certain category of the society (those who owned the technicalities in recycling and environmental field) and they advocated the idea of the recycling cooperative to those who were convinced by the notion of collectiveness over the for-profit alternatives. AM also started from the same motivational point, which is continuing the revolution spirit to make the change tangible. He realized how powerful he can be in implementing his ideas if he studied the legal framework of cooperatives well, and then used his knowledge to fight back the constraints faced in the legal process.

The awareness of the time influence factor in this case led the group to utilize the revolution momentum. They started the work process and the advocacy for the cooperative before it was legalized, so they could build on the heightened motive for action after the revolution. Parallelly, they worked on getting the cooperative legalized, as AM explains, "We would experience one day of hardship with ignorant public servants and grasp the lesson in the next day and strategize around it." He printed out more copies of paperwork than required, carried a hard copy of the law, and was continuously ready and aware of the constraints.

The recycling cooperative still operates successfully through the changing political atmosphere after the revolution. They have managed to sustain its success, however, their initial hopes to expand to other areas of Egypt cannot be actualized for the time being.

The third case, visualized the structural constraints early on and its founder decided to resist the framework altogether. The founders did not encounter much hardship in the social realm; they were offering a service that was met with strong societal need. Potential groups of working women (street vendors) responded well to the cooperatives principles: "Although they are illiterate, they easily saw the shared benefit and developed simple ways of running their work and calculating the surplus and distribution," says MH. He adds: "We decided to let go with all this bureaucratic corrupted system governing cooperatives early on when we went to the office of 'The Regional Union for Consumption Cooperatives' and found it has been closed and abandoned for years."

In parallel to their cooperative activity, this group also decided to file a case against the unconstitutional cooperatives' law. They chose to confront and attempt to fundamentally change the whole structure of cooperatives' law. This resistance strategy was different from the first case, where they depended on the member's collaboration and protest action (such as threatening to protest), or from the second case of taking a nonconfrontational attitude toward government employees and the legal process. This difference was influenced by the ideological orientation of the members in this case. MH and his peers are leftist activists, lawyers, and university professors who took part in different opposition movements.

This last case shows again how the imagined future could be sought of collectively in different forms. MH and his group were not personally suffering from the immediate problem of poverty in Fayoum, but they had a vision to fight poverty through engaging the disadvantaged into a bottom-up collective action while simultaneously fighting the legal structure from a top-down approach. This is a unique case to look at imaging collective futures through collective initiatives that serve and empower other collectives.

Conclusion: Social Change Between Hope and Despair

On society and individuals, Anthony Cohen (1994) portrays their relationship as dance partners: "Each tries to cover the moves of the other; sometimes they merge, at others they separate. Society creates the illusion that it ultimately controls the dance, for it provides the music and the stage. But, to coin a phrase, it takes two to tango. To focus on only one of the partners is to take a very skewed look indeed." Following this view, cooperatives could be seen as an exercise between collective agency and sociopolitical structural constraints, with a perspective of power within society as distributed rather than centralized.

The concept of cooperatives dates back as far as human beings have been organizing for mutual benefit. Tribes were organized as cooperative structures, allocating jobs and resources among each other, only trading with the external communities. Looking at cooperation as the norm for communities makes cooperatives a platform for effective mobilization and sustainable social change in societies. The three case studies show no recipe that could be applied fully to actualize and sustain the imagined future that was inspired by the revolution. Change process is seen in the continuous trials and errors and the different resistance strategies used to maneuver between the collective agency and the structural constraints at play. Cooperatives set the stage for a pathway to take the prefiguration of protests into collective action that challenges established structures and power dynamics.

Imagination was the key process that bridged the gap between the rebel against the present conditions and the ability to think collectively for actions oriented toward an alternative future. This highlights the collective aspect of imagination and, how even in individual trajectories, imagination does not happen in isolation (Zittoun & Gillespie, Chap. 2, this volume). Imagination opens up venues for action when individuals realize that the past is not deterministic on the present, and its force could be counteracted. Imagination opens our eyes to whatever we choose to act on today through accumulating only the experiences from yesterday that were given power to. This may require temporarily living beyond memories of failure and disappointments (Power, Chap. 11, this volume).

Imagination was not only seen in the cooperatives' aspired social change, but also in the capacity of its founders to empathize and form solidarity with other people in the community and find solutions that makes the life of the disadvantaged better even when founders did not personally suffer from the same struggles as those disadvantaged. This empathy motivated a collective action toward a shared future of social justice.

This speaks of the essence of social development initiatives, which is to imagine beyond one's needs, to have the empathy to understand what struggles the wider community suffers from, and to create solutions that caters for the collective. There was a common social development goal between the three cases to deconstruct different hierarchical coercive power structures and reconstruct a socially just society. The three cases were an outcome of protests, which are normally seen in negative lights of vandalism and irrational crowd behavior, but the cases show the potentiality of sustainable collective action coming out of temporary collectives. In spite of the disappointment in the anticipated political changes of the revolution to bring about a democratic equal society, everyday politics resembled in such cooperatives could help us recognize—and give us hope—that individuals could act upon their desired change rather than wait for a savior or resort to violence (Bayat, 2013).

The cooperative initiatives in Egypt, especially in the postrevolution time, materialized what people really aspired for as a collective future as well as what they believed they were capable of amidst the uprising. It built political awareness for its initiators and their teams and experience of practical versus aspired change once it was brought to the ground. Their initiatives, in spite of their varying degrees of success, brought new dynamics to the here-and-now situation by eliminating the top-down power from the equation of production and consumption decisions and replacing it by distributed power in a vision of a future collective society. Data provided good examples to look at the dynamics between the capitalist structures of the society managed by a central power and collective agency in creating autonomy in circles outside of that control. Those trials in their successes as well as failures promise decentralized and multi-localized venues for everyday forms of resistance and change as opposed to mass revolution and violent seizure of state power.

With the challenges facing Egypt today, social change will require reconciliation within a very polarized society postrevolution. Imaging a shared collective future requires the willingness of individuals to exchange positions and perspectives with the aim of reaching some form of consensus (Glăveanu, Chap. 5, this volume). It also requires a relative "freedom" from the here and now and a space for freedom of thought and expression, which is tightly restricted under the current regime, posing security risks for any collective assembly or action.

References

Aboud, S. (2015). *Cooperatives as a tool for liberation and advancement*. Cairo: Al Mahrousa Publishing.

Agustín, Ó. G. (2015). *Sociology of discourse: From institutions to social change* (Vol. 61). Amsterdam: John Benjamins Publishing Company.

Attride-Stirling, J. (2001). Thematic networks: An analytic tool for qualitative research. *Qualitative Research, 1*(3), 385–405.

Bandura, A. (2006). Toward a psychology of human agency. *Perspectives on Psychological Science, 1*, 164–180. Sage Publications.

Barakat, M., & Maarek, E. (in press). *One hundred years of cooperatives in Egypt*. Cairo: SSIPD/Sefsafa House.

Bayat, A. (2013). *Life as politics. How ordinary people change the Middle East* (2nd ed.). Stanford: Stanford University Press.

Boggs, C. (1977). Marxism, prefigurative communism, and the problem of workers' control. *Radical America, 11*(6), 99–122.

Cohen, A. P. (1994). *Self consciousness: An alternative anthropology of identity* (1st ed.). London: Routledge.

Cornejo, C. (2017). From fantasy to imagination: A cultural history and moral for psychology. In B. Wagoner, I. Bresco, & S. H. Awad (Eds.), *The psychology of imagination: History, theory, and new research horizons*. Charlotte: Information Age Publishing.

Epstein, B. (1991). *Political protest and cultural revolution*. Berkeley: University of California Press.

Glăveanu, V. P. (2018, this volume). Perspectival collective futures: Creativity and imagination in society. In C. de Saint-Laurent, S. Obradović, & K. R. Carriere (Eds.), *Imagining collective futures: Perspectives from social, cultural, and political psychology* (pp. 83–105). London: Palgrave Macmillan.

Graeber, D. (2002). The new anarchists. *New Left Review, 13,* 61–73.
Leonard, S. (2014). Back to Utopia. *Dissent, 61*(1), 30–32.
Maeckelbergh, M. (2011). Doing is believing: Prefiguration as strategic practice in the alterglobalization movement. *Social Movement Studies, 10*(01), 1–20.
Power, S. (2018, this volume). Remembering and imagining in human development: Fairness and social movements in Ireland. In C. de Saint-Laurent, S. Obradović, & K. R. Carriere (Eds.), *Imagining collective futures: Perspectives from social, cultural, and political psychology* (pp. 221–235). London: Palgrave Macmillan.
Reicher, S. D., & Haslam, S. A. (2012). The role of social identity; cognitive alternatives and leadership in group mobilization and social transformation. In B. Wagoner, E. Jensen, & J. A. Oldmeadow (Eds.), *Culture and social change: Transforming society through the power of ideas.* Charlott: IAP.
Vygotsky, L. (1987). *The collected works of L.S. Vygotsky. Vol. 4: The history of the development of higher mental functions.* New York: Plenum Press.
Yates, L. (2015). Rethinking prefiguration: Alternatives, micropolitics and goals in social movements. *Social Movement Studies: Journal of Social, Cultural and Political Protest, 14*(1), 1–21.
Zittoun, T., & Gillespie, A. (2016). *Imagination. Developing culture and minds.* Coll. Cultural dynamics of social representation. London: Routledge, 2015.
Zittoun, T., & Gillespie, A. (2018, this volume). Imagining the collective future: A sociocultural perspective. In C. de Saint-Laurent, S. Obradović, & K. R. Carriere (Eds.), *Imagining collective futures: Perspectives from social, cultural, and political psychology* (pp. 15–37). London: Palgrave Macmillan.

11

Remembering and Imagining in Human Development: Fairness and Social Movements in Ireland

Séamus A. Power

The ways in which people remember the past have implications for how they act in the present (Bartlett, 1932; Halbwachs, 1992; Power, 2016, 2017; Wagoner, 2017; Wertsch, 2008). People use the past. They use the future too (Power, 2017; Vygotsky, 1931; Wagoner, Brescó, & Awad, 2017; Zittoun & Cerchia, 2013; Zittoun & Gillespie, 2015; Chap. 2, this volume). Remembering and imagining can be understood as dynamic sociocultural processes that are simultaneously individual and collective. In this chapter, I utilize the theory outlined by Zittoun and Gillespie (2015; Chap. 2, this volume) to conceptualize imagining as a dynamic sociocultural process that can occur on both individual and group levels. In particular, I draw on their "looping metaphor" to illustrate the ways in which imagining futures is a form of escape from the immediate present, often by reflecting on the past, to inform versions of possible futures. They state: "We propose that imagination is disengaging from the here-and-now of a proximal experience, which is submitted to causality and temporal linearity, to explore, or engage with alternative, distal

S. A. Power (✉)
University of Chicago, Chicago, IL, USA
e-mail: seamusapower@uchicago.edu

© The Author(s) 2018
C. de Saint-Laurent et al. (eds.), *Imagining Collective Futures*, Palgrave Studies in Creativity and Culture, https://doi.org/10.1007/978-3-319-76051-3_11

experiences, which are not submitted to linear or causal temporality. An imagination event thus begins with a decoupling of experience and usually concludes with a re-coupling. Thus, imagination is a loop" (Zittoun & Gillespie, 2015, p. 40).

I elaborate their approach in two ways. First, I conceptualize remembering and imagining as dual processes of human development that can be thought of as being linked like an infinity symbol. There is a continuous looping from the past to the future, and back again, always converging on the focal point in the center. This elaboration does not imply symmetry regarding the equal weight both the past and the future have on appraisals, perceptions, thoughts, and actions in the present. Rather, the metaphor is meant to illustrate the continuous temporal interconnections between remembering and imagining and the impact these dual processes have on the present, as well as how the past and future are understood and used. Second, I illustrate the ways moral appraisals in the present—specifically, how people judge what are and are not considered fair and unfair economic practices—are informed by remembering and imagining.

I draw on ethnographic observations and interview data to illustrate how remembering and imagining motivated civic engagement and discontent in the context of the economic recovery following the 2008 financial collapse in the Republic of Ireland. Specifically, I examine the role these dual processes had in galvanizing, justifying, and maintaining social movements when people imagined water services would be privatized. In the Irish case, perceptions of increasing unfairness of distribution of income and wealth are central to imagining a more problematic future Irish society. Protesters felt justified in demonstrating to mitigate this immoral projection. They want a fairer and more equal future.

Remembering, Imagining, and Perceptions of Fairness

Recalling the past occurs at the intersection of the mind and society, between people and the world they inhabit. People use the past. And because the past is reconstructed—intentionally or not—it involves an element of imagining. This is because individuals, and societies, remember a version of what occurred, not the actuality of it. In this way, collective remembering is a dynamic sociocultural process (Bartlett, 1932; Halbwachs, 1992; Power, 2016, 2017; Wagoner, 2017; Wertsch, 2008). This view of remembering is influential in conceptualizing how and why people recall, and for what reasons (Wagoner, 2013, 2017). In contrast, relatively little has been written about how and why people imagine both the past and future, and the impact of what is imagined on their psychological functioning in the present.

The future is not a tableau rasa; it is not a blank canvas (Pinker, 2003). There are always tensions between realities and possible futures. This is particularly relevant because people live in hierarchies (Sidanius & Pratto, 2001). Asymmetries and injustices about how power and economic resources are distributed can underlie people's conceptualizations for what the future should look like. Consequently, different social groups can have different conceptualizations of the future from their past and present social and economic orientations. In this context, perceptions of what is and is not fair play a key role. Fairness is a ubiquitous moral principle (Haidt, 2012, 2013; Jensen, 2015; Power, 2017; Starmans, Sheskin, & Bloom, 2017). Yet, different social groups, who live in hierarchical societies, differ on what is and is not considered fair. Even if the fundamental desire of people's imaginations is to make the world a better place, visions for a morally good life vary across time and cultures (Power, 2011b; Shweder, 1991, 2003). The problem is when these visions of the future clash.

However, imagining the future can be motivating and pragmatic for different social groups. Imagining protectionist policies, the curtailment of civil liberties, or privatization of natural resources, such as water, can motivate protests against perceived unjust or unfair executive orders, policies, or government and corporate intentions. Imagining societies where these policies and orders are not curtailed, where democratic means are not used to restrain a monopoly on power, can justify protests and the development of social movements.

Projections, in the form of views of the collective economic misfortune, are just one example of how thoughts of the future can inform reactions and attitudes in the present. Imagining possible dystopian futures for a person's version of the good, moral, meaningful life is another. Images of a perceived unfair future lead to civic discontent in the near present. In Bolivia, for example, the government's privatization of the country's water supply at the turn of the millennium was met with street protests and the overthrowing of the government. Bolivian citizens imagined their water supply being controlled, monetized by outside corporations, to the exploitation and detriment of ordinary citizens. This was deemed unfair. They rejected this future that was becoming ever more likely. Protesters can be seen as modulating the decisions—and their perceived future implications of these bills, laws, and orders—via civic engagement, like demonstrating.

In this way, individual imagining of collective futures, much like collective remembering of the past, is a contested phenomenon. James (1880/2001) stated: "There are imaginations, not 'the Imagination,' and they must be studied in detail" (p. 170). One way to examine imaginations is to consider the moral foundations underlying visions for the future and their consequences for how people act in the present.

This is because the leaving of the present—via the process of imagination—has transformative implications for the here and now. People use the past and the future to sculpt their subjective realties. This temporal account of activity—highlighting the role of remembering and imagining—has implications for how we understand human development. More specifically, it provides a framework for conceptualizing the dynamics of social movements. It provides a model to think about the moral motivations behind, justifications for, and projections of demonstrations, democratic engagement, and social change.

Deprivation—Protest Paradox: Anti-water Protests in the Republic of Ireland

Ireland was adversely affected by the 2008 global financial collapse. In prior work, I identified the *Deprivation—Protest Paradox*: when the economy collapsed, the Irish generally accepted harsh austerity without protesting. However, when Ireland had the fastest growing economy in Europe in 2014 and 2015, there had been frequent demonstrations, clashes with the police, the refusal to pay taxes, and other forms of civic unrest (Power, 2015, 2016, 2017, 2018, forthcoming-a, b; Power & Nussbaum, 2014, 2016). Data from interviews with public elites and unemployed Irish youth illustrated common cultural and moral patterns of thought, appraisal, and action—steeped in remembering Irish history—that were used to explain and justify the passive response to hardship and suffering caused by austerity. People remembered violent aspects of Irish revolutionary history. They purposely distanced any potential utility of protest or riots as legitimate acts to generate change as the economy collapsed. People used the past to create a peaceful present. The focus of this chapter, however, is the water protests, which began to arise in 2014 during a period of rapid economic growth.

On December 28, 2014, Michael D. Higgins, the current president of the Republic of Ireland, signed a controversial Water Services Bill into law. For the first time in their history, the Irish public would have to pay directly for the water they consume in the form of quarterly bills.

Ireland previously had water charges that were abolished by the Labour Party in December 1996; afterwards, Irish citizens paid for their water through general taxation. In 2010, as part of a €85bn EU-IMF bailout, the Irish government agreed to reintroduce water charges in three years. At that time, water charges were ubiquitous around the world. Until their reintroduction in 2014, Ireland was one of the few countries in the Organization for Economic Cooperation and Development not to directly charge for water consumption.

The Labour Party initially opposed directly charging Irish citizens for water services. Yet, after the 2011 general election, their stance shifted. They formed part of a coalition government, led by Fine Gael, and this coalition drafted a new bill to again directly charge the public for water services. They did not lower other tax rates that were previously increased to pay for water services. A semi-state company, Irish Water, was established to oversee the introduction of water services in 2013. It was part-owned by the Irish government, and by implication, the Irish people. It also had private shareholders. The founding of Irish Water coincided with a sharp economic recovery.

The Irish had endured austerity as the economy collapsed. They expected to reap the benefits of an economic recovery. However, only some people profited from the economic upturn. This was deemed very unfair. People felt deprived relative to other groups in Irish society. Instead of feeling the effects of an economic recovery, Irish people had to pay for the water they consumed. In the context of an economic recovery, people had less money. Therefore, the enactment of the water services law was met with strong opposition from sectors of the Irish public, most visibly in the form of demonstrations.

In this chapter, I illustrate how anti-austerity protesters in Ireland, following the 2008 global economic crisis, draw on the past to motivate and justify their actions in the present, and to articulate their visions for a more economically fair and equal nation. In this sense, the way people draw on the past has implications for how they orientate toward, and act to achieve, their collectively imagined futures. My analysis of interviews with anti-austerity protesters at a series of national protests in Dublin, Ireland, and interviews and urban ethnographic observations with a core group of anti-water-charge protesters in a small Irish city reveal imaginings of an immoral future where water is privatized. This privatization is seen as a further manifestation of unfair austerity and a further step toward a widening gap between the rich and the rest. Protesters use this dystopic projection to loop back from imagining this future and feel motivated and justified to protest in the present. Their aim is to create a more equal and fair future society.

Remembering and Imagining the Privatization of Water

I spoke with a young man in his early 20s as we walked together on one demonstration in January 2015. He told me he went to earlier protests in Ireland aimed at highlighting the importance of having a referendum on gay marriage. A referendum did take place, legalizing gay marriage in Ireland the previous year. That was his first engagement with demonstrations, although he said, "I have been political all my life." Like the majority of my respondents, he too identified a gap between a rosy narrative he was hearing in terms of economic recovery, and his lived reality (see

Power, 2017, forthcoming-a, b). He went to university during the economic recession—paid for by himself, he said—to study accountancy. Weathering austerity in the sanctuary of university, he believed he would reap the rewards of his hard work. On graduating, he found full-time and permanent work impossible to find. He told me he works on a controversial "job-bridge scheme." This program requires people to accept jobs that are offered to them for a slight pay increase on their core social welfare payments. The disjunction between expectations for an imagined future and lived subjectivities in the present creates frustration (Power, 2018 forthcoming-a, b). The Irish protested during an economic recovery when a new charge on water was introduced. It was the final straw. When I asked this respondent why he was protesting today, he told me:

> The aim of today's protest is to stop the privatization of essential services. This has been an agenda that has been followed throughout this country over the past twenty years an agenda that has roots in neoliberal economics, which is a doctrine that preaches that the state should not have assists, that the state should not provide services, everything should be left to the private market, which I feel is completely wrong because the private market cannot provide essential services to the poorest people in society. Because, why does a business exist? To produce, to make a profit, you cannot make a profit for providing services for people who do not have money. So that is the aim here. Water is an essential service, no human being can live without it, and it should not be in the hands of the private sector.

This response reveals how the dual processes of remembering and imagining inform moral judgments that legitimize and justify protest. This interviewee begins answering my question about the aims of the protest by leaving the here and now and by articulating a future scenario where the Irish government sells the semi-state Irish Water (the company set up to administer the water charges in Ireland) to a private corporation. My respondent imagines a continuation of a recent historical trend in Ireland: the privatization of state owned companies. For example, the Irish government sold the semi-state airline company, Aer Lingus, in the mid-2000s. He made a moral judgment when he said, "I feel (this) is completely wrong." Imagining the privatization of the "essential" water services in Ireland, by drawing on neoliberal policies of the past, he justifies the aims of the protest: stopping Irish Water now, before an essential service is out of the control of the State, and by implication, out of the control of Irish people.

Imagining the privatization of Irish Water is an omnipresent theme across my interviews with demonstrators. I spoke to a married couple, who told me they were both retired, meaning they were over the age of 65. During the course of our interview, the woman spoke more, although the man chimed in to agree and extend points his wife made. I spoke to them as a protest got underway: people began marching from Connelly train station in Dublin toward the city center. When I asked, "Why are you guys here today?" the woman told me:

> We are protesting about the water charges. They (the government) brought it in, it was set up as a company (Irish Water), with shares in it, but what is going to happen, in a few years down the road, they will be forced to sell it to repay the company and this thing happened in Bolivia a couple of years ago and the people could not afford (to pay), they wanted a loan from the IMF (International Monetary Fund), the IMF gave them a loan on the condition they privatize their water and the water got so expensive that the people couldn't afford water. There was a revolution in the country, the government had to leave the buildings by helicopter, and the company was thrown out of the country. People don't want to see this happening to this country.

The answer provided by this woman chimes with that of the previous respondent, and also elaborates on his future projections. This retiree also uses imagination and memory to justify her reasons for being on the protest. She initially spoke in the present tense: "We are protesting about the water charges." But in her next sentence, she draws on the past and projects in to the future to explain her opening statement. In the recent past, the government established the semi-state Irish Water company, yet suggests that in the future it will be privatized. There is an implicit moral judgment articulated by the respondent: the privatization of water is morally wrong. She imagines a revolutionary scenario occurring in Ireland similar to the one that happened in Bolivia. When water services were privatized in that country, the corporation overseeing water and sanitation services charged prices for water consumption that some citizens deemed unfair. When this natural resource is threated—a "fundamental human right," as many of my respondents referred to it—violent protest can occur. My interviewee implies a similar future awaits Irish people if water services are privatized. Therefore, it is imperative to stop this imagined privatization in the present. Memories of the Bolivian situation inform how this respondent imagines a future Ireland that leads to democratic action in the present. I heard a common chant at these national protests that confirms an anti-privatization sentiment: "From the rivers to the sea, Irish water will be free!"

Remembering the past informs imagined representations of the future and can impact thoughts and behaviors in the present. This line of logic extends beyond the concrete representations of what the future holds—such as the privatization of water services—to a more general articulation of an unfair and dystopian society.

Once the national demonstrations reached their end point, there were a series of speeches given by left-wing politicians, community activists, poets and musicians, and trade unionists. Each speech reflected some of the discourse from the interviews: people highlighted a variety of social injustices beyond water charges. In one speech, a community activist drew on a violent past to generate a picture of a more dystopian future and to raise the possibility of a utilitarian society. He stated:

> Irish water is a symptom, the IMF (International Monetary Fund) is the disease. And until everyone here has realized that, and joined the dots, and realizing that this isn't just about the water, it's about the prostitution of this island…it's about how they bought and sold us like cattle at a market, and we swallowed what they told us and tore ourselves apart. It is meant to be divisive; it's not about them and us. Instead we should unite again, to stand as men, women and children, whose time has come to say the system isn't working and there must be a better way. There must be a fairer future where our children won't be forced to leave, where they find a future where they believe this island will belong to us once more and not the corporations that have risen to the fore. But for all that we march, we need to keep this in perspective: that the privatization of water is an IMF directive. And

the IMF themselves, for those who cannot yet see, are trying to write the manuscript for modern history. So it's not as simple as demanding that water charges are abolished, to my understanding it is their objective to demolish the notion of a nation-state for all that it once stood for.

This activist created two competing visions for the future. First, he draws on the past privatization of Ireland to project an image where there is continued "prostitution" of Irish resources, including water. This makes an inequitable Ireland: a division between "them and us," between those that benefit from neoliberal privatization espoused by the IMF and those who do not. Increased corporate influence in Ireland, he warned, will erode the nation-state, and by implication, increase inequality. But he also imagines and articulates a future where all citizens "unite" to create a more moral and "better" system. In this more moral framework, which is difficult to precisely visualize, he imagines that "our children" will have a "fairer future." One concrete effect of this more moral nation-state is to mitigate waves of historical migration from Ireland during times of economic hardship (see Power, 2015, 2016, 2017).

In the localized Irish context, imagining the future is informed by the past. It galvanizes, legitimizes, and drives protests in the present. Interviews and ethnographic data reveal imaginations of the future are proximal and distal. The two interview extracts are proximal: the imaginings are specifically grounded in immediate fears of privatization of Irish water. The speech extract reveals a distal imagining: it is a general articulation of dystopian effects of neoliberal policies: the eroding of the nation-state, and country specific ways of living a moral life. A second distal narrative for a future society was articulated: a more utopic and fair society, a return to the moral norms, of a fair, and inclusive, nation-state.

Conclusion

Protesters articulate what ought to happen in order to make Irish society more equitable. It is the leap from what is happening, to what should be happening, that motivates and justifies protest in order to realize their imagined Ireland. In order to add legitimacy to their idealized future society, they locate their imaginations by detailing past examples where privatization of resources, both in Ireland and abroad, are remembered and are used to articulate what they perceive will happen in Ireland. The imaginings of current protesters assist in realizing the next step of these previous ambitions for a fairer Ireland where there is social and economic equality for all. In the Irish case, however, protesters recall the past to strive toward their imagined social worlds.

Leaving the here and now through the process of imagining, is a dynamic cultural psychological process (Zittoun & Gillespie, 2015; Chap. 2, this volume). As my discussion of the Irish case illustrates, the content of imagining is informed by localized sociocultural, historical, economic, and legal contexts. The analysis dovetails with previous research that suggests imagining and remembering are dynamic sociocultural processes (Bartlett, 1932; Halbwachs, 1992; Power, 2016, 2017; Vygotsky, 1931; Wagoner, 2017; Wagoner et al., 2017; Wertsch, 2008; Zittoun & Cerchia, 2013; Zittoun & Gillespie, 2015; Chap. 2, this volume).

Imagining and remembering are two interrelated and fundamental psychological processes of human development that inform how people think, feel, and act in the present. Specifically, these processes impact people's motivations and justifications for making moral appraisals and participating in social movements. In the localized Irish context, people remember past privatizations of essential resources, and imagine the same fate for water services in Ireland. They articulate these imaginations and loop back around from these projections to act in the present. They protest to mitigate imagined efforts to privatize water. The content of their imaginations is informed by history. People draw on related historical examples of perceived unfair neoliberal agendas, such as the privatization of water in Bolivia, and highlight their detrimental effects, to inform their imagination of a likely scenario playing out in the Irish context.

Imagining is not necessarily a moral enterprise. But it can be. In the Irish case study, people's conceptualizations of the future are informed by moral judgments. They articulate imagined immoral societies, with greater economic inequality, social injustice, and unfairness. They use the future. Once they create this image, they loop back to the present to justify their social movement. The Irish respondents I spoke to are demonstrating in order to effect social, political, and economic change. Their aim is to create a fairer, decent, and inclusive society. Imagination is one process used to articulate moral societies and to actualize them. These visions of the future are grounded in imagined interpretations of past blueprints for Irish society. Although people live in hierarchies with uneven distributions of power and resources (Sidanius & Pratto, 2001), imagining more economically equal societies is a way people try to mitigate perceived unfair social systems. There is not one best version of society to strive toward (James, 1880; Zittoun & Gillespie, 2015; Chap. 2, this volume). There is no consensus on one good, true, beautiful, meaningful, and efficient way to live (Power, 2011a; Shweder, 1991, 2003). Perceptions of what is, and is not, considered fair also vary between groups (Haidt, 2012, 2013; Power, 2017). Therefore, imagining possible futures is a contested process. Perceptions of increasing unfairness, unequal power dynamics, and greater economic inequality lead to imagining a dystopian future.

This helps explain why my respondents imagined more unequal and dystopian versions of Ireland if water, and other essential services, continued to be privatized. It also explains why they imagined alternatives: ways to stop morally repugnant visions becoming a reality. Imagining increased social injustices caused by neoliberal free-market privatization, and acting in the present to stop free-market forces by demonstrating, is an articulation of a moral agenda. It is morality in action: an attempt to create a future society that's fairer for generations to come. "I'm here today for my grandchildren. I don't want them to be left with the burden," one respondent told me.

The looping metaphor outlined by Zittoun and Gillespie (2015) can be elaborated. Based on the evidence presented here, remembering and imagining can be conceptualized as being like an infinity symbol. There is a continuous looping from the past to the future, and back again, always converging on the focal point of the present. This is meant to illustrate the continuous temporal interconnections between remembering and imagining and the impact these dual processes have on how people think, feel, and act in the present.

Unacknowledged by the respondents quoted here is an alternative moral agenda for the future. Proponents of free-market democracy might argue unequal economic development is still progress. The rising tide lifts all boats. Industrial capitalism has generated economic value that has lifted hundreds of millions of people out of poverty, increased life expectancy, and increased educational opportunities in a short period of historical time. Privatization can lead to better products and services for consumers and stimulate further economic growth. But respondents were ubiquitous in their condemnation of privatization of water. There was no space to engage with alternative narratives of capitalism or alternative versions of moral societies (see Power, 2017).

There are as many versions of the future available as there are people to imagine them. Maybe even more. But the reality of achieving these societies is curtailed by what can be imagined. This is informed by the weight of the past: by social, cultural, economic, and historical norms, that impact what should be, can be, and is, achieved. The role of morality—particularly, perceptions of fairness—cannot be underestimated in shaping what is imagined. Protesters in social movements are moral actors. Through the process of imagination, they envisage near and distant futures that are often immoral because they are deemed unfair. Protesters use the future. They articulate immoral futures to galvanize, motivate, and justify actions in the present—always steeped in historical and remembered contexts—to create more moral and utopic societies.

Acknowledgments This manuscript benefitted greatly from feedback from Alex Gillespie, John Lucy, Kelsey Robbins, Richard Shweder, and Brady Wagoner. I thank the constructive comments provided by Constance de Saint Laurent and Kevin Carriere on an earlier version of this manuscript. I acknowledge the support of the Lemelson/Society for Psychological Anthropology Pre-Dissertation Award, made possible by a generous donation from The Robert Lemelson Foundation.

References

Bartlett, F. (1932). *Remembering: A study in experimental and social psychology.* New York: Cambridge University Press.

Haidt, J. (2012). *The righteous mind: Why good people are divided by politics and religion.* New York: Vintage.

Haidt, J. (2013). Of freedom and fairness. *Democracy, 28*, 38.
Halbwachs, M. (1992). *On collective memory* (L. A. Coser, Trans. & Ed.). Chicago: University of Chicago Press (Original work published 1925).
James, W. (1880/2001). *Psychology: The briefer course*. New York: Dover Publications, Inc.
Jensen, L. A. (2015). *Moral development in a global world*. Cambridge, UK: Cambridge University Press.
Pinker, S. (2003). *The blank slate: The modern denial of human nature*. New York: Penguin.
Power, S. A. (forthcoming-a). Actual democracy and a United Europe of States: A case study of Austerity and protest in the Republic of Ireland. In B. Wagoner & I. Brescó (Eds.), *The road to actualized democracy: A psychological perspective*. Charlotte, NC: Information Age Publishing.
Power, S. A. (forthcoming-b). The deprivation—Protest paradox: How the perception of unfair economic inequality leads to civic unrest [Lead article with commentaries and response]. *Current Anthropology*.
Power, S. A. (2011a). On social psychology and conflict. *Psychology & Society, 4*, 1–6.
Power, S. A. (2011b). Towards a dialogical model of conflict resolution. *Psychology and Society, 4*(1), 53–66.
Power, S. A. (2015). To understand the eurozone crisis, consider culture. *Chicago Booth Review*, 63–65.
Power, S. A. (2016). A violent past but a peaceful present: The cultural psychology of an Irish recession. *Peace and Conflict: Journal of Peace Psychology, 22*(1), 60–66.
Power, S. A. (2017). *From the elites to the streets: The psychology of democracy and economic inequality*. Chicago: University of Chicago.
Power, S. A. (2018). Economic inequality and the rise of civic discontent: Remembering and deprivation in the Republic of Ireland. In B. Wagoner, F. Moghaddam, & J. Valsiner (Eds.), *The psychology of radical social change: From rage to revolution* (pp. 29–53). Cambridge: Cambridge University Press.
Power, S. A., & Nussbaum, D. (2014, July 24). The Fightin' Irish? Not when it comes to recession and austerity. *The Guardian*. Retrieved from http://www.theguardian.com/science/head-quarters/2014/jul/24/the-fightin-irish-not-when-it-comes-to-recession-and-austerity
Power, S. A., & Nussbaum, D. (2016, March 15). 'You reap what you sow': The psychology of Irish austerity protests. *The Guardian*. Retrieved from https://www.theguardian.com/science/head-quarters/2016/mar/15/economics-as-a-morality-play-austerity-protest-in-ireland

Shweder, R. A. (1991). *Thinking through cultures: Expeditions in cultural psychology*. Cambridge, MA: Harvard University Press.

Shweder, R. A. (2003). *Why do men barbecue? Recipes for cultural psychology*. Cambridge, MA: Harvard University Press.

Sidanius, J., & Pratto, F. (2001). *Social dominance: An intergroup theory of social hierarchy and oppression*. Cambridge, UK: Cambridge University Press.

Starmans, C., Sheskin, M., & Bloom, P. (2017). Why people prefer unequal societies. *Nature Human Behaviour, 1*, 0082.

Vygotsky, L. S. (1931). Imagination and creativity in the adolescent. In M. J. Hall (Trans.) and R. W Rieber & J. Wollock (Eds.), *The collected works of LS Vygotsky* (Vol. 5, pp. 151–166). New York: Plenum Press.

Wagoner, B. (2013). Bartlett's concept of schema in reconstruction. *Theory & Psychology, 23*(5), 553–575.

Wagoner, B. (2017). *The constructive mind: Bartlett's psychology in reconstruction*. Cambridge: Cambridge University Press.

Wagoner, B., Brescó, I., & Awad, S. H. (Eds.). (2017). *The psychology of imagination: History, Theory and New Research Horizons*. Charlotte, NC: IAP.

Wertsch, J. (2008). The narrative organization of collective memory. *Ethos, 36*, 120–135.

Zittoun, T., & Cerchia, F. (2013). Imagination as expansion of experience. *Integrative Psychological and Behavioral Science, 47*(3), 305–324.

Zittoun, T., & Gillespie, A. (2015). *Imagination in human and cultural development*. London: Routledge.

Zittoun, T., & Gillespie, A. (2018, this volume). Imagining the collective future: A sociocultural perspective. In C. de Saint Laurent, S. Obradović, & K. R. Carriere (Eds.), *Imagining collective futures: Perspectives from social, cultural, and political psychology* (pp. 15–37). London: Palgrave Macmillan.

12

Creating Integration: A Case Study from Serbia and the EU

Sandra Obradović

With recent developments in Europe, issues of integration, division and sociopolitical cohesion have come to the fore in both public and private discourses. Events such as the Crimean Crisis and Brexit have opened up important questions of belonging, and how nations imagine their future in increasingly uncertain sociopolitical worlds. This chapter takes a close look at one such country, Serbia, and explores how its politics of integration into the European Union (EU) have raised questions regarding the extent to which the country can remain true to its national "essence" while modernizing and integrating into a globally interconnected community. It will be argued that imagining the future of the nation becomes increasingly hard in times of political change, particularly if that change is seen as causing a rupture from, rather than continuity with, the past.

The chapter is structured into three parts. First, I briefly consider the sociopolitical context of Serbia and its relationship with the EU, delving into some of the hurdles that have marked the integration, and possible

---

S. Obradović (✉)
London School of Economics and Political Science, London, UK
e-mail: S.Obradovic@lse.ac.uk

© The Author(s) 2018
C. de Saint-Laurent et al. (eds.), *Imagining Collective Futures*, Palgrave Studies in Creativity and Culture, https://doi.org/10.1007/978-3-319-76051-3_12

future, of Serbia in the European Union. Second, I place these discussions in the context of the theoretical literature on identity, perceived collective continuity and compatibility, emphasizing what this literature has to offer for unpacking the case of Serbia. Lastly, I draw on empirical data from Serbia to illustrate some of the arguments made in the previous sections. I conclude by considering how the interrelated processes of maintaining continuity and promoting change place limitations on the process of imagining the collective future of a nation.

Serbia and the EU: From In-Between to Being a Part

Serbian history, marked by turmoil, conflict, instability, unification and disintegration, is a complex one that becomes increasingly hard to unite under one narrative (for a more comprehensive overview, see Azulovic, 1999; Ćirković, 2004; Cohen, 1996; Judah, 2009; Pavlowitch, 2002). However, there is an important element that has emerged from this history, which authors have discussed as a sort of identity and cultural "inbetweenness" (Russell-Omaljev, 2016; Živković, 2011). This "inbetweeness" refers to Serbia as a nation built on contrasts and differences, bridging both East and West, tradition and modernity, and experiencing a simultaneous belonging and isolation from the larger European community (Ristic, 2007; Todorova, 1997). This inbetweenness has also permeated Serbia's political choices, both domestic and foreign, as well as elite and public discourses on the nation and its identity.

Therefore, when Serbia began its official talks concerning its membership into the EU in January 2014, it was considered a crucial moment for Serbia, as a European path (or perhaps Western path) had been chosen, supposedly marking a historical turning point for the country. According to the prime minister of Serbia at the time, January 21, 2014, was, by all accounts, memorable:

> *[A] historic day that cannot be ignored [...] this is in the historical sense, the most important event for Serbia after World War II. In strategic terms, this day*

determines the future path of Serbia and the values which it strives for and for which it stands. (Ivica Dačić quoted in Blic Online)

The beginning of talks between Serbia and the EU was also seen as a symbolic victory in Serbia, a recognition of the hard work and progress of the country in fulfilling the requirements of membership conditionality. However, this victory is the result of a prolonged process spanning over a decade, pointing to the many political challenges that Serbia faced (and continues to face) in joining the EU.

While I cannot consider all of the issues that have arisen over the past decade, a couple become crucial in supporting the argument that politics become intertwined with the psychological continuity of a nation. These relate to (1) the pressures on Serbia to face its recent past and (2) the role of Kosovo in Serbian psychology and politics. Each will be briefly discussed below.

First, Serbia's role in the fall of Yugoslavia (1990–1999), and the antagonistic relations with neighboring countries that followed, led the EU to place pressure on addressing the conflicts of the past and normalize relations with countries such as Croatia and Bosnia and Herzegovina. By enforcing these changes, the EU communicated to Serbia the importance of integrating into not only a political community but also a community that shared a similar historical perspective. Serbia was expected to cooperate with the International Crime Tribunal of Yugoslavia (ICTY), and when it failed to do so, negotiations for the country's integration into the EU were frozen for over a year. This, in turn, indicated the normative power of the EU in shaping Serbian politics in dealing with its past (McMahon & Forsythe, 2008). Consequently, in doing so, Serbia was forced to come to terms with a troubling past, a challenge that, in many nations, is met with ambivalence (for another example, see Jovchelovitch & Hawlina, Chap. 8, in this volume).

Second, the issue of Kosovo is perhaps the biggest hurdle toward better Serbia–EU relations, highlighting the importance of issues of national identity, history and continuity in contexts of political change (Economides & Ker-Lindsay, 2015). Kosovo, a region in southern Serbia that proclaimed independence in 2008, holds a prominent identity position among Serbs as the territory on which the Battle of Kosovo took place in 1389, a battle which would later become the foundational myth of the modern Serbian nation (Bieber, 2002). The battle can also be seen as shaping the historical charter of the nation. A historical charter, Liu and Hilton (2005) explain, binds the past, present and future of a nation by defining the historical mission of a group and providing it with its "essence," a uniqueness that sets it apart from other nations. The Kosovo battle has become the core theme from which a Serbian identity has been built, emphasizing a people who are simultaneously resilient and victimized (Subotic, 2011; Obradović, 2017). I return to the meaning of this in the next section.

Although the EU is said to hold no position toward the independence issue, a majority of its members have recognized Kosovo, and in Serbia, it is believed that giving up Kosovo will be the final requirement for EU membership, an act that is considered too big a sacrifice, both by the Serbian public and by its politicians (Begovic, 2014). The EU has placed demands on Serbia to normalize relations with Kosovo, another EU demand which has been considered a threat to Serbia's sovereignty (Obradovic-Wochnik & Wochnik, 2012). From the perspective of the EU, the issue of Kosovo has become a second chance to rectify past failures with the integration of Cyprus as "many European leaders had signaled their determination not to import any more border disputes into the future" (Ker-Lindsay, 2009, p. 6).

Serbia's relations with the larger European community through organizations such as the ICTY and the EU (but also NATO, the UN and the Interactional Court of Justice, ICJ) have thus tended to position Serbian politics as conflicting, or diverging, from those of the EU. This, in turn, has influenced the image of Serbia in the eyes of both EU politicians and the public. In a 1996 Eurobarometer survey, EU citizens were asked to rank which countries they felt should be part of the EU by 2000. In the ranking, Serbia came in third to last (of 28 countries). The results from this survey, though conducted more than 20 years ago, speak for the "many ethnic, religious and historical factors at work in molding the image which people have of the future development of the Community, and, presumably, as a corollary of its identity" (Breakwell, 1996, p. 23). They further speak to the importance of taking into consideration not only economic and political benefits of EU integration, but also how feelings of compatibility and continuity come into play. Particularly so as these seeming incompatibilities can lead to feelings of nonrecognition of the national identity and culture in the larger, supranational community. As political changes are made to fulfil the requirements of integration in Serbia, questions arise as to how these changes will influence the culture and psychology of the people, and thus how society at large might become transformed into something new, and different.

I now turn to consider how these seemingly political issues can be understood better by drawing on insights from social and political psychology. Vast theoretical literatures have been developed addressing issues of identification, belonging, globalization and intergroup relations. Thinking more specifically about the case of Serbia, I focus on theoretical knowledge that can help us understand how these seemingly incompatible political goals shape the ways in which everyday citizens given meaning to, and envision their future in, the European Union.

Belonging "There" While Remaining "Us": Identity and Continuity

Serbia's EU integration is a case that requires us to understand not only the political processes at play, but also the psychological ones, as the changes taking place become linked to the promotion of a particular vision for the future. Specifically, by exploring how issues of perceived collective continuity and sociocultural compatibility become intertwined with seemingly political phenomena, we can unpack the importance of identity in providing a source of stability and essentialism for collectives, particularly in times of sociopolitical change. I do so by first unpacking what is meant by identity in this context.

In 1960, historian Rupert Emerson published *From Empire to Nation*. In the book, Emerson argues, "the simplest statement that can be made about a nation is that it is a body of people who feel that they are a nation" (1960, p. 102). In his definition of the nation, Emerson emphasizes a key component in the creation of a nation-state. That is, the nation as a group becomes real when the people who are part of the nation *feel* part of it as well. In other words, when they identify with the nation. When discussing the concept of "identity," I therefore draw on Emerson's definition and its subsequent utilization by Henri Tajfel in the development of the social identity theory. Tajfel (1981) considered a social identity (of which a national identity is an example) the sense of self which individuals derived from the knowledge that they are a member of a particular social group, from both an emotional and cognitive perspective.

From this definition, it is not hard to see that imagination plays a crucial role in the construction of social identities. A sense of identity is, to a great extent, created by the ability to both experience it and imagine it over time. Namely, a social identity is simultaneously social and individual; it is a part of who "I" am, but it is also bigger than that as it encompasses people from the past, and is assumed to extend beyond my lifetime into the future. The process of imagination is thus bidirectional; we both imagine by remembering (and reconstructing) the past, but also through envisioning the future of our group. The temporal component also gives us further evidence that identities are inherently social. Namely, the symbols that we use and the cultural practices we share as part of our identities are not always rooted in direct experience but are culturally transmitted to us over time and generations. This is particularly true for national identities.

Theoretically, this temporal component has been explored through the concept of perceived collective continuity (PCC; Sani et al., 2007; for a discussion on the temporal dimension of imagination, see also Zittoun & Gillespie, Chap. 2, this volume). PCC refers to how, as members of social groups "we see ourselves as parts of an endless chain, a body that transcends us not only in space, but also, and perhaps more importantly, in time." (Sani et al., 2007, p. 1118). There are two main components to PCC perceived cultural continuity and perceived historical continuity. The first dimension refers to the belief that core cultural values (norms, beliefs, traditions and mentalities) are transmitted over generations, while the second dimension refers to the ways in which events and periods in a group's history are seen as casually linked. In simpler terms, while the former provides an "essentialist" dimension to group identity, the later constructs a coherent historical narrative of the group's past (and its role in the present). Combined, these dimensions allow for identities to be experienced as fixed, essential and continuous. Building on these two dimensions, Smeekes and Verkuyten (2014) illustrate that the essentialist dimension of group continuity (more so than the narrativist) tends to lead to in-group identification. They explain this finding by arguing that preference is given to "essentalism" as it more strongly satisfies the individual's need for self-continuity, thus drawing a link between the individual's psychological needs and how these are derived from social group belonging. The "essentialization" of identities becomes particularly evident in contexts of intergroup conflict, where narratives of identity become intertwined with both constructions of the in-group as stable over time, but also as the out-group as a stable, and inherently different, enemy (see Nicholson & Howarth, Chap. 9, this volume).

Because of this sense of stability gained from group identification, in contexts of change, perceived threats to identity continuity frequently lead to resistance to (or lack of support for) the proposed change (Jetten & Hutchison, 2011; Sindic & Reicher, 2009). For example, research on group mergers has illustrated how manipulating the perception of (dis)continuity can increase (or decrease) resistance to change. When change is proposed within an existing group as well, we find similar trends in regard to the importance of continuity. Namely, when tensions in relation to change come to an extreme, they can lead to group schisms. As Sani (2008) explains, "What triggers a schism is not a disagreement on change in the group doctrinal corpus per se, but a disagreement about the supposed implications of the change for the group identity." (p. 720). Sani's (2008) research on group schisms in the Italian Communist Party during the 1990s and the Church of England illustrates that a change that is seen (by some) as threatening a group's core values and norms has consequences for the extent to which these individuals will continue to identify with the group and perceive it as a coherent and united collective.

It could be argued, then, that in order for groups to perceive change as continuous with a group's past, a sense of compatibility must be supposed between the in-group identity and the imagined future of the group (as brought about by the intended change). Compatibility can come from a shared history or similarities in culture (such as traditions, language and norms) or a shared goal for the future. It is important to note that when discussing concepts such as in-group continuity and compatibility, while these might be perceived as fixed, they are, in fact, continuously being renegotiated and managed (for an example, see Tileagă, Chap. 8, this volume). In other words, scholars exploring the links between past, present and future in general, and the contributors within this volume in particular, do not take a deterministic approach toward human behavior, whether individual or social. Rather, there is a clear awareness of the ways in which essentialist characteristics of a group identity depend on the continued reproduction, and reconstruction, of these elements (Reicher & Hopkins, 2001). Without these efforts, identities would not remain relevant over time, and change is a natural part of any life cycle, be it that of one person or a collective. For example, Hopkins (2011) illustrates how two seemingly incompatible identities—Muslim and British—were renegotiated by British Muslims to create a new, unique way of being which emphasized the dual identities as complementary, rather than clashing.

Thus, in times of sociopolitical change, those who promote change face the challenge of framing their agenda as one that actually promotes, rather than hinders, perceived collective continuity. In this sense, managing which elements of an identity become seen as "essential," and also how they are seen as essential, becomes a powerful political tool in shaping the ways in which the social group comes to imagine its future.

In other words, when exploring sociopolitical change, we must consider how this change is perceived, and the implications this has for how the future is imagined, and whether it is supported or resisted. I turn to some empirical findings from research conducted in Serbia to illustrate these points.

Creating Integration: The Importance of Compatibility and Continuity

In three recent studies, qualitative data was collected to explore how politicians and citizens in Serbia made sense of the political changes taking place in the past two decades, and how these related to a sense of perceived collective continuity of the nation. These studies explored discourses on continuity and change in both top-down and bottom-up contexts, focusing in particular on how identity becomes politicized to legitimize and justify certain collective actions for the future.[1] Due to limitations of space, I will focus mainly on the data on public discourses, with links drawn to the political discourses where appropriate.

In the studies exploring public attitudes, it was found that there was an inherent tension embedded in conceptualizing a Serbian future in the EU (Obradović, 2017). Namely, while individuals recognized the structural and organizational benefits of the EU, themes of cultural and psychological difference emerged to outweigh these benefits. As participants discussed their future in the EU, they also elaborated on their fears and anxieties regarding their abilities to practically exercise their "Serbianness." These discussions ranged from macro-constraints in relation to national sovereignty, to more micro-level concerns regarding banal, everyday practices. Consider the following two examples taken from a recent qualitative study on lay understanding of EU integration in Serbia:

Excerpt 1
Ana: The standards, we want EU standards, but to say to a farmer from Sumadija [region known for the production of plum brandy, Serbia's national drink] "you can't make your own brandy," he'll say "Who, me? What do I need the EU for?"

Excerpt 2
Ivan: Our people, an average citizen with a High School education says "we'll get this and that [benefits], that's great!" but when you tell him "you can't park your car wherever you want, man," then it's "Oh, what, the EU? What's the point?"

Imagining Serbia in the EU thus entailed imagining Serbia as less Serbian. This fear that their national identity would be undermined, or even denied, within the larger common in-group, speaks to the impor-

---

[1] For details of the specific studies, see (Obradović & Howarth, 2018; Obradović, 2017).

tance of compatibility with other in-group members, but also the perceived continuity of the nation's history and culture into the future. Research by Sindic and Reicher (2009) in the context of Scottish attitudes toward the United Kingdom illustrate similar findings, arguing that when a national identity is seen to be undermined within a supranational context, there will be more resistance toward being part of it (and more mobilization toward leaving). This is also clear in the quotes above as they illustrate how continuity becomes linked to resistance to change ("What do I need the EU for" / "What's the point?").

These concerns have not been lost on either Serbian elites or EU officials, as various initiatives have been put into action to emphasize both the civic and cultural commonalities Serbia shares with the EU (Cox, 2012; David, 2014; Vos, 2012). For example, political discourses around political change and EU integration have attempted to alleviate these fears by emphasizing EU integration as a civic project to promote democratization, modernization and progress, thereby constructing it as a political change which affects only the civic (i.e., financial, structural and political) realm of the nation, safeguarding any threats to cultural continuity (Obradović & Howarth, 2018). Furthermore, by analyzing changes to the Serbian national calendar, David (2012) argues that impression management techniques have been utilized to construct ambivalent readings of the calendar intended to satisfy both international and domestic needs. Mainly, he argues that the strategies used function to construct commonalities with European history and culture at large, while simultaneously remaining ambiguous with regard to the nation's role in the Yugoslav wars, thereby maintaining preexisting narratives of past victimhood within the domestic context.

Despite these efforts, bigger issues of the past have led to concerns for the future. This is perhaps most evident in discourses around the future of Kosovo. The Kosovo battle, as discussed earlier, conceptualizes the core of "Serbianness" and thus functions to provide the national identity with a "timeless essence." However, the construction of Kosovo as an essential part of national identity has occurred by not only defending its significance in the presence, but also reimagining the past to construct it as a central and continuous part of Serbian history. Consider the following quotes:

Excerpt 3
Jovan: I think the question [of the political status of Kosovo] becomes important in Serbia because it represents the territory on which the first Serbian state was constructed in the 7th century. It is the cradle of today's national identity, and from there, that was, how do I put this... a key territory which was Serbian, from where, no matter how much Serbia expended or narrowed, it originated.

Maja: You know what, theoretically that sentence, "Kosovo is not Serbia" no one will say that, but everything else beyond that has been done. So, what does that mean to you when you publicly don't say it but you have a liaison officer to communicate with them, you have borders, I mean, I think we've already recognized Kosovo, only that we're not saying it....

Ema: I don't think there was every a big problem saying like "Kosovo is lost". But it's what comes after that. –

Maja: It's not lost; it's its own state, that's different.

Ema: But no, no, you can always add after that "currently". So, there's always that, this moment of the current constellation in the world, Europe, and so on, so that simply that's the reality now, but I don't think anyone thinks that it's something final.

Within these discourses, it becomes telling that the symbolic importance of Kosovo has remained constant over time, similar to the political discourses, and that even in the present context where the reality of Kosovo is one of independence and separation from Serbia, there is still a language of possibility utilized to construct this as an indefinite reality. Thus, imagining the future in a way becomes a coping mechanism for dealing with a perceived historical rupture in the present and uncertainties of how these will continue to develop. While participants were vocal about the reality of Kosovo in the present, politicians have taken a more hardlined approach within their discourses on Serbian future, arguing that "Serbia is not going to recognize Kosovo's independence under any circumstances, and that I all that I can say today, tomorrow and the day after that. That position is not changeable" (Tadic, 2012, as quoted in Obradović & Howarth, 2018). However, as some politicians have critically argued, these promises mean little when the actions of the state speak a different language. Consider the following quote from Vojislav Kostunica, the (then) prime minister of Serbia, in 2008:

Excerpt 4

Our first objective must be to defend Serbia, which means to defend Kosovo. And when we would agree to only defend Kosovo literally, while using alternative routes by signing various agreements to gradually allow for the implementation of Kosovo's independence, then without a doubt, that same foreign actor would assert that we are good and that we are committed to European integration. The DSS will never accept that pro-European means paying with 15% of Serbian territory. Nor will we ever accept that we are not for Europe simply because we are for all of Serbia in Europe.

What this quote illustrates is the supposed "trade-off" between Kosovo and EU membership and the normative pressures perceived to be placed on Serbia by the EU in order to recognize Kosovo's independence. We also see the use of a defensive language, positioning Serbia as under threat, and the need to unite and protect the nation. The future envisioned here is one where "all of Serbia" is "in Europe" and the EU, a future which is seen as only discursively entertained by other politicians in order to gain (international) political points. It is further important to note that it was during this year (2008) that a schism actually occurred in the Democratic coalition (of which Kostunica was a part and subsequently left), due to the inability to agree on how to proceed with the issue of Kosovo and EU integration. Thus, the politics around Kosovo have, in both political and public discourses, become a core "essentialized" part of Serbian identity in relation to which continuity must be constructed, and change compatible.

Another way in which temporal links were utilized was by using the past to imagine the future, arguing that the history of the country clearly illustrated that it was a country doomed to struggle in vain for future fortunes. Consider, for example, the following exchange when participants in Belgrade were asked what they expected to have changed by the year 2020 (focus group conducted in 2015):

Excerpt 5

Darko: Nothing will have changed.
Petar: Maybe it will, but only for the worse.
Mirko: I think that by then some third world war will have started, and again Serbia will be in trouble because it will be on the fence about who to

join. *In every world war we have been like a trigger, but we haven't [actually been], I don't know, Serbia is always [in the middle].... We don't allow them to pass through Belgrade so they bomb us. And now Serbia is in between Russia and the EU. I really think that before then, it doesn't have to be a world war, but I do think that there needs to be some bigger turmoil for it to happen.*

By referencing Serbia's role in World Wars I and II, the participants construct a negative continuity between Serbia's past and its potential future ("I think that by then some third World War will have started, and again Serbia will be in trouble"), thus reaffirming the belief that Serbia is doomed to be a country of conflict and victimhood. In doing so, these participants come full circle in expecting their past and present struggles to continue into the future, in a sense ironically reassuring themselves that their Serbianness (and the "inbetweeness" of it) will remain intact. In contrast, the EU has continuously challenged this notion of victimhood so engrained in the national sentiment, as it has placed demands on Serbia to face, and reconcile, its responsibility in the Yugoslav wars (Dragovic-Soso, 2012, p. 173). In complying with these, public outcry has emerged as these processes directly risk to sever the ties between Serbia's version of the past and its importance in the present, and its links with the future. This was particularly evident in discussions on values, morals and traditions, where many participants felt that supposed progress in the EU was equated with a lack of moral integrity and collective consciousness. Consider the following quote:

Excerpt 6
Aleksandra: Although in the last year I have to admit that everyone is increasingly influenced by the West.
Filip: Earlier it used to be that marriage was a sanctity, it was holy. Whatever the husband did, whatever the woman did, they never divorced, no way. But in the past few years that's been happening more and more.
Aleksandra: Definitely
Igor: But that's coming from the West.
Filip: Western influences
Igor: And that whole Western system.
Aleksandra: That you don't respect your parents for example...

Lea: Nothing good has come from the West.
Igor: Marriage, as an institution, is no longer respected.
Filip: That's right. It's not like before, okay, we are still humanitarian today, but the humanitarianism of before, the socializing, there's none of that. I see that in us, there's no way. Earlier, and it wasn't linked to having money nor a specific period of years, but simply, the system has changed.

What this quote illustrates is the fear that the present—and inadvertently, the future—is one of change for the worse. The quote is further telling of the belief that joining the EU means accepting, and internalizing, a Western perspective on life, one which is seen as less humanitarian and social than a Serbian way of life. It is thus interesting to see how political change becomes intertwined with concerns not only of maintaining a sense of continuity with the past, but also how a group will be able to, both materially and symbolically, exercise their way of life in the future.

Imagining the future in a context of sociopolitical change and uncertainty thus becomes increasingly pessimistic, as participants worry about issues ranging from the ability to practically realize their identities on an everyday level, to the extent to which the national borders will become reconfigured, the domestic politics stifled by EU control, and the larger, collective values replaced by more individualistic worldviews.

Conclusion

In considering how individuals, and elites, imagine the collective future of the nation, we see the importance of both taking into consideration current processes of change, but also how these processes become embedded in larger discourses on national identity, history and continuity. In particular, research on how individuals and groups imagine their collective futures can tell us a lot about how they experience their identities in the present and in relation to others. This becomes crucial when considering how to promote political change, how to successfully mobilize groups around an imagined future, and finally, how to fulfill the individual need for self-continuity through the construction of perceived collective continuity.

Drawing on Serbia as a case study, and thinking about the larger literature, both empirical and theoretical, on supranational integration, national identity and political change, this chapter has highlighted the need for considering also the role of compatibility and continuity, particularly from the subjective viewpoint of the individuals experiencing tangible change as their nation goes through the steps of conditionality.

The process of imagining the collective future of Serbia, as it continues to strive toward EU integration, is rather bleak. In one study mentioned (Obradović, 2017), it was clear that uncertainties and fears regarding the future were embedded in discourses linking the past, present and future. Namely, individuals conceptualized the future in the EU as a symbolic and historically shaped one, where drawing on the past helped to illustrate the bad fortunes that are part of the nation's essence in a way. Thus, as Serbia's past, both distant (the Kosovo battle) and recent (Serbia's global image post-Yugoslavia), entailed events of conflict which left Serbia devastated, isolated and victimized, it was expected that this bad streak would continue to follow the country into its future as well.

Thus, when considering integration, be it local, regional or global, we need to consider more closely how issues of belonging and recognition become embedded in concerns about continuity and compatibility, and how these, in turn, shape what we are able to imagine for our group's future. As nations strive for a sense of historical and cultural continuity (Sani et al., 2007), threats to group identity and their way of life are not only threats to the way things are now but how they are perceived to have always been "forever." These fears in turn create a worry regarding what the future of the collective holds, and whether it will entail a break from the past, and in turn, the assumed "essence" and uniqueness of the group.

References

Anzulovic, B. (1999). *Heavenly Serbia: From myth to genocide*. New York: New York University Press.

Begovic, B. (2014). Economic benefits and costs of Serbian accession to the EU: Is there an alternative? In T. Lunden (Ed.), *Sweden-Serbia and Europe: Periphery or not?* (pp. 84–95). Stockholm: KVHHA, The Royal Swedish Academy of Letters, History and Antiquities.

Bieber, F. (2002). Nationalist mobilization and stories of Serb suffering: The Kosovo myth from 600th anniversary to the present. *Rethinking History, 6*(1), 95–110.

Blic Online. (2014, January 21). *Otvoreni pregovori sa EU:Srbija gleda u buducnost, ceka nas mnogo posla* [Negotiations open with EU: Serbia looks towards the future, a lot of work awaits us.]. Retrieved from http://www.blic.rs/Vesti/Politika/436130/Otvoreni-pregovori-sa-EU-Srbija-gleda-u-buducnost-ceka-nas-mnogo-posla

Breakwell, G. M. (1996). Identity processes and social changes. In G. Breakwell & E. Lyons (Eds.), *Changing European identities* (pp. 13–27). Oxford: Butterworth-Heinemann.

Ćirković, S. (2004). *The Serbs* (The peoples of Europe). Malden, MA: Oxford: Blackwell Pub.

Cohen, P. (1996). *Serbia's secret war: Propaganda and the deceit of history* (Eastern European studies; no. 2). College Station: Texas A&M University Press.

Cox, W. (2012). Soft power and stigma: Serbia's changing image in the eyes of the European Union. *Place Branding and Public Diplomacy, 8*(2), 170–180.

David, L. (2014). Impression management of a contested past: Serbia's evolving national calendar. *Memory Studies, 7*(4), 472–483.

Dragovic-Soso, J. (2012). Apologising for Srebrenica: The declaration of the Serbian Parliament, the European Union and the politics of compromise. *East European Politics, 28*(2), 163–179.

Economides, S., & Ker-Lindsay, J. (2015). "Pre-Accession Europeanization": The Case of Serbia and Kosovo. *JCMS: Journal of Common Market Studies, 53*(5), 1027–1044.

Emerson, R. (1960). *From empire to nation: The rise to self-assertion of Asian and African peoples.* Cambridge, MA: Harvard University Press.

Hopkins, N. (2011). Dual Identities and their recognition: Minority group members' perspectives. *Political Psychology, 32*(2), 251–270.

Jetten, J., & Hutchison, P. (2011). When groups have a lot to lose: Historical continuity enhances resistance to a merger. *European Journal of Social Psychology, 41*(1), 335–343.

Jovchelovitch, S., & Hawlina, H. (2018, this volume). Utopias and worldmaking: Time, transformation and the collective imagination. In C. de Saint-Laurent, S. Obradović, & K. R. Carriere (Eds.), *Imagining collective futures: Perspectives from social, cultural, and political psychology* (pp. 129–151). London: Palgrave Macmillan.

Judah, T. (2009). *The Serbs: History, myth, and the destruction of Yugoslavia* (3rd ed.). New Haven: Yale University Press.

Ker-Lindsay, J. (2009). *Kosovo: The path to contested statehood in the Balkans* (Library of European studies). London: I. B. Tauris.

Liu, J. H., & Hilton, D. J. (2005). How the past weighs on the present: Social representations of history and their role in identity politics. *British Journal of Social Psychology, 44*(4), 537–556.

McMahon, P., & Forsythe, D. (2008). The ICTY's impact on Serbia: Judicial romanticism meets network politics. *Human Rights Quarterly, 30*(2), 412–435.

Nicholson, C., & Howarth, C. (2018, this volume). Imagining collective identities beyond intergroup conflict. In C. de Saint-Laurent, S. Obradović, & K. R. Carriere (Eds.), *Imagining collective futures: Perspectives from social, cultural, and political psychology* (pp. 173–196). London: Palgrave Macmillan.

Obradović, S. (2017). Who are we and where are we going: From past myths to present politics. *Integrative Psychological and Behavioural Science*. Advanced online publication. https://doi.org/10.1007/s12124-017-9410-x.

Obradović, S., & Howarth, C. (2018). The Power of Politics: How political leaders in Serbia discursively manage identity continuity and political change to shape the future of the nation. *European Journal of Social Psychology, 48*(1), 25–35.

Obradovic-Wochnik, J., & Wochnik, A. (2012). Europeanising the 'Kosovo Question': Serbia's policies in the context of EU integration. *West European Politics, 35*(5), 1158–1181.

Pavlowitch, S. (2002). *Serbia: The history behind the name*. London: Hurst & Co.

Reicher, S., & Hopkins, N. (2001). *Self and nation*. London: Sage Publication.

Ristic, I. (2007). Serbian identity and the concept of Europeanness. *Panoeconomicus, 54*(2), 185–195.

Russell-Omaljev, A. (2016). *Divided we stand: Discourses on identity in 'First' and 'Other' Serbia. Social construction of the Self and the Other*. Stuttgard: Ibidem-Verlag.

Sani, F. (2008). Schism in groups: A social psychological account. *Social and Personality Psychology Compass, 2*(2), 718–732.

Sani, F., Bowe, M., Herrera, M., Manna, C., Cossa, T., Miao, X., & Zhou, Y. (2007). Perceived collective continuity: Seeing groups as entities that move through time. *European Journal of Social Psychology, 37*(6), 1118–1134.

Sindic, D., & Reicher, S. (2009). 'Our way of life is worth defending': Testing a model of attitudes towards superordinate group membership through a study of Scots' attitudes towards Britain. *European Journal of Social Psychology, 39*(1), 114–129.

Smeekes, A., & Verkuyten, M. (2014). Perceived group continuity, collective self-continuity, and in-group identification. *Self and Identity, 13*(6), 663–680.

Subotic, J. (2011). Europe is a state of mind: Identity and Europeanization in the Balkans. *International Studies Quarterly, 55*(2), 309–330.

Tajfel, H. (1981). *Human groups and social categories: Studies in social psychology.* Cambridge, UK: Cambridge University Press.

Tileagă, C. (2018, this volume). Troubled pasts, collective memory, and collective futures. In C. de Saint-Laurent, S. Obradović, & K. R. Carriere (Eds.), *Imagining collective futures: Perspectives from social, cultural, and political psychology* (pp. 153–172). London: Palgrave Macmillan.

Todorova, M. (1997). *Imagining the Balkans.* Oxford: Oxford University Press.

Vos, C. (2012). Negotiating Serbia's Europeanness. On the formation and appropriation of European heritage policy in Serbia. *History and Anthropology, 22*(2), 221–242.

Zittoun, T., & Gillespie, A. (2018, this volume). Imagining the Collective Future: A Sociocultural Perspective. In C. de Saint-Laurent, S. Obradović, & K. R. Carriere (Eds.), *Imagining collective futures: Perspectives from social, cultural, and political psychology* (pp. 15–37). London: Palgrave Macmillan.

Živković, M. (2011). *Serbian dreambook: National imaginary in the time of Milošević* (New anthropologies of Europe). Bloomington: Indiana University Press.

13

History Education and the (Im)possibility of Imagining the Future

Mario Carretero

History Education as a Relation of Past, Present and Future

This chapter deals with the contribution of both formal (schools) and informal (museums, exhibitions, etc.) history education to the possibility of imagining the future. It is highly probable that most readers of this chapter would be surprised to even consider that possibility because history education is supposed to consist of the teaching of the past and, to some extent, its relation to the present. This chapter will try to show that is not the case. On the contrary, history education, as history itself, is about the full relation between the past, present, and future (Guldi & Armitage, 2014). I will also consider that the relation of these three aspects has a number of important implications not only for educational practices but also for society in general.

M. Carretero (✉)
Autónoma University of Madrid, Madrid, Spain

FLACSO, Facultad Latinoamericana de Ciencias Sociales, Tucumán, Argentina

Therefore, I will show how this relation plays an important role in the way historical contents are represented by both citizens and institutions. Also, from a theoretical point of view, I will argue that George Orwell envisaged this relation between past, present, and future in his classic novel *1984*. I think it is worth analysing this contribution about the nature of this triad (past–present–future) because Orwell was able to develop a pioneering idea much earlier than some influential social science developments. Also, I will try to show that both formal and informal present practices of history education should be revised in order to promote a full comprehension of the relation past–present–future. This revision is necessary because most of those practices are based very often on an essentialist and romantic view of the past, which does not allow for understanding either the present or the future.

The chapter is organized in the following manner: first, I will draw on two recent, public examples to illustrate the continued importance of the relationship between the past, present, and future in debates about how history is remembered and commemorated. Second, I will draw on Orwell's novel *1984* to argue that the narrative of the book pioneered an interesting idea regarding the political power of shaping the past, present, and the future, while also providing a serious critique of the consequences of the abuse of this power. By analysing Orwell's work, I argue that it stands as a soft metaphor for how history is taught, both formally and informally. Third, by drawing on Orwell's novel, I will argue that there are two mechanisms through which control over history is exercised: (1) by constructing history education to present an idealized and romanticized, yet unreal, representation of the nation's past, and (2) by maintaining this version of the past as the only legitimate, and thus unchallenged, version, in turn preventing alternative constructions of the past, but also the future. I conclude by considering some of the consequences of these simplified constructions of history in both formal and informal educational practices.

History and Its Tensions in the Present

Let us present the first of our two examples. While writing this chapter, news about the Museum of Gdansk in Poland was being discussed. For example, in *The Guardian,* the British newspaper, it appears as "Dispute over 'patriotism' delays opening of Gdansk's new war museum" (Szyndzielorz, 2017). The case is about a dispute between the officials of that museum and the present Polish government, which considers that museum as not "Polish enough" and as lacking patriotism and nationalism. This debate could look as an old-fashioned one and certainly is reminiscent of the end of the nineteenth century, when history started appearing as part of the school curriculum. At that moment, the objectives of history education were basically the same in many nations. This is to say, the main goal was to indoctrinate the students about the glories of the nation in order to develop future citizens very willing to defend their homeland even by war.[1] As a matter of fact, in the period between the World Wars I and II, educational authorities of several European nations seriously considered eliminating history education from the curriculum because it was full of extreme nationalist ideas. Unfortunately, at least some of this intuition was right. Therefore, this present debate about the Gdansk is indeed rather worrying, but also very intriguing. It is worrying because it clearly indicated that unfortunately both extreme nationalism and populism are back. But it is intriguing because it shows how informal history education has essential mechanisms, which deserve our attention as social scientists. One of them is about the relation between the past, present, and future. In other words, this museum has been censored and even its opening has been postponed because the present Polish government does not agree with museum officials, who are very prestigious historians—not only about the past representation but about what would be the goals of the museum to educate future generations. In this vein, this chapter is an attempt at unpacking that relationship and contributing to the growing literature on imagining the future.

The second example also deals with a representation of the past through an informal context—and it is a scene of the popular series

---

[1] Elsewere (Carretero, 2011), I have considered these goals as romantic because of the close relation of Romanticism and nationalist ideas. Present approaches of history education objectives as conceptual tools to critically understand social and political problems through disciplinary developments is something rather recent which started its development by the 80s of the last century approximately.

House of Cards. While fictional, it could perfectly be a real situation.[2] The scene reproduces a visit of Frank Underwood, Vice President of the United States of America, to a living history site[3] devoted to the commemoration of one battle of the American Civil War (1868). The whole scene takes place in a historical re-enactment of that battle. In this case, Frank Underwood is a privileged spectator of that re-enactment along with thousands of people. He is invited to speak for the official closing ceremony of this public historical activity and he clearly and explicitly mentions the goals of most of activities related to informal history education as re-enactments, commemorations and similar ones.[4] Thus, Vice President Underwood says: "Here began the last bloody march toward Appomattox, where General Grant met General Lee[5] for the first time, and *brave men bled to set the course of history*. I'm so honored to be here celebrating the 150th anniversary… Today, we break earth… *so that generations to come will fully absorb the importance of this hallowed ground*" (emphasis is mine). In sum, this commemoration of the past is not about the past itself, but about determining the future through the education of "generations to come." Interestingly, one of the two armies of this battle were, according to the Vice President of the United States, "brave men", even though the Southern army was defending the permanence of slavery.

In sum, the previous examples clearly illustrate how constructing the past becomes a powerful political tool in shaping and imagining the future. And this is what George Orwell was able to show through his famous novel *1984*. Today, his contribution is so widespread that some of his quotes from *1984*, and also in other works as *The Animal*

---

[2] *House of Cards.* Season 2, episode 5, min. 45., ss. 5.

[3] As can be noted, the expression "living history" is indicating, by itself, a clear connection of past, present, and future because if something belongs to the past, how is it living at the same time?

[4] Historical re-enactments are presently a very fascinating area of study (DeGroot, 2016; chapter, 4; also Agnew, 2007) in the fields of historiography, heritage and cultural studies.

[5] At the moment of revising this chapter, hot controversies and even strong political fights have been produced in the United States about precisely the statue of General Lee, who was the military leader of the South. President Trump has criticized the possibility of taking out symbols of slavery as an institution like the statue of General Lee (https://elpais.com/internacional/2017/08/17/actualidad/1502980445_259315.html). Are similarities between Trump and Underwood a pure coincidence?

Farm (1946), are part of our everyday language. For example, sentences such as "All animals are equal, but some animals are more equal than others" and "Big Brother is watching you" were able to denounce the falsity of communism, but can also be applied to the present and future capitalist societies as recent Netflix series such as *Black Mirror* show.[6]

However, the ubiquity of his ideas may perhaps overshadow how much Orwell was ahead of his times. Definitely he was ahead of the dominant ideas of psychology, sociology and education during the 1940s and 1950s. His novel *1984* was published by 1949, and at that time, most of social sciences were not able to realize how influential and powerful the relationship between the past, present, and future could be on the representation of human beings.

Orwell's *1984* as a Pioneering Contribution to Social Sciences

1984 is a novel whose essential core is about how modern states control both the behaviour and the past, present, and future representations of people. Therefore, a number of both internal and external mechanisms and technologies of control are analysed in detail. Unfortunately, on this occasion, I cannot pay attention to all of them even though some are extremely fascinating, particularly for a sociocultural and psychological analysis.[7] Instead, let us examine the components specific to the focus of this chapter. The first sentences of the novel state that "who controls the past, controls the future. Who controls the present, controls the past" (Orwell, 1949). This statement could be rephrased the following way: whoever has control over both formal and informal history education, as

---

[6] See, for example, Episode 1 (Season 3) in relation to the first sentence and Episode 3 (Season 3) in relation to the second one.

[7] For example, the way Orwell looks at the relation of language and thought is also fascinating because he considered many Vygotsgy (2012) positions and also he anticipated many issues discussed later by contemporary research, specifically about the relation between language and thought. This is to say, for example, according to the Party State of *1984*, to change the language being used in the present would definitely influence not only its future use but the thought associated with it.

a way of presenting a specific version of the past, has also control over how the future is imagined. This chapter will try to show that this control is based essentially on two mechanisms. On the one hand, both formal and informal history education are based on an idealized, essentialist and romantic, but not existing, view of the nation's past (Carretero, 2011). On the other hand, history education also maintains and perpetuates this view as the only possible one for the future. In this way, it prevents an alternative view of imagining how things could be. But before we get into these two mechanisms, one clarification is necessary. History education is a theoretical and applied research field, which has achieved important developments in the last two decades (Carretero, Berger & Grever, 2017; Seixas, 2004; Wineburg, 2001; Thünemann, Zülsdorf-Kersting, & Koster, 2014). Therefore, an important number of progressive and renovated educational practices have been developed. On this occasion, my criticisms are mostly related to traditional practices, which unfortunately still are alive in many educational contexts.

The two classic sentences of Orwell have been traditionally considered as a kind of incomplete syllogism. The fact that Orwell's sentences are so popular has probably contributed to this. Thus this syllogism is considered nowadays a kind of tautology or a self-evident truism. However, as a matter of fact, it is not. Thus, I think this matter deserves a careful examination. Having the political control over the present no doubt provides enormous opportunities for determining the future. This is probably the reason why most political leaders attempt to achieve power. This is to say that when they do strive for power, their goal is to have political power not only today but also in the future. Both previous examples clearly show this. But if the control of the present provides such an influence over the future and this influence is carried out from the present moment, why then is the past so crucial in this process? Definitely here comes the genius of Orwell in providing a truly original answer. That is, according to the Orwellian dictum, the best possible way to get and keep political power is first to conquer the present; second, the past; and third, the future. In other words, what Orwell is proposing could be expressed in this counterintuitive manner: if you would like to control the future, you have to modify not just the present, but also the past.

History Education and the (Im)possibility of Imagining the Future 261

But where did Orwell get these ideas? It is well known that he was inspired by a real experience and not just by a completely imagined situation.[8] He was a member of the International Brigades, which fought against the fascists in Spain defending the Spanish Republic, but he also had the opportunity to experience the communist repression in Barcelona over both the anarchists and Trotskyists and to write lucidly about it (Orwell, 1938). Therefore, he was very sensitive to dictatorial violence, and he had both the political courage and the clear determination to denounce human rights violations, such as freedom of speech, within the USSR.[9] But this violation not only consisted of censoring; USSR officials used more sophisticated mechanisms, such as the frequent practices of modifying the past through massive changes of both images and texts being part of textbooks, encyclopaedias, newspapers and other documents (King, 1997; Schlogel, 2008). He describes in detail how photographs were changed in such a way that main characters either appear or disappear according to the convenience of the Party-State. As a matter of fact, several historians have documented how this transformation of images really happened during the Stalinist years in the Soviet Union (Figes, 2007; Judt, 2015). Of course, not only were the images changed, but also the narratives about the past, and this includes the main characters, their purpose and consequences (Carretero, 2018). Interestingly enough, this process of changing the representation of the past has an essential goal and this is not just the political control of the present but also the establishment of just one possible future—the future conceived by the Party-State. This is very clearly shown when Winston Smith, the main character of the novel, is being interrogated and tortured by O'Brien, a Party-State official. O'Brien says, "If you are a man, Winston, you are the last man. Your kind is extinct; we are the inheritors. Do you

---

[8] It has been considered that Orwell was inspired by the novel *We* by the Russian writer Zamyatin (https://www.theguardian.com/books/booksblog/2009/jun/08/george-orwell-1984-zamyatin-we). In his novel, he described a society where the houses are made with transparent crystal. Therefore, all the people are seen by others and by the State all the time and there is no privacy. This idea was re-elaborated by Orwell through the analysis of the influence of the mass media, and particularly TV, on present lives.

[9] As a matter of fact, Orwell had serious difficulties publishing *1984*. As it was a strong critique of the Soviet Union, both USA's and UK's political establishments preferred not having confrontations with their former ally in World War II.

understand that you are alone? You are outside history, you are non-existent." It is clear that in this case, "history" means the past, the present, and the future at the same time.

In addition, it is extremely important to mention that *1984* is not only a novel, not only a political argument criticizing the situation in the USSR in the 1940s, but also what could happen in the future in any society. By 1991, that is to say 43 years after the publication of this novel, the Soviet Union collapsed and the communist system was abolished all over the planet.[10] But nevertheless, this did not affect the validity of *1984*. To some extent, the critical view of Orwell can be applied to our present times. In other words, *1984* was able to predict the future of both communism and capitalism. In this vein, Orwell's ideas are profoundly historicist. His novel has been considered a dystopia, but I think it is definitely a historicist dystopia, which is using the future as a metaphor, which has a highly predictive and explanatory power.

To some extent, it could be said that Orwell pioneered social sciences theories about the importance of social identities (Tajfel, 1967) and the enormous influence of the past on their construction. As a matter of fact, he developed his social thought (Ingle, 2006) about two decades before some influential social psychologists of our time. Scenes of the novel such as those related to the "two minutes of hate" showed how efficient it is to produce a systematic social intervention devoted to people's interiorization of the invention of both the in-group and the out-group. Also, his contributions about the importance of both external and internal mechanisms of control were made about two decades before Foucault published his significant views in, for example, *Discipline and Punish* (1975).

This is to say, he was a thinker with an incredible ability to anticipate the importance of a number of symbolic mechanisms and devices, which can be of enormous influence on human beings.[11] The importance of the

---

[10] Officially, China and Cuba are still communist countries, but it would be much more accurate to consider them as state capitalist countries. The first has allowed capitalist practices several decades ago and the second has a *nomenklatura* which is the owner of most of the country.

[11] Probably one of the most interesting from a psychological and cultural point of view is his argument of a *newspeak*. The relations of this idea with soviet psychology of the 1930s is very clear and it deserves a careful exploration.

past is clearly one of them. This is really essential and can be seen to be related to the difference between authoritarian regimes and purely dictatorial ones. The first one tries to control the present by prohibiting certain ideas and their representations and implementations through a very strict censorship (Moghaddam, 2018). But dictatorships try to go one step further by attempting to modify people's internalization processes.[12] And here is where the past plays an essential role. The past is our main reservoir for future actions. If a person has established an interpretation of her own past, individually and as a member of a community, this will orient her future actions. Her imagination of how that present could be changed and, presumably, improved, will find in the past models and suggestions. For this reason, traditions have such a strong influence on our lives. In other words, what Orwell realized and showed through *1984* is that once a narrative about the past is established as the right version of what has happened, it is extremely difficult to generate one that could contradict the established narrative, regardless of its veracity. This is to say that it is possible to modify the content of the narrative to some extent. For example, modifying its main characters or even establishing a counternarrative is possible, but it is extremely difficult to generate a very different type of grand narrative.[13] I mean a narrative based on a very different type of characters and events.

1984 as a Soft Metaphor of History Education

One particular and very prominent case of this can be seen at historical master narratives (Carretero, 2017; Carretero & Bermudez, 2012; Wertsch, 2002), which play an essential role in history education because, to some extent, they are its centre. As stated earlier, since the beginning of the public educational system, history has been considered an essential component of the process of imagining the nation, according to the classical ideas of both Anderson (1983/1991) and Hobsbawm and Ranger

---

[12] The case of Victor Klemperer (2006) who studied how the language was censored and extremely controlled under the Nazi regime is also very clear.
[13] Wertsch (2002) has alerted us about how very often counternarratives are very close to official narratives in the sense of just having a different content but the same structure.

(2012). Other crucial components are national festivities, commemorations and traditions in general, such as historical re-enactments mentioned in the example from *House of Cards* mentioned earlier. Both authors concur implicitly with the ideas Orwell anticipated more than 40 years before in his novel about the intriguing relation of past, present, and future analysed earlier, by arguing that historical master narratives are invented explanations about the past, which try to have an impact not only in the present, but mostly on the future. The example of the Gdansk museum mentioned at the beginning of this chapter is a clear example of how powerful and resistant to change these narratives could be. Also, both examples show how important these scenarios and narratives become for the political power in order to maintain its control over the population. In sum, I am arguing then that the great novel of Orwell, plus some other ideas included in his political essays,[14] could be considered a soft version of a metaphor of history education. Of course, a hard view would be very difficult to justify except in extremely authoritarian contexts. The last few decades have shown very worrying cases of seriously censoring and modifying in history textbooks in countries such as the United States and Japan[15] (Carretero, 2011; Hein & Selden, 2000) and, lately, Russia (Korostelina, 2017; Tsyrlina & Lovorn, 2017). For example, the Vietnam War was very much hidden in American textbooks (Wineburg, Mosborg, Porat, & Duncan, 2007); the responsibility of Japan has also been disguised in Japan for decades; and presently, President Putin himself is actively defending a grandiose view of the Russian past, which even includes the positive role of Stalin. Therefore, it is highly plausible to predict that the way the citizens of these three countries could imagine

---

[14] For example, let us consider Orwell's ideas about the importance of nationalism when he says: "One cannot see the modern world as it is, unless one recognizes the overwhelming strength of patriotism, national loyalty. In certain circumstances, it may crumble; at certain levels of civilization, it does not exist; yet as a positive force, there is nothing comparable. Next to it, Christianity and international socialism are weak as hay. To a great extent, Hitler and Mussolini rose to power in their own countries because they were able to understand this fact, whilst their opponents were not".

[15] Even nowadays, an important part of present politicians denies the role played by the Japanese army in World War II. For example, they deny the well-established historical research about the 200,000 so-called comfort women, mostly from Korea, used as forced prostitutes for the Japanese army.

their future has been much influenced by the top-down, or institutional, views of the past.

Let us continue with this idea of *1984* as a soft metaphor of history education. In this vein, all over the world, formal history education is national in at least half of their contents. In the case of informal history education, the percentage is probably higher (Grever & Stuurman, 2010). This is the logical consequence of the role of history education on the process of the construction of the nation. Elsewhere, I have analysed how students and citizens of Argentina, Greece, and Spain represent their national master narratives (Carretero & Kriger, 2011; Carretero & van Alphen, 2014; Lopez, Carretero & Rodriguez-Moneo, 2015; Kadianaki, Andreouli & Carretero, 2016). Some clear themes appear in these different contexts. These include:

a) Continuity of the nation based on a lack of differentiation of past and present;
b) Idealization of the past;
c) Moral obligation towards the past;
d) Homogeneity of the nation.

These four themes have also been found by applying different methodologies by researchers from various fields, including social psychology, education, and cognitive and historical studies (Psaltis, Carretero & Cehajic-Clancy, 2017; Smeekes, 2014). As a matter of fact, these four themes are very much supported by numerous collective memories based on everyday representations (LeGoff, 1990; Wertsch, 2002). Nevertheless, they represent clear misconceptions about historical processes because historiographical research clearly shows that nations' developments are rather discontinuous and heterogeneous. Therefore, a continuous and homogenous representation of the national past is simply an idealization, which finally produces an imagined moral obligation (Obradović, 2018 Chap. 12, this volume). As Van Alphen and Carretero (2015) note, idealization of the past leads to perceiving the past as a moral example to follow in the present and the future. All these four themes are important to fully understand the relation of past, present, and future because they have a strong relation among them. On this occasion, I will focus on providing a more detailed analysis of the first one to illustrate this point.

Formal and informal history education is supposed to consist of the teaching of the past as a tool to understand the present. An adequate and complex representation of this causal relation between past and present is supposed to provide a more reliable and counterintuitive comprehension of the present state of affairs. For this reason, this relation is frequently included in the official objectives of the school curriculum. They are mentioned also in the everyday representations of historical events as well—for example, in newspapers, museums, and other informal opportunities of getting in touch with the past. But in reality, most educational practices in both formal and informal history education do not really offer many opportunities to properly learn such mid- and long-term causal connections between past and present because of a very static view of historical time.

For example, let us imagine that a high school student is receiving a history class about the colonization of America by European empires. It is highly probable that both causes and consequences of that historical period are included in its syllabus. Obviously, the causes are about the past and the consequences are about the present. But what is the present in historical terms? It is essential to consider that the present is not only nowadays, but it also could be any other moment in the past, depending on what historical period is being considered. For example, the very well-known sentence of "Columbus discovered America" could be strongly criticized not only because of its Eurocentric perspective (Axtell, 1992; Zea, 1989) but also for at least two additional reasons.[16] First, Columbus had no awareness at all of where he had arrived, being persuaded that Cuba was Japan. As a matter of fact, his original project was to arrive in Asia through a West-oriented way instead of through an East-oriented one. As Columbus never explored most of the American lands, he understood neither what he really did through his five voyages nor that a whole

---

[16] Recent events in New York and Los Angeles (http://www.latimes.com/nation/la-na-columbus-new-york-20170902-story.html) have indicated how controversial this historical figure is who is producing continuous debates in at least the last two decades in both North and South America.

continent was located between Europa and Asia. Second, Columbus was not considered the so-called discoverer of America until 1800–1900. On the contrary, he was rather ignored for centuries. He became a significant historical figure when European national master narratives started having an influential role in the beginning of the nineteenth century as cultural tools were named as myths of origin. But probably most of the students and citizens who have studied Columbus through both formal and informal contexts have thought that he was considered the "discoverer" of America since the end of the fifteenth century. This is to say, they have a very static representation of the relation of past and present, considering the past just as 1492 and the present as simply nowadays, without taking into account the existence of the in-between periods. It is important to consider that this simplistic way of looking at the relation between past and present is a very powerful mechanism to determine the way citizens look at the future, as Orwell realized in his novel. Thus, to either introduce or to eliminate Columbus in textbooks, encyclopaedias, and newspapers as an influential character who was always in the past can be perfectly compared with the job Winston Smith—the main character of *1984*—carries out every day at the Ministry of the Truth. In this vein, once Columbus has been introduced, it definitely contributed to the formatting of the imagination of the future. For example, colonial adventures are legitimized from a moral and political view, and probably colonialism is easily represented as a "natural" historical process. In sum, if both formal and informal present history education practices could ever overcome the soft metaphor provided by *1984*, major changes will be necessary. Probably an initial and very fundamental change will be to understand that history education is not just about the past, as Orwell very lucidly showed us as early as in *1948*.

Conclusion

Traditional formal and informal history education are supposed to consist of the teaching of the past and its relation to the present. This is a rather common conception both in and out of the school. But unfortunately, it forgets that historical knowledge is about the relation among past, present, and future. To illuminate this issue, an analysis of classic novel *1984* has been analysed as a soft metaphor of history education. In this vein, I have tried to show how Orwell was advancing a pioneer idea because whoever has control over history education, as a way of presenting a specific version of the past, also has control over the imagination of the future. This chapter has tried to show that this control is based basically on two mechanisms. On the one hand, history education is based on an idealized and romantic, but not existing, view of the nation. On the other hand, history education also maintains this view as the only possible one for the future. In this way, it prevents a productive process of imagining the future.

Acknowledgements This chapter has been possible because of the support of the Project EDU-2015-65088P, from the Ministry of Education (Spain), and Project PICT-2016-2341, from ANPICYT (Argentina) coordinated by the author. My acknowledge also to Candela Carretero because of her comments about the series *Black Mirror*.

References

Agnew, V. (2007). History's affective turn: Historical reenactment and its work in the present. *Re-thinking History, 11*, 299–312.
Anderson, B. (1983). *Imagined communities*. New York: Verso. New and revised edition 1991.
Axtell, J. (1992). *Beyond 1942: Encounters in colonial North America*. New York: Oxford University Press.
Carretero, M. (2011). *Constructing patriotism. Teaching history and memories in global worlds*. Charlotte, CT: Information Age Publishing.
Carretero, M. (2017). Teaching history master narratives: Fostering imagi-Nations. In M. Carretero, S. Berger, & M. Grever (Eds.), *Palgrave handbook of research in historical culture and history education* (pp. 511–528). New York: Palgrave Macmillan.
Carretero, M. (2018). Historical representations as contributions to the road towards actualized democracy. In B. Wagoner & I. Bresco (Eds.), *Interdisciplinary views on the roads to actualized democracy* (pp. 259–278). New York: Springer.

Carretero, M., Berger, S., & Grever, M. (Eds.). (2017). *Palgrave handbook of research in historical culture and history education*. New York: Palgrave Macmillan.

Carretero, M., & Bermúdez, Á. (2012). Constructing histories. In J. Valsiner (Ed.), *Oxford handbook of culture and psychology* (pp. 625–646). Oxford, UK: Oxford University Press.

Carretero, M., & Kriger, M. (2011). Historical representations and conflicts about indigenous people as national identities. *Culture and Psychology, 17*(2), 177–195.

Carretero, M., & Van Alphen, F. (2014). Do master narratives change among high school students? A characterization of how national history is represented. *Cognition and Instruction, 32*(3), 290–312.

DeGroot, J. (2016). *Consuming history*. New York: Routledge.

Figes, O. (2007). *The whisperers: Private life in Stalin's Russia*. New York: Macmillan.

Foucault, M. (1975 [1983]). *Discipline and punishment*. New York: Basic Books.

Grever, M., & Stuurman, S. (Eds.). (2010). *Beyond the canon*. Basingstoke: Palgrave.

Guldi, J., & Armitage, D. (2014). *The history manifesto*. Cambridge: Cambridge University Press.

Hein, L. E., & Selden, M. (2000). *Censoring history: Citizenship and memory in Japan, Germany and the United Sates*. New York: M.E. Sharpe.

Hobsbawm, E., & Ranger, T. (Eds.). (2012). *The invention of tradition*. Cambridge: Cambridge University Press.

Ingle, S. (2006). *The social and political thought of George Orwell: A Reassessment*. London: Routledge.

Judt, T. (2015). *When the facts change: Essays, 1995–2010*. New York: Random House.

Kadianaki, I., Andreouli, E., & Carretero, M. (2016). Using representations of the nation's past to construct citizenship boundaries: An analysis of Greek citizens' discourse about immigrants' rights. *Qualitative studies in Psychology*. Retrieved from https://doi.org/10.1037/qup0000087.

King, D. (1997). *The commissar vanishes: The falsification of photographs and art in Stalin's Russia*. New York: Metropolitan Books.

Klemperer, V. (2006). *Language of the Third Reich: LTI: Lingua Tertii Imperii*. New York: A&C Black.

Korostelina, K. (2017). Constructing identity and power in history education in Ukraine: Approaches to formation of peace culture. In M. Carretero, S. Berger, & M. Grever (Eds.), *Palgrave handbook of research in historical culture and history education* (pp. 311–330). New York: Palgrave Macmillan.

Le Goff, J. (1990). Preface. In A. Brossat, S. Combe, J. Potel, & J. Szurek (Eds.), *l'Est, la memoire retrouvée (Found memory in the East)*. Paris: Éditions La Découverte.

López, C., Carretero, M., & Rodríguez-Moneo, M. (2015). Conquest or Reconquest? Students' conceptions of nation embedded in a historical narrative. *The Journal of the Learning Sciences, 24*(2), 252–285.

Moghaddam, F. M. (2018). The road towards actualized democracy. In B. Wagoner & I. Bresco (Eds.), *Interdisciplinary views on the roads to actualized democracy*. New York: Springer.

Obradović, S. (2018, this volume). Creating integration: A case study from Serbia and the EU. In C. de Saint-Laurent, S. Obradović, & K. R. Carriere (Eds.), *Imagining collective futures: Perspectives from social, cultural, and political psychology* (pp. 237–254). London: Palgrave Macmillan.

Orwell, G. (1938). *Hommage to Catalunya*. London: Space.

Orwell, G. (1946). *Animal farm: A fairy tale*. New York: Harcourt Brace.

Orwell, G. (1949). *1984*. New York: Harcourt Brace.

Psaltis, C., Carretero, M., & Cehajic-Clancy, S. (Eds.) (2017). Conflict transformation and history teaching: Social psychological theory and its contributions. In Ch. Psaltis, M. Carretero, & S. Cehajic-Clancy. *History education and conflict transformation*. Basingstoke: Palgrave Macmillan.

Schlogel, K. (2008). *Terror und Traum: Moskau 1937*. München: Hanser.

Seixas, P. (Ed.). (2004). *Theorizing historical consciousness*. Toronto: University of Toronto Press.

Smeekes, A. N. (2014). *The presence of the past. Historical rooting of national identity and current group dynamics*. Doctoral dissertation, Utrecht University.

Smith, 1991.

Szyndzielorz, J. (2017, January 28). *Dispute over 'patriotism' delays opening of Gdańsk's new war museum*. Retrieved from https://www.theguardian.com/travel/2017/jan/28/gdansk-second-world-war-museum-delay-patriotism-poland

Tajfel, H. (1967 [2010]). *Social identity and intergroup relations*. Cambridge: Cambridge University Press.

Thünemann, H., Zülsdorf-Kersting, M., & Koster, M. (Eds.). (2014). *History education research. International perspectives and research traditions*. Schwalbach, Germany: Wochenschau Pub.

Tsyrlina, T., & Lovorn, M. (2017). Emotional, moral, and symbolic imagery of modern history textbooks. In M. Carretero, S. Berger, & M. Grever (Eds.), *Palgrave handbook of research in historical culture and history education* (pp. 697–716). New York: Palgrave Macmillan.

Van Alphen, F., & Carretero, M. (2015). The construction of the relation between national past and present in the appropriation of historical master narratives. *Integrative Psychological & Behavioral Science, 49*(3), 512–530.
Vygotsgy, L. (2012). *Thought and language*. Cambridge, Mass: MIT Press.
Wertsch, J. V. (2002). *Voices of collective remembering*. Cambridge: Cambridge University Press.
Wineburg, S. (2001). *Historical thinking and other unnatural acts: Charting the future of teaching the past temple*. Philadelphia: University Press.
Wineburg, S., Mosborg, S., Porat, D., & Duncan, A. (2007). Common belief and the cultural curriculum: An intergenerational study of historical consciousness. *American Educational Research Journal, 44*(1), 40–76.
Zea, L. (1989). E*l descubrimiento de américa y su sentido actual*, México, FCE. (The discovery of America and its present meaning).

14

Conclusion: Changing Imaginings of Collective Futures

Ivana Marková

Individual and Collective Imagination

Imagination is one of the basic mental capacities that define humans as species. In agreement with authors of this volume, I conceive imagination as a feature of the dialogical mind. Dialogical imagination characterizes the mind that is in reflexive interactions with minds of other individuals, groups and communities. More broadly, dialogical imagination involves reflexive interdependencies between minds, institutions and cultures; and between past, present and future events (Marková, 2016). As such, dialogical imagination is intertwined with various forms of thinking and language, such as remembering, making sense of signs and creating signs, with symbolic communication and with judging and evaluating phenomena in social reality. Therefore, imagination can be com-

---

I. Marková (✉)
University of Stirling, Stirling, UK

London School of Economics, London, UK
e-mail: ivana.markova@stir.ac.uk

prehended only in a holistic manner, together with those mental capacities and activities which humans display in their sociocultural and historical contexts.

If, for analytic reasons, this volume singles out collective imagining as a distinct phenomenon to be explored, we should see it as an attempt to *highlight* its collective features within the context of other kinds of social thinking, shared activities and communication. These features might involve, on the one hand, aspirations for desirable common goals and outcomes, and on the other hand, the ways of avoiding problems or conflicts that could threaten the existence of communities. However, collective visions of the future may also refer to collective acceptance of ideological, religious or political doctrines, which groups and communities adopt either thoughtlessly, or due to fear, or indeed due to admiration of such doctrines and of charismatic leaders propagating them.

Throughout the whole of European history, *imagination of the individual* has been both denigrated and celebrated. Disparaged by Plato (1991), it was accepted by Aristotle (1998), and highly acclaimed by Giambattista Vico (1744/1948). Imagination was largely rejected by positivism as a form of irrational thinking (LeGouis, 1997), and Albert Einstein (1931/2009) praised it higher than knowledge.

In contrast, the history of theoretical treatments of *collective imaginations* is relatively short. True, collective imaginary is as old as the history of humankind and we can trace it in all religions, myths and fables. However, explicit theories of collective imagination are linked to the emergence of human and social sciences in the eighteenth and nineteenth centuries. This coincides with dramatic societal changes accompanied by the beginnings of social movements in relation to political and anti-religious protests at the time, and fights against economic exploitations during industrialization.

Alongside these societal changes, the rise of the modern concept of the Self fundamentally contributed to theorization of collective imagination. Let us recall that until the seventeenth century, the concept of the Self was strictly individualistic. Its history goes back to the philosophy of Saint Augustine (AD 354–430), who conceived the Self as the centre of inner incorporeal activity of self-knowing, reflexivity and self-consciousness.

These capacities of the Self, as St. Augustine (397–398/2006) articulated them in *Confessions*, enabled the human soul to reach God. The concept of the Self as a thinker and knower permeated subsequent philosophy for more than a thousand years and culminated in Descartes's "Cogito ergo sum". Such philosophically construed concept of the Self was far removed from the Self as experienced in daily life.

The premodern Self in daily life of the mediaeval society was closely tied to institutions and the existing social structures (Berger, 1973; Marková, 2003). The Self had a stabilized identity that was interwoven into requirements and constraints of the strictly hierarchical mediaeval society. Each social group had a mandatory code of behaviour and of lifestyle to which the Self was submitted.

The breakdown and disappearance of the mediaeval society necessarily led to the development of the modern Self based on new demands. Above all, the post-mediaeval society transformed the relations between the Self and social structures and various forms of Others. These new relations became involved in the Self's search for social recognition, which included the struggle for human rights, dignity and equality. These searches and struggles were also reflected in new philosophical trends, such as those of Fichte and Hegel, and the emphasis on the interdependence between the Self and Others.

The emergence of these socially orientated philosophies and the rise of human and social sciences in the eighteenth and nineteenth centuries were parts of the broadly based societal, cultural and political movements that swept across Europe. They brought about new ideas of nationalism, they encouraged interest in other cultures, and they promoted languages as marks of national identity. These movements, which inspired desires for radical changes in society, called for the democratization of life. They led to diverse formulations of collective imaginations of the future. These imaginations aimed to become the guiding forces of modernity, enabling the development of shared social practices and expectations for the future within a new and legitimate moral order (Taylor, 2002). Most importantly, such practices could be accomplished only in and through understanding the multiple interdependencies between the Self and Other(s).

In building upon ideas about collective imaginations of the future as the guiding forces of modernity, the authors of this volume present a rich spectrum of thoughts ranging from historical to psychological, sociocultural and political approaches. In this concluding chapter, I shall attempt to identify some common themes that permeate this volume and discern some concepts that, to my mind, guide the authors' thinking.

Imagination and Images

Imagination is such a basic capacity of humanity that it cannot be annihilated without destroying the human being *as the* human being. The capacity to imagine can be altered by physiological/biological means (e.g. drugs, stress on the brain, brain injury) or by a mental illness. For example, the loss of memory or of language as a result of brain accident has a destructive effect on imagination and other forms of thought. In contrast, some substances, such as hallucinogenic drugs or narcotics, may temporarily enhance imagination.

While imagination can be altered or destructed only by physiological or biological impact on the brain, images, that is, the processes and products of imagination, are amenable to destruction and manipulation by social means. It is not an exaggeration to claim that, today, we live in the world of images. Rapid advances in communication and technology enable the swift spread of information through media images, artistic products and artefacts. They constantly bombard humans' capacities of coping with the magnitude and diversity of images.

In this section I shall be concerned with two issues. First, I shall discuss how the question 'What is imagination?' is answered by authors of this volume. The answer to this question depends on the problem addressed by the researcher. Second, let us remind ourselves that despite the conceptual difference between imagination as the capacity to imagine, and images, as the processes and products of imagination, these two concepts are often treated as if referring to identical capacities and processes. Yet their conceptual differentiation has an important theoretical and social significance.

Imagination as Decoupling

One way of answering the question 'What is imagination?' is to consider imagination as a mental activity that is separated from the immediate experience, and is concerned with 'what does not yet exist'. This perspective is widespread in social sciences (see Jovchelovitch and Hawlina, Chap. 7, this volume). So conceived, imagination is viewed as wondering about futures that enable creative acting. This perspective is adopted by several authors of this volume who develop theoretical ideas about imagination as a process that is temporarily decoupled from the instant flow of experience.

Zittoun and Gillespie (Chap. 2, this volume) develop a sociocultural model of collective imagination based on their original theorization of imagination of individuals (Zittoun & Gillespie, 2016). They resourcefully extend the three core dimensions of their original model (i.e. time orientation, the semiotic distance of imagining and the plausibility of realization of imagined events) to develop the model of collective imagination. The authors conceptualize in detail these novel extensions. These comprise the degree of centralization of imagining and its emotional valence; these are distributed in collective imaginations of multidimensional spaces in historical and sociocultural fields. Utilizing and developing Zittoun and Gillespie's perspective, Power (Chap. 11, this volume), too, draws on imagination as decoupling of immediate experience.

Other models that seem to adopt the decoupling perspective of imagination are proposed by de Saint-Laurent (Chap. 4, this volume) and Glăveanu (Chap. 5, this volume). De Saint-Laurent proposes a model of collective imagination of the future based on several features of collective memory (see below). Glăveanu explores the construction of collective futures as creative activities of multiple actors and cultural environments. Glăveanu places the relations between the Self and Others in the centre of theorizing creativity, imagination and collective futures. Collective futures are formed both through imagination as an activity of thinking and through creativity as an action-based process.

Decoupling is also involved in utopias. Jovchelovitch and Hawlina (Chap. 7, this volume) critically analyse utopias as strivings for a better future in which there are no conflicts and tensions, and in which the perfect society timelessly flows. The authors argue that utopias tend to be static designs and monologized fictions presenting futures as a kind of blessing for everybody and allowing no alternative. The authors contrast such unrealistic utopias with the forms of collective imaginations that are multifaceted, dialogical and dynamic interactions between Selves and Others.

Brescó (Chap. 6, this volume), too, is concerned with utopias. Specifically, he discusses the Marxist utopia of a classless society that would be achieved through class struggle, and the utopias of nationalist movements in the nineteenth century aiming to create nation states. Brescó uses the notion of 'prolepsis' (see below) to explain the logic of these utopias based on reconstructing the past in order to achieve the required political goals.

In conclusion, while these authors conceive imagination as intrinsic to human thinking and to its related mental activities, they aim to construct specific theoretical models or to refer to particular kinds of collective imagination. Decoupling collective imagination from the immediate experience enables them to bring out the exact features of their theoretical models and of issues they address.

Imagination as Embedded in the Flow of Thinking

Another perspective conceives imagination as part of any form of thinking that takes place in the flow of daily experience, rather than being distanced from it (even if only temporarily). This perspective can be viewed as an extension of Heidegger's (1968) position expressed in his questioning 'What is called thinking?' According to Heidegger's answer to this question, to think means to interrogate oneself, other humans and institutions, as well as to question phenomena in social reality. For Heidegger, to think means to search for a path in an unknown territory. Under such circumstances, the knower does not know where precisely the path might lead, and he/she only has a hunch about the final destination. This may be likened 'to making a first path on skis through new-fallen snow or clearing a way for oneself through dense forest growth' (Gray, 1968, p. xxiv). As Heidegger often repeated, in order to think, 'we must get underway' (e.g. Heidegger, 1968, p. 8). Heidegger considered that thinking and questioning were more or less synonymous capacities.

Imagination, likewise, may be considered as a search for possible routes leading to desirable destinations or at least to outcomes avoiding adverse effects (see Power, Chap. 11, this volume). While one may imagine the outcome, the path to it has yet to be uncovered. According to this perspective, imagination is present in and through most forms of thinking, in particular when humans do not have sufficient information about the relevant issues that might lead to the thought-after destinations. Perhaps only algorithmic thinking and formalistic procedures with rigid techniques and fixed goals can take place without imagination. Otherwise, imagination is involved in learning, questioning oneself and others, searching for a solution, or simply in any attempts to find a path through the unknown terrain. Humans learn in and through making sense of new phenomena, comparing them with past experiences and knowledge, and with what they share with others. In these cases, imagination is part of all kinds of daily thinking and communication, and some authors in this volume adopt this perspective.

Social thinking and dialogical communication involve, above all, the imagining of perspectives of others. It was in this context that Ragnar Rommetveit (1974) introduced the notion of 'prolepsis'—that is, of a conversational move indicating the speaker's anticipation of socially shared commonalities for communication. By imagining the other participant's presuppositions, the speaker proleptically induces a communicatively appropriate response from the other. We can assume that prolepsis plays two roles. On the one hand, and as Rommetveit (1974) suggested, it is closely related to intersubjectivity—that is, to the search for a common ground in order to achieve mutual understanding of the participants. It is this role of prolepsis that was later on developed by Cole (1996) and other researchers in child socialization. On the other hand, by making a conversational move, the speaker has the privilege of controlling the range of appropriate answers from the other, and to that extent, he/she restricts the range of responses from the other participant. Glăveanu (Chap. 5, this volume) touches on this role of prolepsis in discussing 'imagining for others'.

Brescó (Chap. 6, this volume) uses the concept of prolepsis in order to examine collective imagination of the future. He takes as a point of departure the process of a child's socialization, during which parents attempt to lead the child towards their expected goals for their young. Brescó proceeds to build a model of prolepsis in the politics of imagination. He argues that just as parents' cultural past is reflected and extended in the education of their child, so collectively imagined futures are based on multiple ways of reconstructing the past and the present in order to attain the desired political goals for the future. Prolepsis is a part of daily interactions and communication and it explains the spiral logic of social structures that move from and to the past, present and future. Collective imagination, therefore, cannot be isolated or decoupled from daily interactions and communication.

In focusing on collective imagination in relation to literature, Carriere (Chap. 3, this volume) does not use the term 'prolepsis', although the concept of prolepsis permeates his arguments as he claims: 'we imagine the mind of the other and we adjust our interactions based on how we imagine they respond'. Carriere views imagination as being totally enmeshed in the daily social world. It governs intersubjective rules of interaction and beliefs that others share these thoughts and beliefs (Rommetveit, 1974). Like Heidegger, Carriere conceives the ways of approaching the uncertain future through constructing meanings that move across past, present and future. He shows the ways through which literature can propel collective imaginations for intersubjective, as well as for political or creative purposes.

In discussing his model of collective imagination, based on the distinction between imagination and creativity, Glăveanu (Chap. 5, this volume) adopts the position of decoupling imagination from the flow of experience. However, when he is concerned with the question of perspectival collective futures, he views imagination as a feature of the flow of experience and interaction. He outlines three forms of perspectival positions in communication such as the Self for Others, the Self with Others and the Self towards Others. These positions are differentiated with respect to mutuality of perspectives.

Glăveanu's position illustrates that these two conceptions of imagination—that is, imagination as a mental activity distanced from immediate experience and imagination as embedded in daily thought—are complementary. The prioritizing of one or the other conception of collective imagination is given by authors' questions, for example: do they intend to construct a theoretical model of imagination? Alternatively, do they explore imagination in daily flow of thinking, activities and communication?

Images as Products of Imagination

Whichever of these two conceptions of collective imagination one adopts, in the process of imagining, humans produce images. These could be concrete mental pictures or sensorial (e.g. visual, hearing) creations. Although images are produced by the minds of individuals, we assume that they are dialogically constructed in the socially shared social world. Powerful collective images, which are generated in politics and ideologies, shape public decisions. Media images promote the public understanding of science, as well as artistic inventions of humans and computers. Not surprisingly, various forms of collective images are debated across disciplines, such as arts (e.g. Goldbard, 2006), politics (e.g. Bottici, 2011; Czobor-Lupp, 2014) and cultural studies (e.g. Calhoun, 2002; Gaonkar, 2002; Göle, 2002; Lee & LiPuma, 2002). In view of this, it is notable that studies of collective imagination in social psychology have been rare (but see e.g. Arruda, 2014; de Alba, 2004, 2007).

We see in this volume (e.g. Nicholson and Howarth, Chap. 9, this volume) that explorations in social representations, which are based on a sociocultural approach, are closely linked to the studies of collective imagination. Imagination is one of the fundamental concepts of Moscovici's original theory (Moscovici, 1961, 1976/2008) (which however, does not apply to some other social representational approaches). Among joint links between the sociocultural approach to social representations and collective imaginations are, for example, the following: holistic and dynamic perspectives on social phenomena, the emphasis on relations between the past, future and contemporary ideological and political conflicts and their embeddedness in history and culture. Indeed, one may even pose the question as to whether there are any substantial conceptual differences between collective imaginations of the future and sociocultural approaches in social representations, or whether viewing these two fields as separate from one another is a terminological matter.

While imagination is a basic capacity of humanity that cannot be annihilated without destroying the human being *as the* human being, concrete images are subjects of terrific social and psychological influences (Marková, 2017). Dictatorships, totalitarian regimes, modern bureaucracies, markets and political uncertainties have a gigantic power to manipulate and distort images. This happens by channelling thinking, language and symbolic processes through certified routes so that they can serve specific purposes of socialization, whether political, cultural or educational. For example, manipulated photographs by the mass media show genetically modified tomatoes as growing bigger *as if* they were injected by 'genes'. Such photographs, transported from medicine and genetics, stimulate public's ideas and manipulate their images (Wagner, Kronberger & Seifert, 2002). During the HIV/AIDS epidemic in the 1980s, images (by the media) of people infected by the virus formed and transformed collective images or social representations of HIV/AIDS and proved to be much more influential than knowledge of the disease (e.g. Marková & Farr, 1995). Systematic repetitions and re-presentations of images convert them finally into social reality and establish them as truth.

Interdependencies and Oppositions Between the Self and Others

Anthropological evidence shows that already in human prehistory, the categories 'we' and 'they' were fundamental to social life. The preference for one's own group over other groups is one of the basic common-sense assumptions. It is so deeply and unconsciously entrenched in the human mind that it is hard to eradicate, or even to reflect upon it (Benedict, 1942). The Self identifies with the selected Other (a group, nation, or language), and is ready to take part in wars, and to sacrifice oneself for these valued Others. Equally, the Self keeps a distance from unwanted Others, who could be associated with danger, threat and risk. Rather than admitting to oneself one's moral, intellectual and other kinds of shortcomings, the Self attributes them to unwanted Others, rationalizes one's thoughts and conduct, and invents fictitious reasons to justify one's behaviour (Ichheiser, 1951).

This fundamental theme permeates all chapters of this volume, each author focusing on different features of interdependencies and oppositions between the Self and Others in and through rich thematic spectra. The authors portray these interdependencies and oppositions as they take place in heterogeneous political, historical, cultural and psychological events. One possibility is to consider these phenomena in terms of hopes and fears, as images of collective futures rooted in the past, and as semiotic means of collective imaginations.

Collective Imaginations as Hopes and Fears

Some authors present the Self and Other(s) as outright enemies, or as partners trying to establish peace after long battles; as associates making effort to cooperate; or as parties uncertain about one another. The opposing partners differ with respect to a variety of features, such as power relations, trust and distrust and the capacity to negotiate. Collective imaginations of the future involve endless ranges of these dynamic processes.

Tileagă (Chap. 8, this volume) presents the Other in the past communist regime in Romania as having a total power over the Self. After the collapse of communism, citizens, that is, Selves, absolutely isolated themselves from the Other, that is, from communism, which they collectively imagined as an outright enemy disrespecting human rights and national values. Such representation of communism was made explicit in Romania in the 'Tismăneanu Report', a document that reassessed the nature and extent of crimes committed by illegitimate institutions that repressed, and physically and morally abused citizens during the years from 1945 to 1989. Tileagă is well aware of the difficulty in rehabilitating demoralized citizens, many of whom collaborated with the regime. Coping with the past communist Other in the public consciousness is still, after many years, a big challenge for the future. The main problem of constructing the new collective future is to develop ethics based not only on remembering the past injustice but on constructing ethics of trust and responsibility.

Zittoun and Gillespie (Chap. 2, this volume) display representations of communism by the Americans and the Soviets during the Cold War. In contrast to Tileagă's presentation of the Other as an enemy with a total power over citizens, the Soviets and the Americans were outright enemies with relatively equal powers. They both exposed monological collective imaginations of communism, each representing these in totally opposite ways. While the Soviets started from the presupposition of communism as being the bright future of humankind, the Americans created images of communism as an oppression, control and demagogy. However, strategies of coping with local enemies in their own countries in the two regimes were similar. Both the Americans and the Soviets blacklisted individuals who disagreed with the regime and they forbade publications expressing unwanted ideas; censorships and suspicion of espionage dominated their internal and external relations. As Zittoun and Gillespie show, visual images of posters and painting as the forms of control used in both political camps were based on similar, though opposing, contents, of manipulating public images of the past and future of communism.

Future imaginations in protracted conflict and tenuous post-conflict situations are often based on long histories of fights. In such situations, the Self and Other hold to their occasions of fragile peace with a considerable effort. They try to cope with unresolved problems and with the danger that the conflict could restart at any time. Nicholson and Howarth (Chap. 9, this volume) present Israeli–Palestinian protracted conflict in which the two communities are segregated by geographical borders and military powers. Periods of a relative truce and conflict rapidly change as the two parties find it hard to compromise on their geographical, political and economic perspectives. The authors show that the complex intergroup relations and past experiences of both groups remain central to their constructions of collective identities based on unfulfilled images of the future.

Portraying a post-conflict situation after the uprising in Egypt in 2011, Maarek and Awad (Chap. 10, this volume) explore initiatives of cooperatives that mobilized themselves in order to try out new practices that would counter the oppressive past regime and that would put in its place visions of a free and socially just society. Their three case studies show the multifaceted features of collective initiatives, their motives, constraints and the envisaged possibilities for social and political changes. As the authors observe, one cannot provide a recipe 'that could be applied fully to actualize and sustain the imagined future that was inspired by the revolution'. Instead, cooperatives use strategies of trial and error to cope with the unknown terrains. Relations between the Self and the Other in activities of cooperatives can be viewed in two ways. First, in opposing themselves against the Other, that is, the old regime, cooperatives create new visions of the collective future. Second, in order to succeed, cooperatives must coordinate actions between local Selves and Others within the cooperative, place emphasis on self-help and personal responsibility, and so create solidarity and collective imagining of the future.

Obradović (Chap. 12, this volume) poses the question about Serbia's identity as a nation. She observes that Serbia is a country 'in-between' with historical influences from both the West and the East, and so involves considerable cultural contrasts. These issues enter the public awareness with respect to the question as to whether Serbia should become a member of the European Union (EU). As Obradović notes, the Self and Other present themselves as Serbia versus the EU. While there are good reasons for Serbia to become a member of the EU, such as that it will benefit from the economic and political security, the membership in the EU also presents fears of such an alliance; above all, the EU poses a threat to the national identity of the Serbs. Will the Serbs be forced to adopt foreign rules that are discordant with the historical heritage of Serbia? What is Serbia going to gain in terms of national identity by becoming a member of the EU? At present, it appears that citizens are in a pre-conflict situation before starting any negotiations with the EU, which makes it difficult to create a collective imagination of the future. Obradović highlights the importance of Serbia's national compatibility with the EU. This raises the question of the cultural continuity of Serbia's identity. Hopes and fears are likely to dominate future interactions and negotiations with the EU.

In conclusion, incompatible presuppositions between the Self and Others are associated with heterogeneous collective imaginations and identities. The Self and Others as outright enemies clearly define their collective images; The Self and Others in pre-conflict and post-conflict situations have different aims and they face uncertainties in relation to trust and distrust, and hopes and fears for the future. Their collectively imagined futures are constructed in and through their experienced past which is reinterpreted alongside their contemporary conditions.

Collective Futures Are Rooted in the Past

Future imaginations are inevitably embedded in histories, narratives and traditions. The past can be viewed with nostalgia or as a reminder of terror; as a golden age of happiness or as a time of sadness; as a judgement of ethical or unethical conduct of Selves and Others; and so on. Memories are not stable facts to which one can repeatedly refer, but they are imaginative reconstructions and reinterpretations of the past and present, and of future expectations. All chapters thematize, in one way or other, these well-documented phenomena (see also de Saint-Laurent, Brescó, Awad & Wagoner, 2017)

On the basis of her own empirical research, Constance de Saint-Laurent (Chap. 4, this volume) develops a theoretical model involving three roles of collective memory fundamental for the imagination of collective futures. First, she displays two major political narratives, one in the politics of the Right and the other in that of the Left, both having their origins in the French Revolution. These grand narratives, which historically express the opposing frames of reference, still resonate in parliamentary debates and political imaginations in France. Second, the author shows that past experiences serve as examples of analogical events and thus, they guide the logic of historical reasoning. Finally, such examples and their logic augment the possibility of developing general understandings of how the world works and what the future might hold. The author considers these three roles of collective memory, that is, framing, exemplifying and generalizing as mutually interdependent: 'they all participate to the creation and maintenance of general representations of the world'.

These relations between collective memory and the imagination of the future take place in and through language and communication. Constance de Saint-Laurent makes important observations in extending Mikhail's

Bakhtin's (1981) concept of *discursive heteroglossia*. Dialogical participants not only speak in diverse languages at the same time, but they simultaneously refer to several historical situations. This means that *discursive heteroglossia* must be expanded into *temporal heteroglossia*. In other words, dialogue refers not only to the here and now, but it echoes the past, expresses the present and anticipates the future.

In a different context, Jacques Souriau (2013) maintains that a single conversation is part of a 'hyper-dialogue', that is, 'a part of conversations that take place throughout the whole life', recalling memories of the past, co-constructing present experiences and imagining the future. The term 'hyper-dialogue' refers to the very dialogicality and historicity of the human life (Marková, 2016, p. 183).

Seamus Power (Chap. 11, this volume) views imagining and remembering as dynamic processes interrelated with psychological and moral impacts. Specifically, he studies the local Irish context, in which people used analogical thinking in invoking disagreeable memories of the past privatizations of water services in Bolivia. These thoughts contributed to their construction of images for the Irish water services, which were based on a similar incident that took place in another part of the world. The participants in Power's study orientated themselves towards unwanted collective imaginations of past privatizations of basic resources and acted in order to avoid them becoming real. They viewed privatization as an unfair austerity that increases the gap between the rich and poor. Although, as Power maintains, imagination is not necessarily a moral enterprise, people imagine and conceptualize the future using moral judgements. The protestors in Power's study became moral actors for whom the privatization of water was an immoral act, and thus, it motivated and justified their protest actions. More generally, Power concludes, 'protesters in social movements are moral actors'.

Collective Imagination as a Semiotic Process

Sensory images—for instance, visual and hearing images—can take on powerful symbolic roles. In her analysis of Soviet posters during Stalinism, Bonnell (1997) drew attention to visual and verbal symbols expressed in political images and their special semantics combining meanings of words and visual impressions. Political posters skilfully mixed folk culture and symbols of Orthodox religion to create highly effective impressions on the masses. Bonnell commented that visual images were particularly overpowering because most peasants, at whom these posters aimed, were illiterate but they easily understood visual images. Having comprehended this situation, Soviet artists produced truly religious art under the label of politics. In the 1920s and 1930s, the history of the Soviet Union was rewritten using new socialist and communist images (Zittoun and Gillespie, Chap. 2, this volume) which had a tremendous effect on masses. The regime presented 'new images' clothed in old ones. Although masses were not explicitly aware of the substitution of religious images by the political ones, their implicit familiarity reminding religious icons of saints, was effective. For example, on those posters, Lenin had 'qualities of a saint, an apostle, a prophet, a martyr, a man with Christ-like qualities' (Bonnell, 1997, p. 146). Both Lenin and Stalin were presented as super humans whose images were carried on sticks in oval frames just like images of Christ. Another commentator on the relations between Orthodox religion and the Soviet communism, Boris Souvarine (1939, p. 357), remarked that 'Leninism' had become 'a complicated theology with its dogma, its mysticism and its scholasticism' (Marková, 2017).

Zittoun and Gillespie (Chap. 2, this volume), using two examples, also show the importance of visual and hearing images in the competition between the Soviets and Americans during the Cold War. The first example concerns the design of the Soviet satellite *Sputnik 1* that not only orbited the Earth within 90 minutes, but emitted radio signals and thus provided both visual and hearing evidence of its existence. This not only showed the Soviet achievement but brought questions as to whether the satellite was spying or whether it could be carrying a nuclear weapon. The USA and USSR skilfully generated specific images with respect to space competition in designing posters, television programmes, and all possible means of communication and propaganda to influence the public.

Mixing political and religious terminology was another effective means of creating images which the masses easily understood (Marková, 2017). For example, Stalin (1921–1823/1953, 5, p. 73) named the communist party the 'Order of Knights of the Sword' within the Soviet State. Lenin was the 'apostle of world communism' and 'the leader by the Grace of God' (Tumarkin, 1983). Symbols and the semantic significance of images kept changing throughout the history of the regime and this corresponded to its changing ideologies (see Antonova & Merkvert, 1995).

Literature, too, plays a fundamental symbolic role in collective constructions of the future (Carriere, Chap. 3, this volume). Literature allows readers to cross from reality to a magical world and to reflect on these transformations, and thus, what people read, what is promoted or censored by institutions, has a tremendous effect of collective imagination. Forbidden books have always been a particular attraction, secretly circulating among the interested public and shaping the collective imagination. Carriere suggests that there are two main roles of literature. First, it has a psychological function in the sense that it drives action and transforms our social representations of phenomena. It motivates humans either 'to do great deeds or horrible acts of suicide bombings'. Second, it is through literature that humans display themselves as imaginative beings. If we recall again the Heideggerian perspective, 'literature allows us to explore the unknown' and 'to test new boundaries and taboos' (Carriere, Chap. 3, this volume). Literary insights enable humans to imaginatively reflect on their personal and collective self-concepts and to promote changes for the future.

The Future of Collective Imaginations

By bringing together productive and plentiful ideas on imagining collective futures, the contributors to this volume make a major theoretical and empirical advancement in this domain. They explore the main concepts which drive collective imaginings and their dynamic transformations. Yet despite incessant transformations of collective imaginings, the authors appreciate their historical durability and strategic searches for paths in the unknown. For example, de Saint-Laurent shows that the Left and Right in French politics have been forceful in collective imagination since the Enlightenment; collective imaginations of the past communist regimes and Cold War (Zittoun and Gillespie, Tileagă) still resonate in contemporary political and ethical problems; and territorial, religious and political imaginations (Nicholson and Howarth, Maarek and Awad, Glăveanu, Brescó, Obradović, Power, Carretero) do not shake off their historical roots. Collective imaginations express themselves as heterogeneous and multifaceted (de Saint-Laurent); yet on other occasions, they could be articulated as monological utopias (Jovchelovitch and Hawlina, Brescó). The authors have shown the ways in which semiotic processes, mixing visual and hearing symbols, as well as religious and political terminology, abundantly influence the formation and manipulation of images (Zittoun and Gillespie, Carriere, Carretero).

But what about imagining of collective futures? It appears that contemporary dramatic political and economic upheavals all over the world have destroyed the relatively simple dichotomies of rival political parties and of oppositional ideologies that have governed the imaginings of collective futures. Instead, we witness the breakdown of traditional institutions and of established political parties, as well as the increasing distrust and uncertainties over the future of individuals, groups and nations. What role will history and the past grand narratives play in the world dominated by the increasing power of markets, business and self-appointed political leaders? As history and morals become continuously distorted, Carretero's (Chap. 13, this volume) thought of 'the (im)possibility of imagining the future' opens new questions for the future.

Rapid societal transformations do not annihilate imagination. It is images that become more and more volatile, fragmented and unpredictable as they are associated with the breakup of established groups and with re-institutions of new ones. What is dreamt today may be no longer a dream for tomorrow. Yet despite fragmentation and uncertainties of our time, numerous examples show that the dialogical nature of humanity continues to induce solidarity during periods of crises and triumphs, for example, in the public's help to victims of earthquakes, terrorism or disease. Rapid societal changes pose new questions for the creation, maintenance and change of collective images of the future. It is with this in mind that we shall have to search for new ways of rethinking imaginings of collective futures and of understanding the ways images are formed and transformed.

References

Antonova, I., & Merkvert, J. (Eds.). (1995). *Berlin-Moscow*. Moscow: Galart.
Aristotle. (1998). *The Nicomachean ethics* (W. D. Ross, J. L. Ackrill & J. O. Urmson, Trans. and Ed.). Oxford: Oxford University Press.
Arruda, A. (2014). Social imaginary and social representations of Brazil. *Papers on Social Representations, 23*, 13.1–13.22.
Bakhtin, M. M. (1981). *The dialogic imagination: Four essays by M. M. Bakhtin* (M. Holquist, Ed.). Austin: University of Texas Press.
Benedict, R. (1942). *Race and racism*. London: Routledge & Kegan Paul.
Berger, P. (1973). On the obsolescence of the concept of honour. In P. Berger, B. Merger, & H. Kellner (Eds.), *The homeless mind* (pp. 78–89). Harmondsworth: Penguin Books.
Bonnell, V. E. (1997). *Iconography of power: Soviet political posters under Lenin and Stalin*. Beverley/London: University of California Press.
Bottici, C. (2011). From imagination to the imaginary and beyond: Towards a theory of imaginal politics. In C. Bottici & B. Challand (Eds.), *The politics of imagination* (pp. 16–37). Abington: Birkbeck Law Press.
Brescó de Luna, I. (2018, this volume). Imagining collective futures in time: Prolepsis and the regimes of historicity. In C. de Saint-Laurent, S. Obradović, & K. R. Carriere (Eds.), *Imagining collective futures: Perspectives from social, cultural, and political psychology* (pp. 109–128). London: Palgrave Macmillan.
Calhoun, C. (2002). Imagining solidarity: Cosmopolitanism, constitutional patriotism, and the public sphere. *Public Culture, 14*, 147–171.
Cole, M. (1996). *Cultural psychology: A once and future discipline*. Cambridge, MA: Harvard University Press.
Carretero, M. (2018, this volume). History education and the (im)possibility of imagining the future. In C. de Saint-Laurent, S. Obradović, & K. R. Carriere (Eds.), *Imagining collective futures: Perspectives from social, cultural, and political psychology* (pp. 255–271). London: Palgrave Macmillan.
Carriere, K. (2018, this volume). Framing the issue: Literature, collective imagination, and fan activism. In C. de Saint-Laurent, S. Obradović, & K. R. Carriere (Eds.), *Imagining collective futures: Perspectives from social, cultural, and political psychology* (pp. 39–58). London: Palgrave Macmillan.
Czobor-Lupp, M. (2014). *Imagination in politics: Freedom or domination?* Lanham: Lexington Books.

de Alba, M. (2004). Mapas mentales de la ciudad de México: una aproximación psicosocial al estudio de las representaciones espaciales. *Estudios Demográficos y Urbanos, 055*, 115–143.

de Alba, M. (2007). Mapas mentales del centro histórico de la ciudad de México: de la experiencia al imaginario urbano. In A. Arruda & M. de Alba (Eds.), *Espacios imaginarios y representaciones sociales: aportes desde Latinoamérica* (pp. 285–319). Barcelona/México: Anthropos/UAM.

de Saint Laurent, C. (2018, this volume). Thinking through time: From collective memories to collective futures. In C. de Saint-Laurent, S. Obradović, & K. R. Carriere (Eds.), *Imagining collective futures: Perspectives from social, cultural, and political psychology* (pp. 59–81). London: Palgrave Macmillan.

de Saint-Laurent, C., Brescó, I., Awad, S. H., & Wagoner, B. (2017). Editorial: Collective memory and social sciences in the post-truth era. *Culture & Psychology, 23*, 147–155.

Einstein, A. (1931/2009). *On cosmic religion and other opinions and aphorisms.* With an appreciation by George Bernard Shaw. Mineola: Dover Publications.

Glăveanu, V. P. (2018, this volume). Perspectival collective futures: Creativity and imagination in society. In C. de Saint-Laurent, S. Obradović, & K. R. Carriere (Eds.), *Imagining collective futures: Perspectives from social, cultural, and political psychology* (pp. 83–105). London: Palgrave Macmillan.

Gaonkar, D. P. (2002). Toward new imaginaries: An introduction. *Public Culture, 14*, 1–19.

Goldbard, A. (2006). *New creative community: The art of cultural development.* Oakland, CA: New Village Press.

Göle, N. (2002). Islam in public: New visibilities and new imaginaries. *Public Culture, 14*, 173–190.

Gray, J. G. (1968). Introduction. In M. Heidegger (Ed.), F. D. Wieck & J. G. Gray (Trans.), Introduction by J. G. Gray, *What is called thinking* (pp. xvii–xxvii). New York/London: Harper.

Heidegger, M. (1968). *What is called thinking* (F. D. Wieck & J. G. Gray, Trans. and Introduction by J. G. Gray). New York/London: Harper.

Ichheiser, G. (1951). Misunderstandings in international relations. *American Sociological Review, 16*, 311–316.

Jovchelovitch, S., & Hawlina, H. (2018, this volume). Utopias and worldmaking: Time, transformation and the collective imagination. In C. de Saint-Laurent, S. Obradović, & K. R. Carriere (Eds.), *Imagining collective futures: Perspectives from social, cultural, and political psychology* (pp. 129–151). London: Palgrave Macmillan.

Lee, B., & LiPuma, E. (2002). Cultures in circulation: The imaginations of modernity. *Public Culture, 14*, 191–213.

LeGouis, C. (1997). *Positivism and imagination: Scientism and its limits in Emile Hennequin, Wilhelm Scherer and Dmitrii Pisarev*. London: Associated University Presses.

Maarek, E. & Awad, S. H. (2018, this volume). Creating alternative futures: Cooperative initiatives in Egypt. In C. de Saint-Laurent, S. Obradović, & K. R. Carriere (Eds.), *Imagining collective futures: Perspectives from social, cultural, and political psychology* (pp. 199–219). London: London Macmillan.

Marková, I. (2003). *Dialogicality and social representations*. Cambridge, UK: Cambridge University Press.

Marková, I. (2016). *The dialogical mind: Common sense and ethics*. Cambridge, UK: Cambridge University Press.

Marková, I. (2017). From imagination to well-controlled images: Challenge for the dialogical mind. In T. Zittoun & V. P. Glăveanu (Eds.), *The Oxford handbook of imagination and culture*. New York: Oxford University Press, pp. 329–344.

Marková, I., & Farr, R. M. (Eds.). (1995). *Representations of health, illness and handicap*. New York: Harwood.

Moscovici, S. (1961). *La psychanalyse: son image et son public* [Psychoanalysis: Its image and its public]. Paris: Presses Universitaires de France.

Moscovici, S. (1976/2008). *La psychanalyse: son image et son public* (2nd ed). Paris: Presses Universitaires de France. Trans. D. Macey as *Psychoanalysis: Its image and its public*. Cambridge: Polity Press.

Nicholson, C., & Howarth, C. (2018, this volume). Imagining collective identities beyond intergroup conflict. In C. de Saint-Laurent, S. Obradović, & K. R. Carriere (Eds.), *Imagining collective futures: Perspectives from social, cultural, and political psychology* (pp. 173–196). London: Palgrave Macmillan.

Obradović, S. (2018, this volume). Creating integration: A case study from Serbia and the EU. In C. de Saint-Laurent, S. Obradović, & K. R. Carriere (Eds.), *Imagining collective futures: Perspectives from social, cultural, and political psychology* (pp. 237–254). London: Palgrave Macmillan.

Plato (1991). *The Republic of Plato* (Trans., notes, interpretive essay and a new introduction A. Bloom). New York: Basic Books/Harper and Collins.

Power, S. (2018, this volume). Remembering and imagining in human development: Fairness and social movements in Ireland. In C. de Saint-Laurent, S. Obradović, & K. R. Carriere (Eds.), *Imagining collective futures: Perspectives from social, cultural, and political psychology* (pp. 221–235). London: Palgrave Macmillan.

Rommetveit, R. (1974). *On message structure*. Chichester, UK: Wiley.
Saint Augustine. (397–398/2006). *Confessions of Saint Augustine* (E. B. Pusey, Trans.). Teddington: The Echo Library.
Souriau, J. (2013). Comprendre et communiquer avec ceux qui ne parlent pas [To understand and to communicate with those who do not speak]. *Vie Sociale, 3*, 93–116.
Souvarine, B. (1939). *Stalin – A critical survey of Bolshevism*. New York: Alliance Book Cooperation.
Stalin, J. V. (1921–1923/1953). The political strategy and tactics of the Russian Communists. In: *Works* (Vol. 5). Moscow: Foreign Languages Publishing House.
Taylor, C. (2002). Modern social imaginaries. *Public Culture, 14*, 91–124.
Tileagă, C. (2018, this volume). Troubled pasts, collective memory and collective futures. In C. de Saint-Laurent, S. Obradović, & K. R. Carriere (Eds.), *Imagining collective futures: Perspectives from social, cultural, and political psychology* (pp. 153–172). London: Palgrave Macmillan.
Tumarkin, N. (1983). *Lenin lives! The Lenin cult in Soviet Russia*. Cambridge: Harvard University Press.
Vico, G. (1744/1948). *The new science of Giambattista Vico* (T. G. Bergin & M. H. Fisch, Trans.). Ithaca: Cornell University Press.
Wagner, W., Kronberger, N., & Seifert, F. (2002). Collective symbolic coping with new technology: Knowledges, images and public discourse. *British Journal of Social Psychology, 41*, 323–343.
Zittoun, T., & Gillespie, A. (2016). *Imagination in human and cultural development*. London: Routledge.
Zittoun, T., & Gillespie, A. (2018, this volume). Imagining the collective future: A sociocultural perspective. In C. de Saint-Laurent, S. Obradović, & K. R. Carriere (Eds.), *Imagining collective futures: Perspectives from social, cultural, and political psychology* (pp. 15–37). London: Palgrave Macmillan.

Index[1]

A

Activist/activism, 9, 39, 87, 98, 99, 190, 206–208, 215, 229, 230
Alternative/alternative futures, 3, 9, 18, 20, 26, 27, 31, 62, 74, 76, 88, 132, 135, 140–146, 159, 162, 165, 167n9, 170, 174, 175, 183, 187–189, 191, 199–211, 213–218, 221, 232, 233, 256, 260, 278
Analogy, 69–72, 74

C

Case studies per country
   Canada, 92
   Colombia, 89, 94
   Egypt, 10, 199–211, 213–218, 284

EU, 239
France, 27, 66, 67, 286
Ireland, 221–233
Israel, 54, 175, 176, 186, 188, 190
Palestine, 174–176
Poland, 70
Romania, 155n1, 161
Serbia, 237–251, 285
Soviet Union/USSR, 29, 261, 262, 288
Turkey, 9, 98, 99
United States, 9, 264
Change, 3, 5–7, 9, 10, 17, 28, 32, 33, 41, 44, 45, 47, 51–53, 59, 63, 66, 77, 87, 93, 94, 99, 101, 111, 114, 117–119, 124, 130–132, 140–143, 145, 146, 155, 162, 167, 178, 181, 185,

---

[1] Note: Page numbers followed by 'n' refer to notes.

187, 189, 191, 192, 200–207, 209–218, 224, 225, 232, 237–239, 241, 243–246, 248, 250, 251, 259n7, 261, 264, 274, 275, 285, 289, 290
Collective memory, 5–7, 9, 59–77, 84, 91, 110, 120, 137, 153–170, 182, 183, 187, 265, 277, 286
Community, 6, 20, 25, 27, 31, 44, 84, 86–89, 91, 93–98, 100, 120, 131, 135, 137, 139, 155, 156, 158, 160, 166, 170, 180–182, 187, 188, 192, 202–205, 207, 209, 212, 213, 216, 217, 229, 237–241, 273, 274, 284
Conflict, 4, 9, 10, 45, 48, 49, 54, 70, 74, 99, 173–192, 238, 239, 243, 249, 251, 274, 277, 281, 284–286
Continuity, 6, 43, 61, 77, 114, 120, 158, 237–246, 248–251, 265, 285
Cooperatives, 6, 10, 27, 199–211, 213–218, 284, 285
Creativity, 8, 9, 16, 40, 83–101, 131, 277, 280

D

Dialogism/dialogical, 19, 21, 29, 70, 84, 91, 97–100, 174, 177, 180, 184, 185, 190, 273, 278, 279, 287, 290
Discourses/discursive, 18, 65, 71, 75, 76, 94, 110, 116, 156, 160, 189, 192, 229, 237, 238, 245–248, 250, 251

Dystopia, 2, 22, 31, 87, 111, 143, 146, 262

E

Economy/economic, 2, 7, 21, 73, 96, 118, 138, 140, 145, 178, 200, 202, 203, 205, 208, 222, 223, 225–227, 230–233, 274, 284, 285, 290

F

Fantasy, 42, 48, 130, 135–137, 140, 145
Fiction, 2, 26, 27, 43, 44, 46, 49, 50, 53, 61, 75, 278

H

History, 2, 8, 20, 27, 32, 43, 44, 48, 60, 62–67, 70, 70n3, 72–74, 77, 93, 101, 111, 113–116, 120, 124, 155, 157–159, 161, 163, 166, 167n9, 168, 175, 176, 178, 179, 189, 201, 208, 225, 230, 231, 238, 239, 242, 243, 246, 248, 250, 255–268, 257n1, 258n3, 274, 281, 284, 286, 288–290

I

Identity, 5–7, 10, 46, 93, 96, 112, 115, 120, 138, 139, 160–162, 165, 169, 173–192, 201, 238–248, 250, 251, 262, 275, 285
Institutions, 29, 31, 86, 158, 181, 187, 189, 202–204, 211, 250,

256, 258n5, 273, 275, 278, 283, 289, 290
Intergroup, 9, 10, 173–176, 179–192, 241, 243, 248
   interactions, 84, 177–178, 180, 182–188, 190–192, 226, 230, 233, 238, 243, 246, 256, 261, 263–265, 267, 286, 290
Nostalgia, 112, 113, 118–123, 167, 286

J

Justice, 10, 50–52, 123, 153–157, 159, 165, 167–169, 176, 184, 200, 209, 217
   transitional, 160–164, 172, 174–176

L

Lenin, Vladimir, 288
Literature, 2, 5, 8, 16, 17, 28, 39–54, 63, 85, 87, 93, 130, 139, 178, 238, 241, 251, 257, 280, 289

M

Memory/remembering, 4, 5, 8, 20, 60–64, 75, 77n5, 112, 118–120, 136, 154, 156–160, 162, 163, 165–167, 169, 170, 229, 276, 277, 286, 287
Metaphor, 49, 77n5, 221, 222, 232, 256, 262–268

N

Narratives, 9, 10, 53, 54, 62, 63, 65–68, 71, 74, 90, 109, 110, 115, 121, 137, 157, 159, 162n4, 163, 164, 166, 174,

P

Personal World Philosophies (PWP), 60, 72–75, 77
Perspectives, 2, 8, 9, 41–43, 47, 50–53, 63, 70, 84, 85, 88–101, 115, 123n5, 130, 134, 140, 146, 156–158, 166, 167, 167n9, 170, 201, 216, 218, 229, 239, 240, 242, 250, 277–281, 284, 289
   perspective-taking, 10, 15–34, 41, 94
Policy, 27, 44, 51, 53, 54, 69, 70, 89, 93, 132, 154, 155, 168, 175, 223, 228, 230
Political/politic, 2, 5, 8, 10, 15, 16, 20, 21, 26–28, 30, 31, 33, 34, 41, 46–48, 52, 60, 62, 63, 65, 66, 66n1, 76, 84, 86, 87, 91–93, 95, 98–101, 110, 111, 115, 117–120, 122–125, 132, 133, 140, 145, 154–156, 155n1, 158–162, 164–169, 167n9, 174–176, 178, 180, 181, 183, 187, 189, 191, 192, 199–204, 206, 209, 215, 217, 226, 232, 237–241, 244–248, 250, 251, 256, 257n1, 258, 258n5, 260–262, 264, 267, 274–276, 278, 280–286, 288–290

Positions, 66, 66n2, 67, 88–92, 94, 96, 97, 99, 100, 130, 146, 161, 162, 165, 168, 176, 177, 180, 182, 183, 185, 189, 191, 192, 218, 239, 240, 247, 259n7, 278, 280
social, 180
Power, 1, 2, 5–8, 17, 20, 21, 23, 27, 29, 44, 45, 49, 50, 86, 91, 94, 95, 98, 177, 179, 192, 199–201, 203, 204, 206, 207, 210, 212, 216, 217, 223, 232, 239, 256, 260, 264, 282–284
Prediction, 3, 5, 7, 132
Prefiguration, 203
prefigurative politics, 202, 203
Prolepsis, 9, 63, 91, 109–125, 278–280
Protest/protester, 6, 10, 42, 53, 87, 95, 98, 99, 178, 199, 202, 203, 207, 209, 210, 212, 213, 215–217, 222–231, 233, 274, 287

R

Recognition, 94, 186–192, 239, 275
Reconciliation, 157, 160, 161, 191, 218
Recycling/recycle, 209, 210, 214, 215
Remembering and Imagining in Human Development, 221, 223–230

Representations, 4, 7–10, 60, 62, 64, 66, 67, 72–77, 90, 130, 131, 133–135, 137, 140, 142, 146, 154, 165, 167n9, 168, 180, 181, 183, 184, 229, 256, 257, 259, 261, 263, 265–267, 283, 284, 286
social, 69, 174, 180–189, 191, 192, 281, 282, 289
Revolution, 30, 66, 115, 143, 160, 199–201, 206–210, 212–217, 228, 285

S

Self-other, 83, 84, 91, 94, 97
Social change, 39

T

Themata/thema, 9, 174, 184–192
Trajectory, 18, 22, 26, 32–34, 145, 180, 183–185, 188
developmental, 15–16, 22

U

Utopia, 2, 9, 22, 26, 29, 31, 44, 87, 110–112, 115–117, 124, 125, 129–146, 160, 277, 290

CPSIA information can be obtained
at www.ICGtesting.com
Printed in the USA
LVOW13*1735110518
576868LV00015B/412/P